Competitive and Cooperative Macromanagement

NEW HORIZONS IN INTERNATIONAL BUSINESS

General Editor: Peter J. Buckley
Leeds University Management School
University of Leeds, UK

This series is aimed at the frontiers of international business research. Each volume tackles key problem areas in international political economy. The study of international business is important not least because it gives researchers the opportunity to innovate in theory, technique, empirical investigation and interpretation. The area is fruitful for interdisciplinary and comparative research. This series is established as a central forum for the presentation of new ideas in international business.

New Directions in International Business
Research Priorities for the 1990s
Edited by Peter J. Buckley

Europe and the Multinationals
Issues and Responses for the 1990s
Edited by Stephen Young and James Hamill

Multinational Enterprises in the World Economy
Essays in Honour of John Dunning
Edited by Peter J. Buckley and Mark Casson

Multinational Investment in Modern Europe
Strategic Interaction in the Integrated Community
Edited by John Cantwell

The Growth and Evolution of Multinational Enterprise
Patterns of Geographical and Industrial Diversification
R.D. Pearce

Multinational Enterprise and Public Policy
A Study of the Industrial Countries
A.E. Safarian

Transnational Corporations in Southeast Asia
An Institutional Approach to Industrial Organization
Hans Jansson

European Integration and Competitiveness
Acquisitions and Alliances in Industry
Edited by Frédérique Sachwald

The State and Transnational Corporations
A Network Approach to Industrial Policy in India
Hans Jansson, M. Saqib and D. Deo Sharma

Competitive and Cooperative Macromanagement
The Challenges of Structural Interdependence
Edited by Gavin Boyd

Competitive and Cooperative Macromanagement

The Challenges of Structural Interdependence

Edited by
Gavin Boyd

Honorary Professor, Political Science Department, Rutgers University, US and Research Associate, Centre for International Business Studies, University of Montreal, Canada

NEW HORIZONS IN INTERNATIONAL BUSINESS

Edward Elgar
Aldershot, UK • Brookfield, US

Published by
Edward Elgar Publishing Limited
Gower House
Croft Road
Aldershot
Hants GU11 3HR
UK

Edward Elgar Publishing Company
Old Post Road
Brookfield
Vermont 05036
US

British Library Cataloguing in Publication Data
Competitive and Cooperative
Macromanagement:Challenges of Structural
Interdependence. – (New Horizons in
International Business Series)
   I. Boyd, Gavin   II. Series
   338.6

Library of Congress Cataloguing in Publication Data
Competitive and cooperative macromanagement : the challenges of
   structural interdependence / edited by Gavin Boyd.
         p.   cm. — (New horizons in international business)
      Includes bibliographical references and index.
      1. International business enterprises—Management.   2. Strategic
   planning.   3. International business enterprises—Government policy.
   I. Gavin, Boyd.   II. Series.
   HD62.4.C65   1995
   658'.049—dc20   95–6827
                                                                             CIP

ISBN 1 85898 144 1

Printed and bound in Great Britain by
Hartnolls Limited, Bodmin, Cornwall

Contents

Figures

Contributors

Michael Blaine is a Lecturer in the Department of Management and Human Resources, Max Fisher College of Business, Ohio State University, Columbus, Ohio USA. He authored *Cooperation in International Business* (1994), and has published in several business journals, including the *California Management Review* and *Management International Review*.

Peter J. Buckley is Professor of Managerial Economics in the Management Centre at the University of Bradford, UK, and Editor of the Edward Elgar series, New Horizons in International Business.

Joseph R. D'Cruz, Professor in the Faculty of Management at the University of Toronto, is one of Canada's leading authorities on international competitiveness. He has written extensively on corporate globalization and business strategy. He was formerly an Adjunct Professor at IMD International, Switzerland.

Hamid Etemad directs the MBA Programme in the Faculty of Management at McGill University, Montreal. His research areas are international marketing and exporting, strategic alliances, and the management of technology. He has published in numerous business journals, including *Research Policy, Technovation* and *Industrial Marketing*.

Edward M. Graham is a Senior Fellow in the Institute for International Economics, Washington DC. He has written extensively on international trade and technology policies and on the strategies of international firms. With colleagues at the Institute for International Economics he is working on several forthcoming studies of interdependent growth in the industrialized democracies.

John M. Kline is Director of the Landegger Program in International Business Diplomacy at the Georgetown University School of Foreign Service, Washington DC. He authored *Foreign Investment Strategies in Restructuring Economies: Learning from Corporate Experiences in Chile* (1992), *International Codes and Multinational Business* (1985) and *State Government*

Influence on US International Economic Policy (1983). He is a member of the US State Department's Advisory Committee on International Investment.

Alan M. Rugman is a Professor in the Faculty of Management at the University of Toronto. He has held visiting appointments at the London Business School, Columbia University and the Massachusetts Institute of Technology, and was a member of Canada's International Trade Advisory Committee during the US–Canada free trade negotiations. He is the author or Editor of 25 books, and his most recent publications include *Foreign Investment and NAFTA* (1994) and a new text, *International Business: A Strategic Management Approach.*

Alain Verbeke is Professor of International Business Strategy and Public Policy at the University of Brussels. He is the author of more than 60 articles on the strategic management of complex organizations, public and private. His most recent books are *Global Corporate Strategy and Trade Policy* (1990) and *Research in Global Strategic Management*, Vol. 4, *Beyond the Three Generics*, co-edited with Alan M. Rugman.

Preface

This book has been planned as a contribution to international business and international political economy literature. It focuses on trends and issues in the activities of firms and the policies of major states. Some gaps are seen in the research-intensive publications offering advice to managements and policy-makers. Because of these gaps, the significance of certain fundamental problems of interdependent growth tends to be obscured. There is a degree of informational failure in the market for economic advice.

The activities of firms operating internationally are given special attention because they are shaping economic structures on a very extensive scale, while linking them through transnational production and trade. Through all this activity market processes are being altered. Transactions are being internalized within firms expanding across borders and sectors; intrafirm trade is increasing relative to arm's length trade; high volume export substitution is resulting from international production; and market efficiencies and failures are assuming international dimensions.

The changes in markets affect levels and spreads of resulting gains. Intensifying corporate rivalries for global market shares forces weaker firms into decline. Governments are involved in this competition through the implementation of policies intended to benefit national firms, but have different capacities for the promotion of competitiveness in their business communities. Some states, notably the more pluralistic ones, experience major problems of advanced political development: their inferior governance causes difficulties for their firms, while enterprises based in states under more efficient macromanagement are advantaged. The competition between governments is not on a level playing field, because there is considerable use of bargaining strengths, based on size, and for some major states the costs of macromanagement deficiencies are becoming more serious, because of their effects on the corporate competition across borders.

Cautious trade liberalization by governments offers possibilities for increasing gains from commerce, through specialization and economies of scale, with technological advances. Imbalances in the gains, however, tend to set up vicious circles in which losses by less competitive firms in less effectively managed states increase problems of governance which then have further negative effects at the corporate level. Meanwhile, successes achieved by more competitive enterprises in states under more efficient management tend to ensure administrative continuity.

Complex patterns of reciprocal causality between governmental perform-ance and corporate performance are evolving as the internationalization of markets becomes more extensive and as market processes change, with shifts of economic power to firms. Questions about cooperation between govern-ments have to be considered, in the interests of communities and sectors whose fortunes are being linked across borders. These questions relate, in part, to common interests in the resolution of problems of advanced political development, and in moderation of the neomercantilism which tends to develop in the policies of the more effectively managed states. Questions about cooperation between firms, as well as between firms and governments, also have to be considered. Managements can collaborate with each other, restraining their rivalries, with substantial efficiency effects, as has been evident in the practices of Japanese firms. Efficiencies can also result from collaboration which promotes congruence between corporate strategies and the policies of governments. Further efficiencies are clearly possible if the policies of governments are harmonized and thus help to blend corporate cooperation with corporate competition across borders.

The potentials for cooperation at the enterprise and government level are very significant. Use of these potentials could reduce imbalances in gains from involvement in world trade and production, thus moderating strains that tend to intensify problems of governance in the less advantaged states. Im-peratives to plan for cooperation at and between the two levels can be recognized, on the basis of concerns about public goods and about the devel-opment of the international political economy as a whole. Such concerns, in the Triad pattern of industrialized states, have been evoked by the references to social solidarity in the European Commission's 1994 White Paper on *Growth, Competitiveness, and Employment*. The concept of solidarity recalls the painful beginnings of a great enterprise, and can be seen to have a transnational dimension related to the tasks of cooperative macromanagement. Rising structural interdependencies, especially with their current asymmetries, set requirements for cooperative policy mixes that can promise greater effi-ciency and equity, in what would become a multicountry social market economy, with multigroup patterns of corporate cooperation.

Work on this volume has benefited greatly from exchanges with the contrib-uting authors. I am very grateful for their chapters and for insights gained during our exchanges. Readers, I trust, will wish to become more acquainted with the other publications of these distinguished authors. Preparation of the volume was encouraged by Peter J. Buckley, Professor of Managerial Economics at the University of Bradford, Editor of the Edward Elgar Series on New Horizons in International Business. His assistance has been very valuable, and Edward Elgar's support for the project is greatly appreciated. My chapters have benefited very much from discussions with Professor Yale Ferguson of the Political Science Department at Rutgers University, Newark, New Jersey, USA, and with colleagues at meetings of the International Studies Association over the past few years.

GAVIN BOYD

1. Transnational enterprises and national political economies

John M. Kline

The contemporary challenge for effective macromanagement is shaped by an interactive dynamic between transnational enterprises (TNEs) and national political economies. Both manifest rapid and fundamental change, modifying their own character while simultaneously altering their relationship with each other. In this environment, public policy managers perform tasks under increasing time pressures with fewer clear guidelines or broadly effective tools. Business executives respond to complex new demands for competitiveness in a vibrant global market-place that retains significant local differentiation. Academicians struggle to keep pace, increasingly drawn into unfamiliar terrain when events in the observable world fail to correspond with expertise defined by the divisions of traditional academic disciplines. An interdisciplinary effort is needed to assess these systemic changes in order to understand their impact on macromanagement in an interdependent world political economy.

Global commerce transformed nation-state relations in the latter part of the 20th century, particularly after economics further outdistanced military alternatives as the pragmatic instrument for nation-state competition and welfare enhancement. Although this reordering is now well accepted, tension remains between accepted theory and actual practice due to the growing disjuncture between traditional political economy measures of national benefit and competitiveness, and the growing importance of globally adaptive TNE strategies. As national authorities increased their reliance on private economic instruments, business responsiveness to national political direction actually decreased. TNEs became both the symbols and the facilitators of structural interdependencies that diminish the range of effective unilateral national policy options.

The open world trading system built through multilateral political cooperation after World War II has generated unexpected interactive processes that challenge national political sovereignties. International commerce, initially comprised of physical trade across national borders, expanded to include foreign production and private multiparty exchange conducted by multina-

tional corporate agents. More recently, complex transnational business ventures mix and match production locations, commercial functions and benefit
distribution with diminishing regard for national political boundaries.

While these economic changes continue – and in many ways both influencing and influenced by them – numerous nation-states are undergoing political
transformations. Some are involved in regional economic cooperation ventures that weaken national identities and loyalties. Others, including some in
regional economic blocs, are experiencing internal strains associated with
problems of interdependent governance. With all these changes, national
boundaries grow less relevant, and sometimes appear to be hindrances to
necessary macromanagement tasks in an increasingly interdependent world.

This chapter traces the transformation of global commerce and its interactive relationship with evolving nation-state authority. The first section sketches
the evolution of transnational business from nation-based trading patterns to
the emergence of an increasingly integrated international production system
with complex transnational alliance networks. These changes have loosened
connections between TNEs and their home countries while simultaneously
opening most national economies to increased foreign penetration. The next
two sections therefore investigate the impact on political authorities when the
relevance and effectiveness of national boundaries appears diminished. One
response relies on reinforced measures to assert sovereignty and promote
competitive national welfare. Other alternatives lead to enhanced international and regional links, or to decentralized solutions that meet political and
socio-cultural needs. The final section identifies policy issues raised for governments that must respond to the transnational dimensions of new structural
interdependencies, as well as the demands of local polities concerned with
their own immediate economic fortunes and cultural identities.

THE EVOLUTION OF TRANSNATIONAL BUSINESS

From Trade to Foreign Direct Investment

Cross-border trade in physical goods comprised the historical foundation for
international commerce, providing participants with unavailable or less expensive products by exploiting comparative endowment differences between
geographic locations. Although early trade preceded the rise of nation-states,
trading patterns helped to establish or reinforce relative national power in the
international system, sometimes providing the rationale for military action.
International trade also generated linkages between nations, but governments
monitored and regulated physical flows across their own borders, thereby
largely controlling the composition and impact of foreign imports.

Trade in physical goods still comprises a principal element of global commerce; however, its role within the international system fundamentally changed as foreign direct investment (FDI) expanded, portfolio flows increased, and technology, services and business alliance networks broadened the scope of commercial dealings. In particular, FDI, termed by DeAnne Julius (1991) the 'neglected twin of trade', was not properly recognized by most analysts and policy-makers. Global figures for domestic investment, domestic output and FDI all expanded at similar rates throughout the 1970s, but FDI flows rose faster after the early 1980s. Between 1985 and 1990, the nominal average growth rate for world FDI was nearly two and one-half times higher than those for nominal gross national product or merchandise exports (34 per cent versus 12 and 13 per cent, respectively) (UN, 1992, pp. 1, 17).

Early FDI appeared to follow trade patterns as corporations moved to defend and expand their export markets. More recently, trade has followed investment. As a statistical concept, FDI is both a flow and a stock concept, whereas trade (exports and imports) is measured by annual flows. This difference reflects the fact that a corporation's investment stake is cumulative over the years, deepening its commitment to selected foreign locations and influencing both local production and sales patterns as well as increasingly determining export and import flows. By 1992 the global stock of FDI reached nearly $2 trillion, generating approximately $5.5 trillion in sales by foreign affiliates (compared to $4.4 trillion in world exports of goods and non-factor services). Approximately one-third of world trade now takes place on an intrafirm basis (within the same TNE), meaning that prior foreign investment decisions play a major role in determining where and how trade flows will occur (UN, 1993, p. 13).

Sectoral Shifts and Financial Flows

Another basic change in the profile of international commerce has been a shift from FDI concentrated in the primary sector and resource-based manufacturing to technology-intensive manufacturing and services. The expansion of FDI in technology-intensive manufacturing has occurred mainly in the newly industrializing countries, particularly in the electronics and informatics sectors. Technological change, meanwhile, has spurred FDI in services, revolutionizing many businesses including telecommunications, advertising, banking, insurance, transportation, retailing and tourism. From 1970–90, the services component grew from one-quarter of the stock of world FDI to nearly one-half, amounting to about 60 per cent of annual FDI flows. Finance and trade-related activities comprise the majority of investment in the service sector (UN, 1993, pp. 61–78).

Although FDI in services receives less public attention than trade in services (due primarily to discussion of the latter in the Uruguay Round of trade negotiations), international business in the services sector is more intimately related to investment processes than to merchandise trade. Direct consumer services generally require foreign investment to participate in the market (hotels, restaurants) and intermediate producer services may also demand a local presence for effective competition (insurance, consulting). International trends towards deregulation and privatization fuel FDI in services, permitting foreign corporations to compete in many business segments previously restricted to national (often governmental) monopolies. Industrial TNEs also invest heavily in service activities to support their own operations (Dunning, 1993, Chapter 10; Porter, 1990, Chapter 6).

Definitions of FDI vary considerably from nation to nation, making cumulative international analyses and cross-national comparisons difficult. Issues include whether to count reinvested earnings in FDI calculations and whether investments should be valued on an historical cost, current cost or market value basis. An important conceptual distinction is also drawn between direct and portfolio investment. The common, but not universal, definition considers at least 10 per cent ownership as direct investment, implying enough shareholding power to give the foreign investor some element of significant control or influence over corporate operations. Although this consideration is important for macromanagement policies and objectives, the aggregate expansion and potential volatility of other capital flows also significantly affect national and international options.

Reviewing the recent transformation in global finance, a survey in *The Economist* (19 September 1992) profiled some statistics that raise the question: 'has financial interdependence neutered economic policy-makers?':

- the US capital account balance swung from a net outflow of $2 billion in 1979–80 to a net inflow of $129 billion in 1985–88; Japan moved from a $5 billion inflow to a $75 billion outflow;
- international bank lending grew from $324 billion in 1980 to $7.5 trillion in 1991, expanding ten times faster than GDP in the OECD countries;
- US securities transactions with foreigners were equivalent to 9 per cent of GDP in 1980 but 93 per cent in 1990; similar growth occurred in Germany (8 per cent to 58 per cent) and Japan (7 per cent to 119 per cent).

Foreign exchange markets illustrate why the expansion and volatility of private international financial flows raise public macromanagement concerns. The trading volume on London's foreign exchange market expanded by 62 per cent from 1989 to 1992, exceeding $300 billion daily. The US market grew 49 per cent, reaching nearly $200 billion. Total world-wide currency trading is estimated at nearly $1 trillion daily. Such massive flows dwarf the size of government intervention in these markets, which averages $200 million daily (Dominguez and Frankel, 1993, p. 89). In foreign exchange crises, government intervention increases and the intervention's impact can be enhanced if seen as a signal of follow-on economic policy actions. Government resources are, however, limited, and the European Monetary System crises in September 1992 and July–August 1993 demonstrated the difficulties for public authorities of managing broad private market challenges to national, or even regionally coordinated, currencies.

New Strategies and Structures

Profiling TNE activity has been made more difficult by the expansion of non-traditional foreign investments. This category involves a range of low (or even non-equity) business ventures that may exhibit similar qualities and impacts as FDI, but without the same financial commitment and risk. These include arrangements such as franchising, subcontracting, financial or R&D consortia and professional partnerships. An associated development, driven by many of the same cost, technology and marketing factors, is the proliferation of international strategic alliances (Cowhey and Aronson, 1993; US Congress, 1993, Chapter 5). These ventures often mix and match the competitive resources of TNEs from different countries and regions, further confusing the national identities of products and enterprises.

It is becoming more difficult to describe a typical TNE using factors such as size, sector and organization, or even to generalize about a firm's country of origin, location of investment or national identity. The sheer number of these entities has grown enormously. TNE headquarters in major developed nations has more than tripled, from 7,000 in 1969 to nearly 24,000 in 1990. Using definitions based on FDI (and thereby excluding many low or non-equity investments and corporate alliance arrangements), the United Nations estimated in 1993 that a global total of 37,000 TNE parent enterprises control some 170,000 affiliates around the world (UN, 1993, p. 19).

The United States, United Kingdom, Japan, Germany and France account for over one-half of parent TNEs based in developed countries (90 per cent of all TNEs); these same five nations also play host to nearly one-half the developed countries' 46 per cent share of foreign affiliate locations (over 40 per cent of affiliates locate in developing countries, with the remainder in Central and Eastern Europe). Within this core five-nation group, however, specific TNE characteristics have changed. During the 1980s, the numbers and employment of US-based foreign affiliates dropped even as total investment grew; German TNEs increased their affiliate numbers and employment; and expanding Japanese FDI included a growing number of foreign affiliates from small and medium sized TNEs (UN, 1993, p. 22).

Industrial concentration is still relatively high, as the largest 100 non-financial TNEs (three-quarters of them based in the five major developed home countries), account for nearly one-third of world outward FDI stock. The majority of these TNEs are in the petroleum, automotive, chemical and pharmaceutical sectors, but such asset-based rankings are biased towards capital-intensive industries and may not reflect the general importance of TNE commercial activity in other business sectors (UN, 1993, pp. 23–8).

An important corollary finding about these 100 top-ranked TNEs is that their significance for the international economy, implied in the asset concentration figures, is more than matched by the international economy's importance for them. Foreign sales comprise one-half of these companies' total sales. This reliance on business outside the home country is echoed in other rankings that show similarly high proportions of sales and profits coming from commercial activities outside a TNE's base country. Other internationalization signs include the proportion of foreign employment, share ownership, and top management and board composition of major TNEs (Holstein *et al.*, 1990).

With each successive change, evolving TNE structures move further away from an early pattern in which single (principally US) parent corporations directed wholly owned foreign affiliates engaged principally in serving previously established export markets or securing production inputs. A desire for rationality and order, understanding and prediction, thus impels analysts to seek replacements for the original concept (Grosse and Behrman, 1992; Vernon, 1992). The variations are legion, often shaped by whether one begins research with an enterprise behaviour or public policy framework. Most observers recognize the interactive dynamic between these two perspectives, but disciplinary training or experience usually sets the initial approach, and it is admittedly difficult to develop research involving interactive causality. There is an ongoing debate over whether discernible market and public policy trends favour globalization, regionalization or fragmentation in TNE structures (Porter, 1986; Doz, 1987; Morrison and Roth, 1992).

Influenced heavily by the work of John Dunning, the concept of an emerging integrated international production system (IIPS) among TNEs offers a particularly useful bridge to these approaches. This concept grows out of the evolution of TNE strategies and structures from initial stand-alone (multi-domestic) operations to simple integration (outsourcing) to complex international production (with regional core networks). The complex IIPS involves those TNEs whose integrated global production, as well as trade in goods and services, organizes cross-border value-added activities through FDI and other control mechanisms. Governmental and intergovernmental policies influence this commercial coordination, but TNEs can also 'create new parameters for Governments and, in many instances, lead rather than follow Government actions' (UN, 1993, pp. 113–17).

The IIPS concept encompasses decentralization as well as centralization forces, both in terms of TNE organization and intergovernmental relationships. Competitive pressures can lead TNEs to disperse both decision-making and specific business functions to regional or national locales throughout their complex networks, thereby becoming more responsive to continuing differences in culture, economic conditions and governmental regulations. Flexible production technologies enable firms to fill market niches without suffering from loss of scale advantages. New communication technologies permit the higher degree of centralized coordination among business functions within a TNE network, necessary to achieve the deep integration of corporate activities that marks the IIPS. Within this environment, TNEs require innovative and flexible organization and human resource management approaches in order to compete (Bartlett and Ghoshal, 1987; Pucik, Tichy and Barnett, 1993).

DEFINING, DEFENDING AND DIRECTING NATIONAL POLITICAL ECONOMIES

Governments find themselves torn between continuing past policies favouring internationally open markets, working for regional economic integration, and coping with interests that traditionally favoured protectionism but now sometimes use international economic linkages to escape national control. The choices are related to issues about the evolving role of national and international regimes and how they relate to the TNE changes described in the previous section.

Political units are essentially territorial in nature; they define, defend and promote the interests of constituencies located within their specified boundaries. Nation-state systems define political sovereignty in relation to recognized physical borders, with only the most powerful states asserting extraterritorial rights that nonetheless often prove impractical or ineffective in implementation. The defence and promotion of constituent interests therefore constitute a national government's principal duty. Associated notions of national welfare are judged not just by security from external physical threats, but also by a citizenry's real and relative standard of living. Fostering economic prosperity thus becomes a major objective on any government's policy agenda, and measures of national economic growth and competitiveness serve as important indicators of government performance.

The determination of a national government's international economic role traditionally rested on two presumptions fundamental to the functioning of contemporary nation-states. The first was that welfare considerations should be measured at the level of the national territorial unit. The second was that national governments are both responsible for how international economic forces affect their citizens and are the main agents able to manage that impact. Both of these presumptions are being challenged as evolving TNE networks alter functions and structures within national political economies.

Measuring and Promoting National Welfare

Trade statistics offer a good illustration of the difficulty with territorial-based measurements of national economic well-being and competitiveness. The historical public policy debate revolved around whether national welfare is better served by export-oriented mercantilism seeking a favourable balance of trade, or consumer-oriented access to a variety of low-priced import goods that may result in a trade deficit. Alternative responses were to seek balanced trade or to adjust trade objectives to a nation's stage of economic development. Now the question as posed is less relevant because the basic territorial measure is losing its meaning (Julius, 1991).

The United States records massive trade deficits, the majority deriving from a bilateral imbalance with Japan: a fact that causes serious political friction between the two governments. However, Kenichi Ohmae argues that, '[T]he data that attract so much political attention are unreliable... The flows of economic activity measured by official trade statistics represent a tiny and steadily decreasing share of the economic linkages between the two nations' (Ohmae, 1994). This conclusion, largely correct, stems from changes in the composition of trade flows, as well as from the increased importance of FDI and offshore production.

Services and technology-intensive product exports are fast-growing segments of global trade and US exports, but they are undercounted because they are so different from the traditional manufactured goods and commodity exports on which trade statistics were based. For example, the US Commerce Department valued software exports in 1993 at $385 million, although Microsoft Corporation alone registered five times that amount in international sales. Official export statistics include the value of instruction manuals and blank discs but not the software program itself, meaning that a $300 sale may count for only $5 to $10 on the national trade ledger. Software exports alone may be $4 billion higher than recorded, while some estimates suggest that total US exports are undervalued by as much as 10 per cent – roughly the size of the trade deficit (Gleckman, 1994).

Expanded overseas production adds another difficult element to measuring national business competitiveness. Exports from affiliate operations based in third countries do not affect bilateral trade measures, such as Japanese purchases of US trademark sportswear sewn in Taiwan or semiconductor chips fabricated in Malaysia. These products may nonetheless be associated with the parent firm's home nation. Ohmae claims that, since the mid 1980s, Japanese consumers have bought at least four times as much per capita 'American' products than US consumers have purchased 'Japanese' products. He rejects traditional trade measures to assess bilateral relations, in part because trade balance results, 'are the result not of government policies but of strategic choices made by individual companies operating in the global marketplace' (Ohmae, 1994).

Attempts to include the broader international performance of US TNEs in a measure of US competitiveness yields results in striking contrast to the standard trade deficit. A National Academy of Sciences' calculation measured companies' total global sales, regardless of territorial production sites, and found that the 1991 US deficit of $28 billion would turn into a $164 billion surplus. A more conservative approach proposes counting the overseas profits of US TNEs as US exports, arguing that these funds will result in more US domestic investment and R&D. Under this measure the 1991 deficit would turn into a $24 billion surplus (Davis, 1994a). Problems exist with both alternatives, but the main argument is that trade balance statistics provide an incomplete and potentially very misleading picture of the competitiveness of a nation's enterprises – unless national enterprises are defined as only those firms producing fully within the nation's territorial borders (including, for example, the US affiliates of foreign TNEs but not the foreign affiliates of US firms). In short, national territorial borders and traditional trade measures no longer match well the transnational organization and operation of global business.

National and Enterprise Competitiveness

This new business reality lies behind two recent public policy debates. The first reached the popular media as a battle within the Clinton Administration regarding how to define and rank companies in terms of eligibility for government support. The key disagreement concerned whether to support the interests of US affiliates of foreign TNEs over foreign affiliates of US-based TNEs. Labour Secretary Robert Reich favoured promoting exports and high-skill jobs for workers in the United States regardless of a company's purported nationality. Chair of the Council of Economic Advisers Laura Tyson reportedly argued that US-based TNEs better serve US interests because they locate most key business functions in their home country (Davis, 1993; Bradsher, 1993). Of course, the real issue was neither so simple as portrayed in the media nor so narrow in its application to public policy.

Although related to the question of setting US government priorities, the second debate focuses on broader issues of how TNEs relate to the objectives and interests of national political economies. This debate came to a head in mid 1994 in a dispute carried in *Foreign Affairs* regarding the use of national 'competitiveness' measures to inform and guide public policy goals. Paul Krugman (1994a) challenged notions that the global economy has become so important that a nation's economic fortunes are determined by its competitiveness on world markets. He argued that such a belief fosters the concept of a zero-sum competition between nations, leading to wrong and even dangerous public policy decisions and actions. Lester Thurow, Stephen Cohen and others defend the utility of certain competitiveness measures and concepts, arguing that global commerce has moved beyond the reach of traditional comparative advantage theory and that, regardless of particular measures of international penetration of domestic economies, '[T]hose who don't compete abroad won't be productive at home' (Thurow, 1994).

Much of this second debate centres around problems of measurement, providing much evidence that traditional economic statistics are simply outdated and constitute unsatisfactory reflections of real-world business activity and its differential impact on national territories. Certainly this conclusion holds for the importance of simple trade balance figures, and the same appears true for the comparative application of productivity and value-added statistics between evolving business sectors and across international boundaries. However, while disagreement exists about which admittedly inadequate statistical measures to use in evaluating national economies, the critical part of the *Foreign Affairs* debate concerns whether and how to apply the competitiveness concept in the context of a national *political* economy. Cohen (1994) regards competitiveness as an organizing concept for a broad set of indicators, none of which is singularly satisfactory, while the interaction between them is not (yet?) explainable. Krugman (1994b) despairs of this economic imprecision, pointing out that the resulting ambiguity leaves a broad field for rhetorical use, and abuse, of competitiveness concepts in a policy debate.

The disagreements in *Foreign Affairs* regarding how TNEs relate to national political economies are related to the Clinton Administration's debate over how to treat US and foreign TNE affiliates. Companies compete in world markets, but does a TNE's nationality matter in determining the distributive territorial effects of its commercial activities? The answer to this question is important if the general results of global commerce are distributed in a zero-sum fashion among national economies. If so, then political leaders should perhaps also engage in the competition to secure the largest share of benefits for their citizens, and resulting policy interventions will attempt to discriminate in favour of national firms. If TNE nationality does not matter for distributional purposes, national politicians should be guided by selected measures of territorial economic impact (employment, exports, location of R&D), irrespective of the nationality of the business agents involved.

Both competitive options face practical difficulties. The evolution of transnational business, as discussed in the previous section, makes it increasingly difficult to distinguish the corporate entity involved in commercial activities, much less establish its national identity. However, measuring and valuing comparative economic impacts on national territories is just as difficult, partly because of interrelated effects of TNE business changes. The growing magnitude, complexity and importance of intrafirm TNE activities, added to the blurring effect of expanded international strategic alliances, makes it harder to discern and measure the national impacts of TNE operations.

SHIFTING POLITICAL BOUNDARIES

While global economic changes influence national political options regarding economic management, they also play a role in a more fundamental reorganization of national political economies. The nation-state is often taken as a given in examining the relationship between TNEs and national political economies. However, there is a significant reshaping of national systems, with internationalization, regionalization and decentralization trends all operating in response to interactive political and economic forces.

International Institutions and Agreements

Internationalization and regionalization both involve transferring some elements of political sovereignty to institutions larger than the nation-state. The concepts are also related in that regionalization may be seen as either an interim stage before broader internationalization or as a potential obstacle to its achievement. The basic explanation for both tendencies is that transnational economic activities are no longer susceptible to effective national control, and that attempts to promote unilateral national advantage, particularly in a competitive, zero-sum fashion, will be self-defeating and will jeopardize international welfare.

Promoters of internationalization urge greater authority for multilateral economic organizations. Ratification of the Uruguay Round Trade Agreement, replacing the General Agreement on Tariffs and Trade (GATT) with a World Trade Organization (WTO), is in line with this approach. The WTO will incorporate a broader range of economic activities (trade in services, intellectual property rights, trade-related investment rules) while strengthening its multilateral decision-making processes. Much domestic US opposition to the pact springs from charges that US sovereignty will be lost when the nation can no longer veto the findings of a multilateral trade panel, even though the enforcement mechanism will remain the same as the process used by GATT to sanction national retaliation for an uncompensated violation of trade rules.

Diminished national powers over transnational economic events appear to justify additional forms of international cooperation and coordination. The October 1987 crash of world stock markets highlighted the close interconnections between global financial centres where enormous unregulated flows of private capital move constantly around the world, 24 hours a day. The Bank of Credit and Commerce International, whose scandal-ridden collapse reportedly affected 1.3 million people world-wide, provided further evidence of the limited reach of national regulatory authorities. This crisis overwhelmed national regulators faced with a banking network that employed 14,000 individuals from 83 nationalities in more than 400 offices spread across 73 countries (Kline, 1992a).

Global environmental problems with the production and use of chlorofluorocarbons (CFCs), transfer-pricing techniques used by TNEs to avoid national taxation or escape exchange controls, and instances of both economic and social 'dumping' across international boundaries, all point to the need for a greater internationalization of political authority in order to catch up with the globalization of TNE operations. However, this is made difficult by the reluctance of national authorities to give up elements of sovereignty to international institutions that lie beyond their control. In certain cases, regionalization appears to offer a more immediately practical and potentially safer solution, ceding selected elements of sovereignty to more known geographic neighbours.

The Triad's Regional Blocs

Regional alignments can both promote and respond to increased economic integration. The European Union (EU) represents the most advanced regional arrangement, dating from the Treaty of Rome in 1957. In this case, early policy initiatives created a Common Market encouraging intraregional trade and some integrated production activity, which in turn showed the need for a Single Market initiate to encourage greater investment and a deeper integration of business activity (UN, 1992, pp. 35–40). Although economic integration is still not complete, and political integration lags well behind, member states have ceded significant sovereignty, particularly over international and increasingly over national economic processes, to EU institutions.

A far more limited initiative in 1965 promoted trade integration between the United States and Canada in automotive products. The 1989 bilateral Free Trade Agreement and the subsequent trilateral North America Free Trade Area (NAFTA), incorporating Mexico, were arguably more a response to economic integration already being fostered by TNE activity. The agreements promote further integration and break new ground in covering some items related to trade in services, intellectual property rights and investment issues. Further policy initiatives in the Asian Pacific region may also be required to respond and potentially reinforce economic interdependencies being led by TNE-related business activities (Boyd, 1993).

These policy developments in the so-called 'Triad' regions parallel certain investment-based regional organization patterns formed by large TNEs (UN, 1991). Whether TNE activity leads or responds to regional integration policies (or both), the implications for national political economies are significant. Although few analysts predict that national governments in other regions will soon match the level of political integration attained by the EU, deeper economic integration inevitably leads member states into coordinated or cooperative activities that have notable political implications. For example, having committed itself to NAFTA, the United States was quick to provide Mexico with standby financial reserves when the Chiapas rebellion and the assassination of a leading Presidential candidate threatened to unleash international financial pressures that might undermine Mexico's economy and further destabilize its political situation (Mathews and Behr, 1994).

Regionalization, however, could produce a future world economy organized and led by three powerful blocs dominated by Northern hemisphere industrialized countries. Although nations in Latin America are also signing many – sometimes overlapping – trade agreements, most are probably more anxious to align with NAFTA than with Southern hemisphere neighbours. The principal unresolved debate over regionalization concerns whether the major blocs will adopt restrictive or exclusionary policies to promote their own competitive advantage, or utilize their regional policy harmonization to build a more cooperative global economy that encourages transregional integration (UN, 1992, pp. 44–5).

Drifts Towards Decentralization

While most eyes are focused on analysing whether global economic developments might lead to enhanced regional or international economic policy-making, some evidence points towards a decentralization of national authority either through political fragmentation or a conscious devolution of governance responsibilities. The 1990s ushered in a broad reorganization of nation-state power in the wake of the Soviet Union's dissolution. As political and sometimes territorial boundaries are redrawn into smaller units across Central and Eastern Europe, economic considerations weigh heavily in calculations regarding the practical dimensions of national sovereignty. Newly independent or reorganized states that can establish effective links to global markets, or even to the regional economies of Western Europe, will be better able to sustain their practical political sovereignty.

The importance of international economic integration to small nation-states can be seen in the case of Singapore. One of the fast-growing Asian 'tigers', this nation could not sustain its economic success, nor perhaps long maintain its practical political independence, without an open international economic system. An open global economy can similarly encourage political fragmentation by sustaining the separatist dreams of potential break-away regions that would not be economically viable on their own. For example, the separatist ambitions of Tamil activists reportedly rely on plans to build a free trade zone around Trincomalee harbour to provide essential ties to the world economy that could sustain an independent Tamil state in northern Sri Lanka (Davis, 1994b).

Even regional integration does not always develop along the lines of preexisting national territorial borders or only within the parameters of nation-state agreements. Practical economic integration proceeded along the US–Canada and even US–Mexico borders, often with joint institutions involving state and provincial governments, long before national authorities negotiated the NAFTA agreement (Brown and Fry, 1993). For many citizens of Quebec, the assumed ability to negotiate access to NAFTA and maintain other international economic links nurtures their ambitions for political independence from Canada. Provinces in western Canada, more economically integrated with north-western US states than with eastern Canadian provinces, are also becoming attracted to further political decentralization, or even independence, if Canadian national leaders move too far to appease Quebec's desire for greater autonomy.

Global and regional economic pressures may also lead to decentralization in the form of a devolution of governance responsibilities when national governments are perceived to be less capable of protecting or promoting the economic interests of particular constituent regions. These tendencies are most evident in federalist systems where the forces of global interdependence penetrate domestic boundaries and overlap significant powers exercised by subnational governments (Hocking, 1993; Duchacek, 1986).

In the United States, state and local governments now operate foreign offices, promote exports, attract and regulate FDI, and participate actively in policy-making on international economic issues. This involvement can generate international disputes such as the controversy over state use of unitary taxation methods (Kline, 1992b). The GATT trade talks even produced a government procurement agreement that permits US states to decide individually whether or not to subscribe to the code, effectively giving them as much, if not more, effective power as national governments for whom the code is binding (Kline, 1994).

These changes all suggest that governance in the nation-state political units long responsible for shaping the international system are not so static and stable as might be assumed. In assessing the relationship between TNEs and national political economies, one should therefore take into account possible changes in national political units as internationalization, regionalization and decentralization pressures all play out simultaneously on these entities. In the interactive dynamic set in motion by the mismatch between transnational economic processes and national policies, both political and business players may be reshaped.

GOVERNMENT POLICY ISSUES

Five types of policy issue for governments arise from the national political and TNE restructuring changes outlined above. The first set of issues relates to the basic question of whether and how national governments compete against each other, with discriminatory treatment of non-national enterprises. Since it is impossible to aid 'us' but not 'them' without knowing who 'we' are (Reich, 1990), governments need to establish definitions for corporate nationality that can sort through increasingly complicated TNE networks. Simple ownership criteria will not guarantee any certain territorial division of business benefits. When governments commit fiscal resources to promote national business competitiveness, political pressures will mount to attach restrictions mandating that employment, revenue, technology or other benefits accrue to the sponsoring country. These restrictions will, of course, limit corporate flexibility to utilize cost-effective combinations of global resources, perhaps thereby negating the competitive advantage being sought.

Closely associated with the task of formulating workable TNE nationality definitions is the challenge of applying reciprocity standards. Reciprocity can be used to grant conditional national treatment to enterprises from nations that treat your own enterprises in a similar fashion. However, where national economic or business systems differ, reciprocal treatment can be difficult to define. The tendency is therefore to look at results rather than treatment, but this approach raises measurement problems and issues about expected effects; that is, should equal treatment yield equal results? These difficulties are already evident in administering the US–Japan semiconductor accord that provides for fair treatment and reciprocal market access. Governments will inevitably begin estimating what free market forces would produce in the absence of systemic distortions or other market failures, leading perhaps to market share allocation by government fiat.

The second policy category encompasses distributive concerns about how TNEs affect key economic objectives, particularly growth, employment, national revenue, the balance of payments and technology enhancement. These concerns are linked with the questions about national competitiveness, and an important related issue involves managing necessary trade-offs among policy goals. For example, promoting advanced technologies may lead to reduced employment, or at least employee retraining and readjustment requirements. National policies seeking increased tax revenue can adversely affect employment and technological innovation, depending on how the policies influence a TNE's options to shift production and R&D activities. The expansion of FDI and transnational business networks increases the capacity to shift TNE operations in response to national policy changes. Hence governmental choices must reflect a deeper understanding of TNE strategies and options as they relate to potential trade-offs between public policy objectives.

Competition policy is a third major issue that merits special attention (Graham, 1993; Hay, 1993; Jorde and Teece, 1992). The evolution of TNE organizational patterns involves consolidation in major industrial sectors and the development of broad intercorporate arrangements, including many among rival firms, that offer collusive potential. Transnational enterprises compete and cooperate among themselves. National competition policies differ among countries in orientation and especially in enforcement. Privatization and deregulation trends around the world offer new opportunities for progress in formulating common standards and working towards cooperative actions in this area. Such initiatives would also help address international problems stemming from national structural differences, such as the effects of Japan's *keiretsu* system. Without prompt and substantial progress, national authorities may soon find themselves lagging too far behind to influence significantly the shape and competitive implications of TNE strategic alliances.

The fourth policy area includes other significant issues where coordinated action beyond national borders is a requirement, rather than an option, if regulation is to be effective. For example, improved international coordination is necessary to manage interconnected global financial markets, as information disclosure, conflict of interest, and trader responsibilities standards differ widely. The growth in international grey market goods also raises significant policy issues relating not only to compensation for property rights, but also regarding product safety standards. Global environmental issues present still more challenges because effective action cannot be confined by national territorial borders: problems such as air and water pollution do not respect these political boundaries.

A final set of issues covers the interactive effects between evolving TNE business patterns and the changing relationships between international, regional, national and subnational political units. Polities and TNEs are both becoming more diverse, changeable, and harder to identify and relate to one another through the use of traditional classification systems and organizational grids. Associated with the problem of systemic analysis is the normative issue that most developing countries could be relegated to the far periphery of an integrated world economy built by TNEs and governments in the developed Triad region. The majority of world citizens could also be left economically disenfranchised if international institutions are dominated by competitive rivalries between rich countries seeking only further self-aggrandizement.

CONCLUSION

Transformations in transnational business may lead national governments beyond their territorially bounded jurisdictions and ambitions into designing expanded roles for adaptive international cooperation. International corporate alliances point towards ways in which rival entities may both compete and cooperate to their mutual advantage, and hopefully to the advantage of all if their actions are restrained by accepted competition policies (Cowhey and Aronson, 1993), Governments must still work to avoid potentially destructive competition in economic management by matching it with cooperation in the management of interdependencies that result from TNE operations and other international commercial activity.

Ongoing TNE changes may soon make transnational business processes too complicated to sort out national identities in the manner needed to foster nation-state competition in a zero-sum game. Cooperation may become not only the normatively better choice, but the default option as well. However, the concluding chapter to this story is far from written. Government policies and TNE strategies interact, with each influencing future options for the other. The best efforts of all parties are required to meet the macromanagement challenges presented by the still evolving relationship between TNEs and national political economies.

BIBLIOGRAPHY

Bartlett, Christopher and Sumantra Ghoshal (1987), 'Managing across Borders: New Organizational Responses', *Sloan Management Review*, **28** (4), Fall, 43–53.
Boyd, G. (1993), *Corporate Planning and Policy Planning in the Pacific*, London: Pinter Publishers.
Bradsher, Keith (1993), 'In Shift, White House will Stress Aiding Foreign Concerns in US', *New York Times*, 2 June, p. 1.
Brown, Douglas and Earl Fry (eds) (1993), *States and Provinces in the International Economy*, Berkeley: Institute of Government Studies Press.
Cohen, Stephen (1994), 'The Fight over Competitiveness', *Foreign Affairs*, 73 (4), July/August, 194–7.

Cowhey, Peter and Jonathan Aronson (1993), *Managing the World Economy*, New York: Council on Foreign Relations Press.

Davis, Bob (1993), 'Clinton Aides Grapple with Definition of a US Company in a Global Economy', *Wall Street Journal*, 2 July, p. A1.

Davis, Bob (1994a), 'World-Trade Statistics Tell Conflicting Stories', *Wall Street Journal*, 18 July, p. A1.

Davis, Bob (1994b), 'Growth of Trade Binds Nations, but it also can Spur Separatism', *Wall Street Journal*, 20 June, p. A1.

Dominguez, Kathryn and Jeffrey Frankel (1993), *Does Foreign Exchange Intervention Work?*, Washington D.C.: Institute for International Economics.

Doz, Yves (1987), 'International Industries: Fragmentation versus Globalization' in Bruce Guile and Harvey Brooks (eds), *Technology and Global Industry: Companies in the World Economy*, Washington D.C.: National Academy Press, pp. 96–118.

Duchacek, I. (1986), *The Territorial Dimension of Politics Within, Among, and Across Nations*, Colorado: Westview Press, Inc.

Dunning, J. (1993), *The Globalization of Business*, New York: Routledge

Gleckman, Howard (1994), 'Uncle Sam's Stats: Call them Unreliable', *Business Week*, 18 July p. 40.

Graham, Edward (1993), 'Multinationals and Competition Policy', *International Economic Insights*, 4 (4), July/August, 26–8.

Grosse, Robert and Jack Behrman (1992), 'Theory in International Relations', *Transnational Corporations*, 1 (1), February.

Hay, Donald (1993), 'The Assessment: Competition Policy', *Oxford Review of Economic Policy*, 9 (2), Summer, 1–26.

Hocking, B. (ed.) (1993), *Foreign Relations and Federal States*, London and New York: Leicester University Press.

Holstein, William, Stanley Ree, Jonathan Kapstein, Todd Vogel and Joseph Weber (1990), 'The Stateless Corporation', *Business Week*, 14 May, pp. 98–105.

Jorde, Thomas and David Teece (eds) (1992), *Antitrust, Innovation, and Competitiveness*, New York: Oxford University Press.

Julius, D. (1991), *Foreign Direct Investment: The Neglected Twin of Trade*, Washington, D.C.: Group of Thirty.

Kline, John M. (1992a), Testimony before the Joint Economic Committee, Congress of the United States, 13 May.

Kline, John M. (1992b), 'Negotiating Limits on Unitary Taxation in the United States', published by The Pew Charitable Trust, Institute for the Study of Diplomacy, Georgetown University.

Kline, John M. (1994), 'State (and Local) Boundary-Spanning Strategies: Political, Economic and Cultural Transgovernmental Interactions'. Paper presented to conference on Centralization in Japan and in the United States: Reinventing Intergovernmental Relations in an Era of Increased Internationalization, Washington D.C., August.

Krugman, Paul (1994a), 'Competitiveness: A Dangerous Obsession', *Foreign Affairs*, 73 (2), March/April, 28–44.

Krugman, Paul (1994b), 'The Fight over Competitiveness', *Foreign Affairs*, 73 (4), July/August, 198–203.

Mathews, Jay and Peter Behr (1994), 'Investors Hopeful on Mexico', *Washington Post*, 25 March, p. B1.

Morrison, Allen and Kendell Roth (1992), 'The Regional Solution: An Alternative to Globalization', *Transnational Corporations*, 1 (2), August, 37–55.

Ohmae, Kenichi (1994), 'US–Japan: Counting What Counts', *Wall Street Journal*, 22 March, p. A14.

Porter, M. (ed.) (1986), *Competition in Global Industries*, Boston: Harvard University School Press.

Porter, M. (1990), *The Competitive Advantages of Nations*, New York: The Free Press.

Pucik, Vladimir, Noel Tichy and Carole Barnett (eds) (1993), *Globalizing Management*, New York: John Wiley & Sons, Inc.

Reich, Robert (1990), 'Who Is Us?', *Harvard Business Review*, **68** (1), January/February, 53–64.

'Survey of the World Economy', *The Economist*, 19 September 1992, pp. 5–48.

Sweeney, Richard (1994), 'Does the Foreign-Exchange Market Beat the Fed?', unpublished article, Georgetown University.

Thurow, Lester (1994), 'The Fight over Competitiveness', *Foreign Affairs*, **73** (4), July/August, 189–92.

US Congress, Office of Technology Assessment (1993), *Multinationals and the National Interest: Playing by Different Rules*, Washington, D.C.: US Government Printing Office.

United Nations (1991), *World Investment Report: The Triad in Foreign Direct Investment*, New York: United Nations.

United Nations (1992), *World Investment Report: Transnational Corporations as Engines of Growth*, New York: United Nations.

United Nations (1993), *World Investment Report: Transnational Corporations and Integrated International Production*, New York: United Nations.

Vernon, Raymond (1992), 'Transnational Corporations: Where Are They Coming From, Where Are They Headed?', *Transnational Corporations*, **1** (2), August, 7–35.

2. Policy environments for corporate planning

Gavin Boyd

In the major industrialized democracies which dominate the world economy, the strategies of national and transnational corporations are influenced by diverse policy mixes with macro and micro objectives, implemented in the public interest and in the interests of vital support groups. Corporate decision-makers are especially conscious of the tax and regulatory measures, the trade promotion and industrial endeavours, and the fiscal, monetary and financial policies that affect overall growth, inflation and the availability of capital. All these, with infrastructure improvements or neglect, affect information flows and costs, production costs, transaction costs and incentives to produce at home or abroad, as well as to engage in rent-seeking or productive activity. Balances between competitive and cooperative business strategies are also affected, especially through government measures affirming or denying values that strengthen or weaken the normative dimension of a political economy. Meanwhile, phases in political business cycles are altered, necessitating adjustments in forecasting for strategic planning.

Changes in policy and policy-induced changes interact with market-induced changes in the operational environments of firms, and this is an extensive transnational process. Markets, with their efficiencies and failures, are being internationalized by high volume trade and multinational production, and policy mixes have external reaches through specific and more general effects on the activities of national and foreign firms. Corporate managements, seeking to expand their shares of markets which they are linking, respond to the opportunities and problems of the policy- and market-induced changes to which they contribute. Their production and trading activities alter the structures of national economies and the interdependencies between those structures, thereby affecting the growth and employment objectives of governments. A national administration can be increasingly advantaged if it receives substantial cooperation from firms with strong home country loyalties. Quests to exploit opportunities in world markets, however, tend to weaken the home country ties of corporate managements. As they expand their global operations they acquire greater flexibility in the choice of production ventures and locations; they increase their knowledge of world markets; they enter into multiple strategic partnerships; and they are able to bargain more effectively with their own and foreign governments to secure subsidies, favourable tax treatment and trade concessions.

The concerns of governments with growth and employment tend to become more active as elements of economic sovereignty are lost to firms that are increasingly free to pursue their own objectives and extract favours. Entrepreneurial collaboration with industrial, trade, competition and foreign direct investment policies becomes more necessary for the development of orderly diversified interdependent national economies. Administrations compete for the necessary entrepreneurial cooperation through efforts to provide superior business environments and through microeconomic measures intended to enhance national location advantages.[1] This policy competition can entail major costs for governments in states with weaker structural competitiveness whose business environments are not attractive.

The competition for corporate cooperation benefits from rivalries between firms, but these rivalries (which are changing the markets that are being linked) are leading to general increases in global oligopoly power as weaker enterprises are forced into decline. The growth of this power is facilitated by the failure of major states to cooperate for the development of international competition policies. Increases in this power are aided more and more by applications of new technology, the financing of which becomes more and more feasible for the oligopolistic firms because of their large resources.[2] In the global corporate rivalry, however, patterns of collaboration between enterprises based on long-term commitments can ensure advantages over larger firms colluding at arm's length for market domination. This has been demonstrated by the Japanese industry groups. Their international market gains have, moreover, evidenced the extent to which national economic policies can be aided by the highly motivated cooperation of an integrated intercorporate system.[3]

Domestic competition for office contributes to the policy competition between governments as they seek to increase growth and employment by acquiring greater direct or indirect influence over the activities of firms. Governments tend to be held increasingly accountable, by voters, for trends in overall economic conditions. Popular beliefs in the efficiency and equity effects of markets tend to decline as foreign import penetration grows, dependence on exports increases, and major externalities are caused by firms shifting their operations to overseas bases. Confidence in market justice diminishes as market processes become internationalized, and justifications are seen for administrative guidance or interventions in the public interest. Effective governmental market involvement, moreover, is seen to require measures countering (if not overwhelming) the rival economic policies of other national administrations. The political fortunes of governments can thus depend on their displays of zealous economic nationalism in pre-election phases of national business cycles.

The national policy environments influencing corporate decision-making reflect asymmetries in policy competition. Some governments are disadvantaged by weak cooperation from their business communities and weak vitality in those communities. Some governments are also disadvantaged by their own macromanagement failures, especially where these result in unsustainable fiscal expansion. Administrations experiencing these or other problems of governance may be unable to make corrective adjustments, but nevertheless may have strong bargaining leverage because of the size of their economies. This leverage can be used to externalize the costs of macromanagement deficiencies, for example through the extraction of trade concessions from smaller and weaker states.[4]

DIVERSITY IN POLICY ENVIRONMENTS

Policy mixes in the major industrialized democracies are shaped, in differing policy styles, by domestic and external factors which interact in conditions of high, complex, asymmetric structural and policy interdependence. The policy styles, reflecting leadership orientations and capabilities, tend to be consensual or conflicted, and holistically rational or reactive, experimental and disjointed. The cumulative effects of continuities and discontinuities in these styles result in differing degrees of integration in each national political economy – in elite consensus, in solidarity within the system of intercorporate relations, and in the alignment of corporate strategies with the administration's policies. The pressures of global market rivalries and of policy competition by other governments, together with internal rivalries for office, oblige each national administration to optimize the management of its economy, for increasing structural competitiveness. Efforts are made to promote the development of balanced, integrated, high growth national economies, capable of increasingly effective involvement in the international trading, production and financial systems. Emphasis has to be placed on encouraging and supporting higher technology specializations under innovative entrepreneurship. Assertions of economic sovereignty become necessary, in cooperation with national firms, to influence if not control external trade and production linkages, so as to maximize their benefits while limiting their vulnerabilities and costs.

The basic contrasts in policy styles tend to be expressed in system-building effects. Consensual and rational decision processes are generally oriented towards building an integrated political economy, through relational collaboration between the administration and national firms, making the state a nexus of informal contracts which sustain the home country attachments of firms. Conflicted and reactive policy styles are less functionally oriented in line with systemic requirements for competitiveness. The individualistic cultures which activate such decision processes obligate administrative aloofness to allow wide scope for market forces. Less integrated political economies thus result from proliferating forms of competition, with little cooperation in the patterns of intercorporate relations.[5] Groups contending for control of the administration moreover tend to become capable of manipulating policy to advance economic interests, while causing policy processes to become further conflicted. Problems of governance resulting from conflicted and reactive policy styles thus tend to be perpetuated. Successes in macromanagement made possible by more consensual and rational decision processes, however, help to prevent the emergence of problems of governance.

Rather comprehensively functional policy mixes tend to result from consensual and rational policy processes. A very important feature of these policy mixes, as has been evident in Germany and Japan, is allocative discipline, made possible by elite commitments to the public interest that restrict politically motivated uses of state resources to secure sectoral or community support. This allocative discipline contributes to economic stability, holds down the costs of government and facilitates long-term corporate planning. Expressing administrative interest in extensive informal cooperation with the business community, these policy mixes activate wide-ranging consultative relationships with managements that open the way for concerted entrepreneurship, with assurances of cooperative adaptation to any adverse trends in foreign markets.[6]

Conflicted and reactive policy styles tend, however, to produce inconsistent policy mixes with inadequate allocative discipline. The lack of such discipline typically necessitates monetary tightening to control the inflationary pressures of fiscal expansion; this, together with the rising costs of government, limits growth, adversely affects the international competitiveness of exporting firms, and encourages firms to produce abroad rather than in the home economy. Industrial measures to enhance the competitiveness of exporting firms tend to be flawed because of the leverage of sectoral interests. Uncertainties about the evolution of these policy mixes moreover discourage long-term corporate planning. Meanwhile major firms managing their operations very independently often disrupt sectors and communities by relocating production activities in order to rationalize their global strategies.

The dysfunctional effects of a conflicted and reactive policy style are evident principally in the USA. Irresponsible legislative assertions of constituency interests in the system of divided government necessitate extensive compromises, in excess of available resources, to make possible budget enactment. Heavy deficit spending during the first half of the 1980s, with sharp currency appreciation caused by monetary tightening, was followed by large, rapid increases in foreign production by US firms for home and other markets.[7] Large trade imbalances resulted from this, from losses in world markets by US exporting firms and from surges of imports from Japan which, like the increased foreign sourcing by US enterprises, responded to the strong consumer demand caused by the heavy fiscal deficits. Recoveries of international competitiveness by US firms manufacturing in the home economy for export have been difficult, despite currency depreciation since the mid 1980s, and production abroad by American enterprises has been growing very much larger than US exports. Adverse balances of payments, resulting mainly from imbalances in merchandise trade, have tended to cause further currency depreciation, that is, in conjunction with the inflationary effects of the large fiscal deficits. Uncertainties about the future of the US economy, moreover, attributable to the unfavourable fiscal outlook and to weaknesses in the nation's financial institutions, have contributed to the currency depreciation, and have provided additional incentives for US manufacturing firms to expand their international production operations.[8]

Complex asymmetries in policy interdependence were altered by the sequences associated with the dysfunctional trend in the US policy mix. Within the USA there were pressures to externalize the costs of adjustment by securing German and Japanese commitments to fiscal expansion, and applying market-opening leverage against Japan. US government endeavours to induce German and Japanese policy changes caused decision-makers in those countries to identify more firmly with the rationales of their functionally superior policy mixes, which were ensuring greater structural competitiveness. These policy mixes were characterized by allocative discipline and the ordering of industrial, trade, foreign direct investment, competition and financial policies towards the support of vigorous foreign market penetration by national firms. The most functional mix was Japan's, which was primarily a consequence of potent synergistic interaction between technocratic authorities and a dynamic integrated intercorporate system.[9] The efficiency effects of this mix were, however, weakened by high volume property speculation that led to a recession in the early 1990s, and were subsequently threatened by cabinet instability. Nevertheless Japan's capacity to cope with US market-opening leverage remained strong because of American dependence on Japanese purchases of US government debt, and growing competition between American states to attract Japanese direct investment.

The German policy mix, more broadly consensual than Japan's, especially because of a well-institutionalized advisory system, was not adversely affected by any regulatory failures, but was implemented with less synergistic interaction between technocrats and the national intercorporate system. This system was less integrated than its counterpart in Japan, and somewhat less dynamic, due partly to the conservative influence of German banks as major participants in the ownership and management of manufacturing firms. Through the early 1990s the policy mix had to cope with the heavy costs of rehabilitating the former East German economy, and the necessary fiscal expansion had to be countered by strong monetary tightening, although this drastically slowed growth in the home economy and throughout the European Union.[10] High German interest rates drew substantial capital flows out of the USA, and these, together with large and rising volumes of US investment in Asian, European and Latin American equity markets, contributed to a slackening of growth in the USA – that is, in conjunction with slack demand in Europe which affected US exports. In interactions with the USA over fiscal and monetary issues, however, Germany had potent bargaining strength as the dominant member of the economically more integrated European Union, which was adding new members and which was able to assert its interests forcefully in confrontations with the USA during the final stages of the Uruguay Round.

The recent history of the American, Japanese and German policy mixes has thus demonstrated how the system-building effects of these mixes are critical for structural competitiveness and for bargaining strength in dealings over market access and the coordination of economic policies. The spread of gains from international trade and production tends to become less favourable for a liberal political economy in which conflicted and reactive policy-making in effect encourages very independent and almost totally competitive behaviour by the enterprises constituting its fragmented intercorporate system.[11] For the liberal political economy, rivalry becomes more difficult with more integrated states whose firms collaborate extensively to concert their operations, in line with the functional policies of their governments, for collective increases in world market shares. Problems of governance in the liberal political economy can then be aggravated, especially because of internal conflicts over methods of adjustment, which can be very divisive due to the accumulating costs of fiscal laxity as well as adverse balances of payments. The rising levels of the adjustment costs, moreover, can meanwhile further reduce structural competitiveness, as well as national and foreign business confidence.

The more integrated states, engaged in more successful competition for world markets, have incentives to maintain the system-building effects of their policies, for domestic political benefit and to achieve further external advantages. Through acquiring stronger positions in the global economy, moreover, they can manage more effectively adversarial trade and investment interactions with the liberal political economies. The internal system-building is aided by broad elite consensus on basic principles of macromanagement, and stronger institutional development (in business associations and in each legislature) ensures functional aggregations of interests. Fiscal discipline is thus sustained, and the home country loyalties of national firms tend to be retained, especially because many of these in the higher technology sectors form dynamic innovative clusters. These become bases for participation in international strategic alliances, often entailing collaboration with firms based in liberal political economies. Such firms, despite large size and resources, can be disadvantaged by the lack of supportive relational contracting in the fragmented intercorporate systems of their home economies.

FISCAL, MONETARY AND FINANCIAL POLICIES

A primary imperative in a policy mix is allocative discipline, in the public interest, that can make the costs of government reasonable for producers and consumers, with reference to the provision of administrative goods and services. Unrestrained, unprincipled value free competition for office can lead to unsustainable neglect of this imperative. In political economy terms, voters have to cope with risks of opportunism, moral hazard and adverse selection when choosing representatives for office, because of information problems: these can be high in a liberal political economy if its aggressive individualism is expressed in the manipulation of information and in institutional manipulation, perpetuating generally low levels of authentic accountability and appraisal. The risks for voters are lower in a more integrated, high trust political economy with a record of fiscal discipline and institutionally more developed organizations for the representation of interests.

With the increasing growth of structural interdependencies, the macro-economic measures of the major industrialized democracies have been inter-acting, directly and indirectly, exhibiting much asymmetrically reciprocal causality, while the domestic sources of these measures have operated according to the dynamics of distinctive policy styles. In the evolving pattern, competitive pressures have in some respects activated a logic of convergence, resulting in considerable awareness of imperatives for fiscal restraint. A very prominent destabilizing feature of the pattern has, however, been the unsustainable fiscal expansion in the USA, which has been partially obscured by inaccurate official estimates.[12] Because of high levels of speculation in the economy as a whole and stresses in its financial sector, as well as because of the migration of industry to which it contributes and the uncertainties affecting the international role of the dollar, unsustainable deficit spending tends to increase the risk of a financial crisis.[13] This would be felt throughout the global economy, and would be difficult to overcome through large increases in the money supply (as was done in 1987) as there would be a greater flight of capital since financial markets are now more internationalized.

Fiscal discipline is politically difficult to achieve in the USA. This acute problem of governance has to be stressed because it activates vicious circles in which the negative effects on growth virtually obligate increases in the deficits. Debt service charges rise, investments are drawn away from productive use, higher interest rates affect the funding of industry and consumer demand, tax burdens reduce the international competitiveness of US exporting firms, foreign sourcing becomes more profitable for US enterprises, and slack growth necessitates higher welfare payments. The gravity of the problem appears to be evident to many in the business elite, and it evidently tends to increase emphasis on working for short-term profits as well as on risk reduction through the use of opportunities for expansion into global operations. Total US government debt rose from 34.34 per cent of GNP in 1980 to 61.56 per cent in 1990.[14]

Monetary restraint, to overcome the inflationary effects of heavy deficit spending, is the responsibility of the Federal Reserve. Although the formally independent monetary authority, it is subjected to criticisms and demands from Congress, the administration, the financial sector and manufacturing interests. Its record suggests shifting emphasis between tacit acceptance of a 'natural' rate of unemployment, as a restraint on wage costs, and obligations to respond to popular hopes for higher growth with lower interest rates. The shifting emphasis occurs with lags after changing conditions that provide rationales for the switches, but these are also affected by fluctuations in the international role of the dollar, influenced by alterations in balance-of-payments deficits which activate speculative exploitations of volatility in financial markets. The Treasury, as the executive agency primarily responsible for exchange rate policy, has to cope with Federal Reserve decisions on monetary loosening and tightening, and with the volatility in world financial markets, as well as with the strains in the US financial sector. The options available regarding interventions in those markets and the use of persuasion in informal dealings with the Federal Reserve are limited, because of the imperatives for inflation control and for the maintenance of foreign confidence in the dollar, but also for increased growth in the home economy and improved US competitiveness.[15]

Financial policy is set basically by legislative enactments of regulatory principles and assignments of regulatory authority. Built-in conflicts tend to result because of opposing and diverging financial sector interests which influence diverse groups of legislators.[16] Regulatory failings are therefore possible, and over the past decade and a half have contributed to a grave deterioration in the health of numerous banks and savings and loan associations.[17] Unresolved regulatory issues related to the pressures for competitiveness in world financial markets have, moreover, affected the efficiency of banks under sound management, and have tended to intensify the interests of those managements in opportunities for foreign rather than domestic operations.

The availability and cost of capital for American industry has been affected by the weaknesses in the financial sector, while the interest of financial institutions in short-term returns – approaching those from investments in higher growth East Asian countries or higher interest European countries – has evidently tended to reinforce the short-term orientations of managements in US manufacturing enterprises. American international manufacturing firms with extensive overseas operations have, however, been less affected than corporations operating entirely in the home economy, because of wider access to sources of funding and the realization of higher overall profits. The factors limiting the choices open to firms operating only in the home economy are significant because, while equity financing is very common, there are tax incentives to use debt financing, as well as related incentives to limit dependence on equity financing by mutual and pension funds. Reliance on debt financing, however, has to cope with volatility in interest rates, and this reinforces the common emphasis on achieving short-term returns. This emphasis, it must be stressed, causes financial management to be given high priority, with diversions of entrepreneurial energies in manufacturing firms away from the management of production functions.[18]

Altogether, linkages between the effects of US fiscal, monetary and financial policies contribute to the evolution of an environment that strains entrepreneurial capabilities, making success depend more and more on aggressive competition while coping with the results of governmental mismanagement. Commitments to this aggressive competition tend to make its pressures more intense, and these pressures are also strengthened by the growing internationalization of the home market and of the foreign markets in which US firms are operating. As Japanese transnational enterprises are especially active in all that market-linking, the external consequences of their home policy environment become evident within the context of the US economy – more so than in any other industrialized democracy.

Japan's fiscal, monetary and financial policies constitute a functional mix, because of substantially rational decision-making based on synergistic technocratic interaction with an integrated intercorporate system. Fiscal discipline is maintained by the dedicated officials of the powerful Finance Ministry, which functions with strong authority that has been accepted by elite consensus over the past five decades. Growth-facilitating infrastructure development and administrative services are provided at moderate cost, making corporate tax burdens relatively light, while government health and welfare costs are limited by extensive managerial paternalism. Monetary policy continues a tradition of moderate restraint, seeking to limit currency appreciation caused by balance-of-payments surpluses. Strong administrative influence on the financial sector is maintained, despite a deregulating trend which has facilitated large-scale involvement by Japanese banks in global financial markets. There is a very active tacit concern to maintain informal restrictions on foreign entries into this sector.

The fiscal discipline has been possible because the intercorporate system's peak business organizations and the largest political party, the Liberal Democratic Party, have well-developed interest aggregating capabilities. These have been used in intensive wide-ranging consultations with officials in the Ministry of Finance. There has been no participation by organized labour in these corporatist processes, and the representation of broad community interests has been possible only through the parliamentary system, in which the Liberal Democratic Party's conservative role has been supplemented by some of the smaller political organizations, and in which a tradition of deference to the Ministry of Finance has remained strong.[19]

The fiscal discipline has, however, been relaxed in recent years to overcome the recession of the early 1990s that had been caused by the fall in inflated property values. This relaxation has accorded with US demands for a fiscal stimulus that would increase consumer demand and hopefully draw in more imports, but the main beneficiaries are national firms with strong domestic market positions. Continued export-led growth has been facilitating a gradual economic recovery, but an emerging issue for long-term fiscal policy is the expansion of foreign production by Japanese firms relative to exports from Japan. There are losses of tax revenue, and some reductions in outwardly oriented domestic employment. The direct investment outflows help, however, to moderate upward pressures on the yen, and the production abroad reduces the trade surpluses that are primarily responsible for these upward pressures.

The international reach of monetary and financial policy has been greatly extended over the past decade by the emergence of several Japanese banks as dominant players in global financial markets.[20] Strong relational ties between these banks, and their extensive links with integrated Japanese regional production systems in North America, East Asia and other parts of the world, enable them to function with concerted strategies. These assume much competitive importance for the expansion of shares in financial markets and for the gradual restriction of opportunities for unwelcome speculation by American- and European-based financial institutions. The strengthening of shares in world financial markets, meanwhile, becomes linked with changes in the fundamentals determining Japan's major bilateral balances of payments. These changes result primarily because Japanese manufacturers of higher technology products continue to acquire larger shares of advanced country markets.

Germany's fiscal, monetary and financial policies follow economic logic similar to Japan's. These policies have been basically outcomes of corporatist processes involving national labour unions as well as peak business associations, in close consultations with central economic ministries shaped in an administrative culture of institutionalized commitment to order and growth. The corporatist processes have been linked with multiple parliamentary functions in the nation's federal system, and this has been possible mainly because of a tradition of cooperation in the public interest between the two main political parties, the Christian Democrats and the Social Democrats. Very broad accountability has resulted, with federal policies under constant review by an independent Council of Economic Experts.[21]

Strong elite consensus has maintained allocative discipline, to hold down costs of government and thus facilitate export-led growth at rising technological levels. Such growth has been possible primarily because of superior competitiveness in the favourable context of European market integration, and the resultant prosperity has tended to strengthen the consensus in support of allocative discipline, which has been complemented by sustained monetary restraint. With the allocative discipline, however, there have been extensive subsidies for national industries and large welfare expenditures to assist the unemployed, whose numbers were roughly 10 per cent of the workforce during the early 1990s.[22]

Monetary policy, while restrictive to hold down inflation, has been managed with tacit concerns to prevent appreciation that could hinder exports. A dominant role in the European Monetary System has helped to restrain upward pressures on the currency caused by surpluses in trade with other European Union members. Fundamentals altered by the weaker trade performance and higher inflation rates of some of those members, however, severely strained the European Monetary System during 1992, causing the exit of certain states, including Britain. Prospects for advancement towards a regional monetary union that would follow the formation of the European Union's Single Market thus became uncertain. Difficult issues were posed for German monetary policy: as the restraints on currency appreciation had been weakened, Union partners were resentful of the deflationary effects of German monetary tightening; and yet it was clear that German influence in a projected regional monetary union could be more than offset by the concerted efforts of other members.[23]

Financial policy maintains and regulates an integrated banking system which is deeply involved in the ownership, funding and advising of manufacturing firms. This involvement gives a high degree of stability to the nation's cohesive intercorporate system and sustains emphasis on long-term planning by manufacturing enterprises. It also contributes to the preservation of strong home country ties in those enterprises, and indeed has been partly responsible for limiting their interest in developing foreign operations. Their emphasis on supplying external markets through exports rather than international production has resulted in a very high volume of foreign trade, with total exports approximating those of the USA. The financial sector's influence on planning in the higher technology manufacturing firms seems, however, to have been somewhat cautious, as these have tended to lag behind Japanese competitors in applications of advanced research and development.[24] The degree of caution has evidently been related to the fairly secure positions of German firms in the markets of other European Union members, where they encounter competitive pressures weaker than those experienced by Japanese firms exporting to the USA.

The preservation of a high degree of integration in the national financial sector has vital importance for Germany's structural competitiveness in the European Union and in world markets. The Union is committed in principle to the establishment of an integrated market in financial services, but the cohesion in the German sector poses high entry barriers, and the competitiveness of financial institutions in other Union members is generally inferior. As rivalries for shares of the Union's Single Market intensify, peak German business associations may well become very active sources of resistance to attempts at penetration of the national financial sector by other Union or by non-European institutions.

France's fiscal, monetary and financial policies have been more conflicted assertions of central power in a less integrated political economy with an intensely individualistic culture. These policies have evolved in competitive cooperation with Germany, on a basis of partnership for virtual joint leadership of the European Union. Weaker structural competitiveness because of a less integrated and less dynamic intercorporate system has tended to motivate strong French use of state power for advanced industrial growth, but with costs that have added directly and indirectly to government debt. (This debt rose from 16.81 per cent to 28.54 per cent of GNP between 1981 and 1991.[25])

Fiscal discipline has been somewhat weaker than Germany's over the past decade and a half, and achievement of the intended growth effects has been hampered by the disunity in the intercorporate system and the dampening influence of bureaucratic authority on entrepreneurship in that system. Overall development in that system, moreover, continues to reflect the adverse consequences of large-scale state sector expansion under a Socialist administration during the early 1980s. Substantial privatization under conservative cabinets in the later 1980s, continuing into the 1990s, has been gradually restoring vitality to the enlarged private sector, but with lags affecting levels of investment in new technology and of competitiveness in the home and external markets.[26]

Fiscal and monetary policies over the past decade have been intended to push inflation to low levels, so as to enhance competitiveness by holding down production costs, but the export gains have been small.[27] In commerce with Germany, the main trading partner, deficits which had become relatively large in the late 1980s were reduced to moderate levels by the early 1990s, while exports to other Union members and to the rest of the world remained substantially below Germany's. Exports to the then European Community in 1992 amounted to US$152,903 million, while Germany's were US$215,773 million.[28] The endeavour to maintain fiscal restraint has had to contend with heavy welfare costs because of high unemployment related to the recession spreading from Germany. Slack demand at home and throughout the Union has meanwhile obligated cautious private sector planning. The need for caution has evidently been greater than it has for German firms because French dependence on exports to the Single Market is roughly 20 per cent higher than Germany's, and because French enterprises have generally weaker resources.

Monetary policy basically follows Germany's, because of the established commitment to partnership which has been given a strong basis in structural interdependence, despite strains deriving from asymmetries in fundamentals related to differences in trade performance.[29] In the projected European monetary union France could receive support from other member states for a common policy less restrictive than that favoured by Germany. However, in the structuring of that union there would be choices that would be difficult for France, because of their implications for German interests and because of uncertainties about the outcomes of negotiating strategies according different priorities to the bilateral relationship.

Financial policy evidences strong concern to maintain the national character of the banking system, especially because of its importance for the funding of higher technology industries. The administrative resolve may well be strengthening because of sensitivity to the increasing competitive pressures of the Single Market, and also because of reactions to the growing Japanese financial presence in Europe, which has been facilitated by the failure of the European Union to require substantial reciprocity by Japan on questions of financial market access.[30]

Britain's fiscal, monetary and financial policies have been shaped in a liberal political economy with a weaker executive, reacting to diverse pressures from legislative groups and from a fragmented intercorporate system, in a context of rivalries between Conservative and Labour Parties. These rivalries have been as divisive as those between the major political groups in France, but over the past decade and a half each executive has had to cope with strong pluralism within its own majority. Technocratic inputs into policy have been weaker than in France, because of a liberal tradition of government aloofness from industry and commerce. The absence of strong peak business associations with broad interest aggregating capabilities has allowed this tradition to persist, but with understandings that interventions are necessary because of losses of competitiveness due to industrial decline.[31]

Fiscal policy has been expansionary over the past half decade because of rising welfare costs associated with high unemployment, the difficulties of reducing burdensome administrative costs, and the influence of political competition for office on allocative and tax decisions. Government debt as a proportion of GDP had risen to 34.67 per cent in 1991, and the fiscal deficit increased to about 8 per cent of GDP in 1993.[32] Imperatives for monetary tightening were becoming stronger as the deficits continued to rise, but there was evidence of reluctance to hinder recovery from the European recession.

Monetary policy had been loosened after Britain's departure from the European Monetary System in 1992. That departure had been forced by speculation against the currency, mainly by American financial institutions, for which opportunities had been provided by balance-of-payments problems. High interest rates to restrain inflation had been responsible for an overvalued currency, adversely affecting Britain's exports. The emphasis on inflation control had been linked with a long-standing bias in monetary policy favouring the nation's financial institutions rather than its manufacturing firms. Since the departure from the European Monetary System there have been uncertainties about British participation in the regional monetary union envisaged in the Maastricht Treaty. It has been clear, however, that Britain's economic growth will depend mainly on involvement in European Union commerce, as other member states receive about 50 per cent of Britain's exports, including about two-thirds of those to industrialized countries.[33]

Financial policy has had a liberal orientation, reflecting preference for a system in which financial institutions are free to pursue their interests as market opportunities provide, without any obligatory regard for the funding needs of the nation's manufacturing firms.[34] German-type financial sector involvement in such funding has not developed, and British financial institutions have made extensive use of their scope for involvement in international financial markets, drawn especially by opportunities in higher growth areas. If there are advances towards monetary union in Europe the development of an integrated regional financial system will become increasingly necessary, in the common interest. Britain's involvement in this may well have to be negotiated on terms acceptable to Germany and France, and these may be expected to evidence concerns with mobilizing more European Union financial resources for the support of European industrial development, and with the control of volatility in world financial markets associated with conflicting pressures on the US dollar.

INDUSTRIAL POLICIES

The intensifying competitive pressures in world markets that are being asymmetrically internationalized are causing governments to become more active in advising and supporting national firms involved in those markets. The types of administrative endeavours conform to patterns evident in the management of fiscal, monetary and financial policies, and are associated with related forms of political change. Structural interdependencies are altered, to the advantage of more integrated states capable of more efficient macromanagement.

The endeavours to enhance competitiveness tend to focus on assisting the development and application of advanced technology by national firms in sectors that have become strategic because of intense rivalries that are leading to increases in international oligopoly power. Discriminatory trade measures often help to protect the domestic market positions of the technologically aided firms, and can also shelter other enterprises whose fortunes are linked with those firms. The strategically most significant industrial policy activity that can be attempted, however, is the promotion of concerted entrepreneurship across a wide range of national sectors in line with designs for structural competitiveness based on aggregated firm-specific potentials. This has become possible in Japan through long-established practices of intensive consultation between technocratic authorities and the integrated national intercorporate system.

Where the intercorporate system is fragmented, and there is a tradition of distrust between it and an internally conflicted authority structure, replication of the Japanese achievement in comprehensive system-building is not possible. As an alternative, a liberal industrial policy can aim at maximizing home country location advantages through infrastructure development, regulatory efficiency, low cost administration and openness to foreign direct investment. Impartial arm's length dealings with firms can then cause their rivalries to have efficiency effects of systemic significance. These firms would, however, remain free to serve the home market and foreign markets through production abroad, responding individually to imperatives to build active presences in all major foreign economies. A liberal industrial policy can thus risk unfavourable shifts in balances of payments, due to migrations of industry.

American industrial policy initiatives have been attempted over the past decade. These have mainly been in line with a political tradition favouring the liberal option, but in response to challenging gains in structural competitiveness by Japan, facilitated in part by the serious deficiencies in US macroeconomic policies. Losses of competitiveness in higher technology sectors have been identified, notably in automobiles, electronic equipment, electrical machinery and computers, while there have been indications that competitiveness has been retained in aerospace, chemicals, non-electrical machinery and drugs.[35] While the losses of competitiveness have been reflected in sectoral trade balances, however, there have been problems of measurement due to large-scale intrafirm commerce, much of it associated with foreign sourcing for the home economy.[36] These problems have surfaced while studies of US international firms have shown that their shares of world markets have been maintained while the home economy has experienced large trade imbalances.

The ventures into industrial policy activism have been motivated to a large extent by administrative interests in sectoral political support, especially where exporting firms have been significantly affected by losses to foreign competitors in the domestic and external markets. The political motivations have tended to limit the scope for technocratic inputs, which have not been based on long accumulations of skills like those in the Japanese industrial policy bureaucracy. Congressional assertiveness on behalf of constituency interests has, moreover, resulted in rising volumes of authorizations that have bypassed technocratic assessments.[37] Broadly functional aggregations of sectoral interests, meanwhile, have been virtually impossible because of the fragmented US pattern of intercorporate relations.[38] This fragmentation has persisted in a context of distrust and aggressive rivalry between firms, and of corporate distrust of government authority.

There has been a persuasive rationale, however, for administrative endeavours to promote and support collaborative private sector research, to balance advantages gained through such cooperation by Japanese firms, and to reduce (if not eliminate) risks caused by anti-trust enforcement which have discouraged even pre-competitive collaboration.[39] Endeavours to develop research consortia have been successful, but large US higher technology enterprises have tended to be interested primarily in forming links with Japanese firms for collaboration in advanced research and development. While participation in the US-sponsored consortia has been restricted to national companies, issues concerning the determination of their eligibility have been difficult to resolve. It has not been possible to prevent leakages of new technology through the international strategic alliances of these firms.

The strong interests of US higher technology enterprises in research collaboration with Japanese corporations reflect awareness of the superior dynamism of Japanese centres of innovation in applied frontier technology. Research consortia sponsored at home by the US administration have less predictable futures, and can have less utility because of anti-trust restrictions on collaborative production which do not hinder such cooperation with Japanese enterprises in their home environment. Corporate interest in the officially sponsored consortia, moreover, is apparently guarded, because of the shifting patronage concerns to be expected under each new administration, and the aggressive involvement of legislators in allocating funds for projects excluded from independent review.

Technology funding has been substantially extended under the Clinton Administration,[40] and has been complemented by trade policy activism to secure designated shares of the Japanese market for US higher technology products.[41] The abrasive methods used to impose this form of managed trade have, however, alienating effects which, for example, could influence the attitudes of Japanese investors towards purchases of US government debt. The managed trade arrangements can also invite deception by American as well as Japanese firms. US enterprises can sell to third country markets by formally routing products through collaborating Japanese firms, thus helping to meet targets for the penetration of the Japanese market. Japanese managements can provide indirect inducements for US firms willing to circumvent the market-opening agreements in exchange for preferential treatment of their other interests, in Japan or elsewhere. Meanwhile, further rapid advances in applied technology by Japanese firms can make managed trade specifications obsolete, and such advances can continue during any subsequent negotiations.

The problem of trade imbalances in high technology sectors which has activated US industrial policy initiatives is related to the effects of corporate preferences for serving external markets through foreign production. The extensive uncoordinated development of industrial capacity abroad for this purpose tends to increase the high technology sectoral trade imbalances. These do not necessarily reflect losses of international competitiveness by US firms, and they are accounted for in varying degrees by the very substantial foreign production of such firms, as well as by relatively high volume exports to the USA from Japanese and other foreign firms less involved in international production. A fundamental issue for US industrial policy decision-makers, therefore, is the relationship between external production by national firms and production in the home economy for export. In this relationship there are trade effects of much greater magnitude than those experienced by other industrialized democracies.[42] For the home economy there is a danger of sectoral deindustrialization and of adverse trade balances.

Japan's industrial policy is basically an administrative partnership with an integrated intercorporate system, and results in much spontaneous but also guided concerting of entrepreneurial energies. Firms compete very actively – but also cooperate very actively – in the intercorporate system, maintaining relational ties with each other, especially in industry groups (*keiretsu*), and with the major economic ministries. The extensive coordination of entrepreneurial activity has wide-ranging growth effects, through ambitious investment and efficient use of industrial potentials (with much information-sharing and risk-sharing), a general lowering of transaction costs, and the continuous building of a system of alliance capitalism.[43]

Technocratic inputs of high quality, based on long experience in the administrative guidance of corporate decision-making, are possible because of a strong tradition of managerial deference and functional responsiveness in continuous intense consultative relationships which align policy and corporate strategies. The process largely bypasses parliamentary activities, which deal with the enactment of legislation framed in general terms that allow much scope for bureaucratic discretion. There is little legislative review of administrative practice, because of customary deference similar to that observed by corporate managements. Technocratic performance is, however, strongly task-oriented, in the general interest, especially because of informal accountability for the maintenance of high quality consultative macromanagement.[44] This accountability extends into the future, as many technocrats obtain managerial appointments after early retirement. There is, however, no review of administrative policy by an independent high status institution such as the German Council of Economic Experts. Such an organization would not fit easily into the Japanese system because of the pervasive respect accorded to technocratic expertise and the informality associated with much policy implementation.

The dynamism of the Japanese intercorporate system, generated especially in its industry groups, results in constant collective enhancement of firm-specific advantages, with gains through collaborative business strategies and technology-sharing. Technocratic guidance through the projection of sectoral potentials and advances in frontier technology is thus facilitated. The provision of subsidies, which could have divisive effects, is unnecessary, because of the large resources gained by many Japanese firms through successful exporting, and because of the services provided for numerous small and medium-sized enterprises by the large General Trading Companies, which are active members of the industry groups. The concerted entrepreneurship, with long-range planning and promises of stability through collaborative adjustment to stresses, offers prospects of continuing growth, with an increasing outward orientation.[45]

Technocratically guided export-led growth has been the principal achievement of Japanese industrial policy. International production for foreign markets is following their penetration through exports, especially because of strains caused by Japanese trade surpluses, and industrial policy is thus assuming an external reach. This reach is considerable because the exclusive quality of Japanese corporate cultures is maintained as integrated foreign production networks are formed. Rotations of managerial personnel ensure the continuation of active links with bases in the home economy that operate within the multiple links between the intercorporate system and the economic ministries.[46] Administrative and corporate preferences are to maintain much research-intensive and high value-added production in the home economy while preserving strong links between it and the foreign production networks.

Administrative sponsorship of collaborative private sector research is a major feature of the overall technocratic coordinating function. Large-scale corporate funding for this research limits the need for government allocations, and is provided in a context of trust in obligations to share new technology. The private sector funding accounts for about 80 per cent of national spending on research and development, and as a proportion of GNP has been higher than such funding in the USA for several decades. Because of the degree of integration in the intercorporate system, there is no administrative or private sector concern about leakages of new technology to foreign enterprises. The research and development has, however, to be undertaken with extensive efforts to gain access to foreign frontier technology, and this requires selective technological sharing, with participation in international strategic alliances. The selectivity can be maintained while Japanese firms continue to achieve faster applications of advanced technology[47] and derive superior bargaining advantages from their collective market strengths.

Germany's industrial policy is shaped in political processes more broadly representative than those in Japan, because of the dynamics of the nation's federal system and the expression of union interests, but the principal outcomes are subsidies. In the absence of a strong technocratic guidance function like that in Japan, there is a pattern of financially based guidance by banks. These have extensive equity participation in German manufacturing firms and assume active supervisory roles through representation on management boards. The bonds are relational, and their stability facilitates long-range planning. There is, however, a degree of conservative bias, which accounts for a relatively lower level of corporate dynamism than that in Japan, and which is reflected in a technological lag behind the more advanced Japanese higher technology firms.[48] Subsidies, authorized under the authority of the Ministry of Finance and the Ministry of Economics, are the results of allocative processes managed with high levels of accountability in the public interest, but are important means of generating political support for the ruling party or coalition.[49]

The subsidies are on a relatively large scale and, in conjunction with the extensive bank financing and the representation of labour interests in the policy process, they contribute to solidarity in the intercorporate system, which is integrated, although not as tightly as Japan's. German firms thus retain strong home country ties, and serve external markets much more through exporting than through international production. High wage costs, however, together with the recession and intensifying competition in the

European Union market, are causing ventures into manufacturing at foreign locations. This is on a modest scale compared with Japan's international production. The principal external market is the USA, where German direct investment on an historical cost basis totalled $29,205 million, while Japan's was $96,473 million in 1992.[50]

The expansion into international production is evidently restrained by the influence of organized labour and, to some extent, by the influence of banks in the home economy. Involvement in the nation's established patterns of corporatist consultations may gradually assume less significance because of the demanding tasks of external management and of related entries into international strategic alliances. Ties with the home economy may, moreover, be weakened to a degree by the gradual elimination of industrial subsidies, which is an obligation for all European Union members. In common with other members Germany is experiencing considerable Europeanization of its microeconomic policies as the integration process deepens within the Union. Intergovernmental interactions are extending the range of policy coordinating functions across the Union; German influence at the Council of Ministers level has to enlist the support of other members; and German interest groups are active in collaboration with those of Union partners in the proliferating lobbying activity directed at the European Commission.[51]

A common industrial policy for the Union is not in prospect, because of strains between the members that have been increased in recent years by the German-based recession and the sharpening of intraregional disparities in the Single Market. The formal German preference is a Union offering wide scope for market forces. In such a context German structural competitiveness would remain superior, but it would be diluted by a common European industrial policy, as this would enhance the efficiencies of firms based in other member states, and the costs would be borne disproportionately by Germany. Union-sponsored regional efforts to develop new technology receive German support, however. These endeavours are hampered by collective decision-making problems and by the interests of many European firms in collaboration with American or Japanese rather than other Union enterprises, but they offer significant benefits through cooperative research.[52] Collaborative technology projects sponsored by groups of European states and managed outside the Union structure are also given German support, and these may well be preferred to European Union projects because of the prospect of more substantial long-term results.

France's industrial policy is a process of strong technocratic activism: it is the work of a constitutionally powerful executive relating to a fragmented intercorporate system, on the basis of shared concerns regarding the nation's structural competitiveness, especially in rivalry with Germany. The policy style tends to be autocratic, because of very limited executive accountability, weak interest representation through the parliamentary system, a tradition of corporate subordination to administrative direction, and the absence of strong independent advisory councils.[53] Entrepreneurial activity in the intercorporate system tends to be weaker than in Germany, and the system's lack of solidarity hinders the development of collaborative corporate strategies. Potentials for synergistic interaction between managements and the technocratic level are therefore quite limited. There is a tradition of technocratic activism to compensate for the relative weakness of corporate resources, but this has tended to induce managerial dependence on state support.

Large subsidies are provided for national firms, which have been sheltered by formal and informal trade barriers. Most of these barriers have been removed in line with the obligations of membership in the Single Market, but they limit non-European penetration of the French economy through exports. The subsidies are intended to assist the attainment of superior international competitiveness by major French enterprises, but under the current administration there is emphasis on giving more scope to market forces in order to increase the competitiveness of all national firms. Membership of the European Union entails obligations to phase out industrial subsidies, but for France this is a more difficult requirement than it is for Germany. French firms mostly lack the kind of financial sector support received by their German counterparts, and lag behind the German enterprises in exports to other members of the European Union and to the rest of the world.[54]

French structural competitiveness has been impaired by the negative growth effects of large-scale nationalizations in the early 1980s under a Socialist government which brought roughly one-third of the nation's industrial capacity into the state sector. Substantial but gradual privatization policies implemented by conservative administrations have reduced state burdens caused by the inefficiencies of the state enterprises, but the private sector has to reckon with the possibility of renationalizations under a future Socialist administration. Ideologically the French Socialist Party is further to the left than the German Social Democratic Party, and can draw considerable support while the economy is in recession.

As strong state power has induced considerable subservience in the fragmented intercorporate system, the current emphasis on freedom for market forces will probably have to be increased and prolonged before there will be any significant improvement in entrepreneurial performance. A technology enhancement programme is being implemented to assist advanced sectors and compensate for relatively low levels of corporate investment in research and development, but it indirectly induces continued dependence on state support. Managements in French higher technology firms have strong incentives to collaborate with state research and development initiatives, but they also have incentives to collaborate and accept partnerships with American corporations. Such ties can offer access to large resources and advanced technology for greater competitiveness in the Single Market, and can also provide improved bargaining leverage in dealings with the French administration.

The evolution of French industrial policy is influenced by the intrusion of European Union issues into national politics, partly with reference to the allocation of Union funds for development in backward areas of France and other members, and partly with reference to Union sponsorship of technology programmes.[55] There appears to be little interest in the formation of a common industrial policy for the Union, because of concentration on problems of French structural competitiveness, and presumably also because of doubts about the capacity of the Union's structures to manage a common programme for regional industrial development.

Britain's industrial policy is implemented by administrations with greater accountability to a constitutionally stronger legislature. There is much more administrative respect for corporate autonomy than in France, but the intercorporate system is fragmented and this prevents coherent aggregation of its interests as a basis for policy.[56] The bureaucracy has a tradition of impartial arm's length dealings with firms and business associations, and alternations in adjustment to interventionist measures favoured by the Labour Party and the free market preferences of the Conservative Party. An ideologically based gap between the policy orientations of these two major parties is narrower than that between the two principal political groups in France, but not as narrow as that between the two leading parties in Germany. The divergence in Britain is a source of uncertainties for firms, especially because of common perceptions that the divergence tends to widen during recessions, and that these can cause electoral volatility. The context is an economy which has experienced considerable industrial decline, explained in part by problems in management–labour relations, but also by the adverse effects of policy-induced currency appreciation on manufacturing for export. There has been large-scale outward direct investment which has contributed to the industrial decline, and thus to weaknesses in the intercorporate system.[57]

Consensus on industrial policy issues is difficult to achieve because of failures in administrative leadership, due to cabinet pluralism; the absence of sustained technocratic activism; and the problems of aggregating intercorporate interests, which reflect strong individualism in the business culture. Conservative administrations, over the past decade, have sought to promote industrial efficiency through the discipline of free market forces, with emphasis on weakening the power of organized labour, especially as a source of opposition to the introduction of new technology.[58] This has tended to make management–labour relations more adversarial, but in recent years management practices at new Japanese manufacturing firms in Britain have had demonstration effects by indicating efficiencies to be gained through the sponsorship of working-level autonomy.

The increased reliance on market forces has received more critical judgement than might otherwise have been expected because of the European recession (during which unemployment has risen to about 10 per cent), while the prospects for effective involvement in the intensely competitive Single Market have seemed very uncertain.[59] Increased structural competitiveness would be possible with greater cooperation between British firms, on the basis of relational dealings like those in Japanese or German industry groups, but there are no indications that such collaboration is developing spontaneously. Stresses in the economy appear to increase individualistic managerial pursuits of market opportunities at home, in the USA and in the European Union. Britain is the leading European source of direct investment in the USA, and the flow, which in recent years has been roughly twice that into the European Union, has been high compared with that from Germany into the USA – despite the larger size of the German economy and the larger volume of German exports to the United States.[60]

COMPETITION POLICIES

The industrial policy measures implemented by the US, Japanese, German, French and British administrations are in varying degrees supported by competition policies. The significance of these policies depends in most cases on the orientations of national firms towards cooperation and competition within each country's intercorporate system. Where there is much relational contracting the shared commitments to this become sources of informal restraints on competitive and also anti-competitive activities. Regulatory agencies then operate with responsiveness to processes of spontaneous reciprocal corporate monitoring. In such a context there can be general acceptance of strong domestic market positions acquired by major firms that respect the independence of small competitors and of their own suppliers. In the absence of self-regulating practices associated with relational contracting, however, government regulatory functions become very demanding. Anti-competitive activities tend to multiply as firms strive to maximize their market shares, and policy-makers confront difficult choices not only in assessing cases of tacit anti-competitive collusion but more fundamentally in determining the relative weight of criteria for equity and efficiency. The enforcement of competition policy in such a context can work against an industrial policy that is intended to help large national firms strengthen their domestic market positions in order to become internationally more competitive.

American competition (anti-trust) policy has wider scope than those of the other leading industrialized democracies, and has significant effects on the nation's structural competitiveness. Policy in this context is expressed by setting guidelines for the enforcement of laws against anti-competitive activity. Vague language in these laws is open to various interpretations, and although most of them were enacted more than 60 years ago legislative revision has not been feasible. Authority for enforcement is vested in the Antitrust Division of the Department of Justice and in the Federal Trade Commission, with restrictive or liberal emphasis according to guidelines set by succeeding administrations.

Large numbers of private lawsuits under the anti-trust laws have resulted in a disorderly assortment of judicial interpretations and decisions. Inconsistencies and reversals of judgements, and the prospect of more to come, pose many uncertainties for firms. At risk are market sharing and price-fixing arrangements, restraints imposed by producers on retailers, the gaining and defence of dominant market positions, mergers resulting in monopoly power, and price discrimination that can be considered predatory. The judicial and regulatory uncertainties are very significant because suing parties that prove injury are entitled to triple damages, and because violations of the 1980 Sherman Act, covering monopoly power and business collusion, are criminal offences.[61] US firms thus have to manage their integration, diversification, production and marketing strategies with much legal advice. This adds to information costs and production costs, discourages various forms of competitive behaviour, and limits interest in long-term planning. The risks and costs can add to the incentives encouraging ventures in international production which offer reduced exposure to possible anti-trust enforcement.

The anti-trust legislation is not a restraint on tacit collusion, for example through informal price-fixing by firms with strong market positions, but indications of such collusion can provoke much investigative activity by regulatory authorities seeking evidence of collusion. The formation of industry groups based on relational contracting is thus discouraged and, in view of the efficiencies which are possible in such groups, changes in US anti-trust legislation have been advocated.

Japan's competition policy, operating in a context of culturally based restraints on competitive and anti-competitive behaviour, does not impose significant restraints on large national firms consolidating domestic market positions. Informal regulatory activity within the intercorporate system is considered to be effective, and strong domestic market positions are felt to be necessary for national firms competing in foreign markets. The interests of leading firms are well represented in the policy process, and this representation ensures continuity in the orientation of competition policy.[62]

The US administration exerts pressure for Japanese adoption of a more restrictive competition policy that would break informal bonds in the nation's industry groups and weaken the domestic market positions of leading firms, but this is resisted. There is pervasive elite support for the preservation of the established pattern of self-regulation in the intercorporate system. The leverage available to the USA, it must be stressed, is limited because of US vulnerabilities related to dependence on the confidence of Japanese investors in the American economy.

The regulatory authorities responsible for competition policy in Japan have much less significance than the powerful Ministry of International Trade and Industry, and its organizational perspectives have been shaped by awareness of the competitive strengths of the nation's industry groups that have been demonstrated in the penetration of the American and European markets. There is clearly little willingness to attempt what would be an unsuccessful struggle against the cohesion of these groups in order to appease the US administration. Moreover, there are no indications of openness to arguments that greater overall efficiency would be possible if the relational ties in the industry groups were weakened.

Toleration of the strong domestic market positions of leading national firms is matched by a dimension of Japanese competition policy which protects the interests of small retailers by restricting opportunities for the establishment of large department stores. American pressure is applied to have the restrictions lifted, but this is opposed because of concerns about the welfare of the numerous small retailers and about the large-scale marketing capabilities of major US retailers, based on their domestic market positions and on their operations in Europe.[63]

European Union firms operate under a common competition policy implemented by the European Commission, as well as under national competition policies. Directives from the Council of Ministers allow the Commission to operate with much discretion, with generally more toleration of monopolistic practices than is permitted in the USA. The Commission has to approve large mergers if the turnovers involved are above 5 billion ECU world-wide or 250 million ECU within the Union. Most of the mergers considered in recent years have been approved. The drive for complete internal market integration has expressed broad elite consensus that this will facilitate the emergence of strong European enterprises capable of gaining competitiveness in world markets. The directives from the Council of Ministers, however, have to be consistent with general prohibitions of anti-competitive behaviour in the Treaty of Rome. Under the Treaty the European Court of Justice is the final authority for settling disputes between firms and between firms and governments over issues of monopoly power.[64]

The competition policies of member governments have varying effects in their national intercorporate systems. These administrations endeavour to maintain their established regulatory arrangements, although they have interests in working towards regional policy harmonization and have to accept rulings by the European Court of Justice, which is working through a long backlog of cases. Each government's domestic concerns obligate efforts to influence the administration of competition policy by the European Commission, and there are significant opportunities for this because the Commission is informally open to much interaction with interest groups as well as with member governments.[65]

Germany's competition policy operates in an intercorporate context similar to Japan's, but with somewhat weaker informal restraints on anti-competitive behaviour. For structural competitiveness the degree of spontaneous self-regulation in the intercorporate system evidently assumes increasing importance as the subordination of national competition policy to the European Union's common competition policy continues. National competition policy is implemented through an independent regulatory structure which operates to maintain stability in the integrated pattern of bank industrial holdings, cross investment and interlocking directorates. This pattern is relatively well protected against takeovers by outside enterprises, and its relational ties in effect allow leading firms to preserve strong positions in the home market.[66]

France's competition policy is implemented with much administrative discretion, in a context of very authoritative dealings with firms. The formal basis for policy is a 1986 law against anti-competitive behaviour, but successive administrations have avoided restrictive interpretations of this that might hinder the emergence of national firms with strong domestic market positions. Firms have no obligation to notify the administration of collaborative agreements that may hinder competition. Scope for mergers and acquisitions within the national intercorporate system is limited because the number of publicly traded companies is relatively small, large holdings are held by banks, other institutions and families, and the positions of established managements are in effect protected by law and by the association agreements on which firms operate. The discretionary implementation of competition policy discourages (and can block) foreign takeovers of French firms.[67] As this power, if challenged, must yield to decisions by the European Commission and the European Court of Justice, however, the concerns with structural competitiveness which are evident in French competition policy are making the promotion of solidarity in the national intercorporate system more desirable.

Britain's competition policy is quite liberal in its domestic and external applications. It is implemented through rulings based on several laws against anti-competitive behaviour, enacted over the past two decades, which allow wide scope for interpretation and which allow assessments of economic benefits to outweigh judgements about the negative impacts of restrictive practices. The regulatory authorities operate under administrative supervision and direction, which can in effect give firms immunity against regulatory proceedings. There is active administrative concern to facilitate the development of internationally very competitive firms with strong domestic market bases, achieved in a context of market discipline, with extensive scope for entries by foreign firms. A wide range of restrictive practices is tolerated, under exemptions allowed by law in numerous areas of the economy.[68] These exemptions are especially significant because there is little self-regulatory activity in the very individualistic intercorporate system and the shareholding pattern gives many firms little protection against takeovers. Roughly 25 per cent of these takeovers since the early 1970s have been hostile.

The implementation of Britain's competition policy is gradually being affected by European Union directives and judgements, especially because of issues posed by collaboration between British and other European firms and by cross-border mergers and acquisitions. The liberal policy orientation and the degree of fragmentation in the intercorporate system are responsible for much openness to European entries, and are permitting intense rivalries between Union firms for which Britain has become a very contestable market. These rivalries are processes in Union-wide struggles for domination of the Single Market which are motivating large-scale rationalizations, new production ventures, and mergers and acquisitions where feasible.[69] Weaker firms are being forced into declines by more efficient enterprises exploiting the different opportunities of markets and policy environments. The structural effects vary across the Union, and for Britain they are posing sharply industrial policy issues that are especially relevant because of the liberal orientation of competition policy. In the evolution of structural interdependencies with major European partners, their policies and the activities of their firms are tending to become more potent factors, causing asymmetries that must be expected to have cumulative effects.

FOREIGN DIRECT INVESTMENT POLICIES

With the general intensification of corporate rivalries for world market shares the management of foreign direct investment policies has increasing significance for structural competitiveness, and in this respect it is linked with the structural consequences of competition policies. Some national administrations seek to enhance structural competitiveness by attracting foreign direct investment into high technology sectors. Governments in states which already have superior structural competitiveness tend to restrain incoming foreign direct investment, while assisting the efforts of their firms to gain larger shares of external markets through international production as well as through direct exports.

An integrated pattern of intercorporate relations, which generally ensures superior structural competitiveness, limits penetration by incoming foreign direct investment, and typically generates informal regulatory arrangements with which outside firms have to conform. If the intercorporate pattern is fragmented this is likely to be evident in a lower level of structural competitiveness. To raise this level, without being able to promote cohesion in the intercorporate system, foreign direct investment policy can rely very much on regulatory methods, to exclude potentially threatening entries and to attract others promising substantial benefits, while guiding (if not controlling) outward direct investment. A liberal foreign direct investment policy can, however, entail acceptance of losses of structural competitiveness if fragmentation is responsible for lower dynamism in the intercorporate system.

American foreign direct investment policy is liberal, and has had a history of confidence in the international competitiveness of US firms. The policy has facilitated much cross-investment between the USA and Europe and, in recent years, rapid large-scale inward direct investment from Japan. Europe has been the main location of US outward direct investment, and the flow has increased since the late 1980s because of the opportunities of the Single Market, which have become more significant with its enlargement.[70]

On outward direct investment the policy remains liberal because of very extensive business interest in its preservation. This interest is based on recognition of related tax benefits, of the advantages of an active presence in each major foreign market, and of the utility of avoiding regulatory exposure and union pressures in the home economy. Issues concerning deindustrialization and employment losses in the USA have been given some prominence in public policy debates, but much greater prominence has been given to questions regarding the structural effects of high volume inward direct investment. Such investment has grown large since the depreciation of the US dollar in the mid 1980s, and the most significant inflows have been from Japan. These inflows have aroused concern in Congress because the Japanese direct investment position has ranked second only to Britain's, and has assumed much strategic significance due to the emergence of an integrated Japanese production system for North America.[71]

Unsuccessful attempts have been made by legislative groups to restrict Japanese direct investment in the USA and to impose performance requirements. Pressure from these groups evidently has some influence on executive use of powers under the amended 1988 Omnibus Trade and Competitiveness Act to block foreign acquisitions of US firms on economic security grounds, but there have been no indications of administrative interest in limiting expansion of the Japanese presence through ventures that do not involve acquisitions. Numerous US states compete to attract Japanese direct investment, and in higher technology sectors Japanese firms have entered into many strategic alliances with US enterprises that extend the local and international links of Japanese subsidiaries in the USA.

The relatively modest US direct investment position in Japan, and the informal restraints on entries by American firms through direct investment, activate persistent US leverage for the adoption of a more liberal foreign direct investment policy by the Japanese administration. The strong cohesion in the Japanese intercorporate system discourages US foreign direct investment, and any increases in US pressure tend to increase that cohesion. In US policy, however, higher priority is given to securing Japanese acceptance of targets for US exports to Japan, and leverage for this purpose relies on threats of restraints on Japanese exports to the USA. Discriminatory measures that might be taken against Japanese direct investment in the United States would risk provoking outflows that would affect overall business confidence.

The strong US direct investment position in Europe, which is greatly undervalued by historical cost figures, is not a source of any significant issues in relations with the European Union. Such issues may emerge, however, if US firms appear to be gaining very powerful positions in the Single Market because of the weak competitiveness of Union enterprises. The European direct investment position in the USA, although it has grown large, is not considered to have strategic significance like that which Japanese firms have acquired through very active involvement with moderate outlays in higher technology manufacturing and with financial sector investment much higher than Europe's.[72]

Japan's foreign direct investment policy, expressing the interests of its industry groups, informally restricts entries by outside firms while assisting the large-scale outward direct investment which in effect extends the integrated national intercorporate system into foreign economies. The efficiencies made possible by relational ties in this system are sources of superior competitive advantages which reinforce corporate interest in maintaining the established orientation of foreign direct investment policy.[73] This entails resistance to foreign demands for reciprocity, but this has been feasible because of foreign competition to attract such investment and because of the vulnerabilities affecting the USA's bargaining potential. Rivalries between European Union members have prevented the development of firm demands for Japanese direct investment reciprocity, while the USA's fiscal deficits (as well as the investment bidding of American states) have become major restraints on the use of pressures against Japan.

Advanced technology needs, however, necessitate discretionary relaxation of the informally restrictive policy on inward direct investment. Technological leads for Japanese firms cannot be guaranteed without ensuring their access to frontier research by American and European enterprises and institutes. Japanese investment in research facilities working closely with these enterprises and institutes has to be made acceptable by allowing American and European investment at centres of innovation in Japan. An important asymmetry in the relationship is the weakness of basic research organizations in Japan, which contrasts with the higher development of fundamental research institutes in the USA and at some European centres. On the Japanese side an advantage is the capacity of many firms to make commercial applications of advanced technology very rapidly, so as to pre-empt new market opportunities.[74]

In financial services Japanese discretionary foreign direct investment policy has made moderate concessions, well short of reciprocity, to US and European requests. Japanese bargaining power in this area of policy has been strong because of the large resources of the nation's major banks and the interests of many foreign firms and governments in access to financing by those banks, which is available at very competitive rates.[75] The development of large-scale funding activities by these banks has become a constraint on US and European resorts to pressure for less unequal access to Japan's financial markets.

European Union foreign direct investment policies are mostly less liberal than the USA's, because of priorities given to national industrial policy objectives and because of interests, shared with national business communities, in limiting external structural penetration. Solidarity in the business community as a restraint on such penetration is high in Germany, and thus affects the significance of formally liberal treatment of incoming direct investment. This solidarity is also a restraint on outward direct investment. Strong formal and informal administrative controls imposed on France's less cohesive business community also limit incoming direct investment, while restraining outflows. Very liberal British policy, in a context of low cohesion in the business community, results in much openness to incoming direct investment and leaves the way open for large-scale outward direct investment.

A common foreign direct investment policy may evolve in the European Union if it advances towards a higher stage of political integration. Pending such an outcome the foreign direct investment policies of member states are affected by the Union's competition policy, its regulation of the Single Market, and its common policy on external trade. The rather liberal competition policy can be given applications that weaken informally restrictive treatment of incoming foreign direct investment in Germany or France, and that limit the scope for discretionary restriction in Britain. In the Single Market an outside firm whose direct investment is accepted by any member state can market its products throughout the Union, although in the absence of a common foreign direct investment policy this consequence of market integration encourages competitive offerings of inducements to non-European firms. Meanwhile the common policy on external trade, which in effect attracts external direct investment, influences the strategies of incoming firms through local content requirements, rules of origin, and anti-dumping directives.[76]

Germany's foreign direct investment policy has the most significant regional effects because the nation's dominant position in the Single Market is sustained by the dynamism of its informally protected intercorporate system. Opportunities for foreign acquisitions of German firms are restricted because of the influence of national financial institutions with extensive industrial interests, the implicit encouragement of economic nationalism by the administration, and the administration's explicit sponsorship of order and stability in the economy. To function efficiently a foreign enterprise has to secure acceptance in the established system of intercorporate relations, in which national firms are advantaged because of wide-ranging informal ties. Outward direct investment, restrained to a degree by the relational bonds of the business community, derives competitive advantages from those bonds and from links with the national administration. Its policy on outward direct investment, while influenced by basic concerns with preserving solidarity and dynamism in the orderly home economy, is more liberal than that of the French administration.[77]

French foreign direct investment policy, implemented with strong administrative control of, and influence on, a less cohesive and less dynamic business community, is restrictive because of interests in limiting external structural penetration and in restraining migrations of industrial capacity. The stock of inward direct investment in 1990 (US$70 billion) was about half the level in Germany, while the French direct investment position abroad (US$115 billion) was about two-thirds of the German total, as a result of outflows that had become very large in the late 1980s. The size of these outflows indicated strong corporate interest in the direct investment opportunities of the integrating European Community market, and may also have expressed the desires of French managements to reduce exposure to administrative direction. A requirement for prior authorization of outward direct investment that had long been in force was terminated in 1986, but administrative interest in exerting some influence over the outflow through discretionary measures has remained active.[78]

Inward direct investment by American firms appears to be preferred to incoming investment from other European Union members, because of the generally greater resources of US enterprises. Issues in dealings with these firms can in most cases be settled bilaterally, but issues arising out of the presence of other European firms in France may involve the complex regulatory processes of the Union. The discretionary openness to US direct investment, however, draws inflows somewhat smaller than those into Germany, where dynamic centres of innovation are strong attractions. Within the Union Germany is a major source of incoming direct investment, and this poses some structural issues because of possible penetration by the integrated German intercorporate system.

Britain's foreign direct investment policy is very liberal, expressing government respect for entrepreneurial autonomy and confidence in the efficiencies generated by free market forces. Strong individualism in the pattern of intercorporate relations tends to ensure that the policy remains liberal, although the volume of outward direct investment is high and has contributed to a significant degree of deindustrialization. The total foreign direct investment position is very large – approximately US$250 billion in 1990, having risen rapidly from US$100 billion in 1985. Because of weak cohesion in the intercorporate system effective entry barriers to incoming direct investment are low, and it is attracted in relatively large volumes from the USA, Japan and the rest of the world. Much of this investment is drawn by the opportunities of the Single Market, and by cost advantages, as Britain has opted out of the Social Policy Protocol of the Maastricht Treaty and has a corporation tax rate much lower than that of Germany, the other main recipient of non-European direct investment.[79]

The liberal policy on inward direct investment is implemented with administrative discretion. This is generally not related to specific industrial policy objectives, but can block foreign takeovers of national firms, depending on judgemental preferences at Cabinet level. Such preferences usually do not discriminate against inward direct investment from the USA, which makes up a very large part of the foreign direct investment position in Britain. Britain is the preferred location for American European investment in financial services and real estate, but despite cost advantages draws slightly less US manufacturing investment than Germany. US firms show strong preferences for Germany as a location for the production of transportation equipment and chemicals. US manufacturing investment in Britain in 1993, on an historical cost basis, totalled $22,855 million, while the British direct investment position in manufacturing in the USA on an historical cost basis was $42,543 million – more than double Germany's, and also more than double Japan's.[80]

Potentials for the development of a common Union foreign direct investment policy are limited because of the diverging interests and policy orientations of the leading member states, which are related to the contrasts between their intercorporate patterns. Intensifying competition between European firms for domination of the Single Market is contributing to more active policy competition between member governments, as their concern with domestic growth and employment are affected by disparities which are tending to increase in the spread of gains from commerce within the Union. The policy competition is a source of reluctance to collaborate for common treatment of foreign direct investment, and of tacit unwillingness to be bound by any Union agreements to work towards the introduction of a common policy. There is recognition of shared interests in limiting the offering of competing inducements to attract US and Japanese direct investment, so as not to restrict opportunities for European firms in their own market. In the absence of a common will to concert measures for this purpose, however, many policy choices are strongly influenced by expectations that national firms will be advantaged by investment from outside the Union, through diverse linkages as well as through joint ventures and mergers.

TRADE POLICIES

Foreign trade policies in the major industrialized democracies tend to be influenced by more active interest representation than their competition and foreign direct investment policies. In those areas of government activity, regulatory functions and uses of administrative discretion generally engage the attention of relatively small business groups, but trade policy issues are widely seen to have extensive sectoral and community implications. The wider scale of interest representation which normally results, and which invites administrative activism, gives trade management much prominence in national decision processes. Basic features of each policy style are given expression, depending mainly on institutional capacities for aggregating corporate and business group demands. These aggregating capacities are determined by degrees of cohesion or fragmentation in national intercorporate systems, which in turn affect the practical significance of trade policies. A highly integrated intercorporate system sets up rather impenetrable entry barriers, as has been evident in Japan.

In policy processes related to the principal Euro-Pacific trade flows, the most prominent issues are commonly regarded as problems in arm's length commerce. However, intrafirm transfers account for a high proportion of these flows, and are related to international production which greatly exceeds the trade flows. Much of this production constitutes high volume export substitution, and is increasing faster than the trade flows because of the advantages which transnational enterprises derive from producing within their major markets. Intensifying competition for shares of the markets which they are linking causes the transnational enterprises to rationalize their national, regional and global operations, resulting in negative externalities for sectors and communities with inferior location advantages. Nevertheless, imbalances in what is generally seen as arm's length commerce tend to assume greater policy significance because of political action by threatened local firms. In the USA, despite very high volume foreign production by American firms, their shifts of operations to external locations provoke relatively little public discussion.

Intrafirm commerce accounts for about 40 per cent of the USA's trade flows, and US exports (arm's length and intrafirm) are about 20 per cent of the volume of foreign production by US firms.[81] In Japan's commerce intrafirm trade is very high, but overseas production is a relatively smaller process of export substitution. Such production in relation to exports (mostly arm's length) is much smaller in the external relations of Germany and France, but somewhat larger in Britain's foreign economic relations.

The fundamentals which pose issues for US trade policy concern the balance-of-payments effects of high volume export substitution through foreign production, and of income-shifting practices associated with that production; and with related forms of intrafirm trade, as well as with arm's length trade, both of which are increasingly linked with international corporate alliances. Change in these fundamentals results mainly from the increasing ratio of foreign production to exports. The politically contested issues are, however, trade imbalances, principally with Japan, as the volume of foreign production is given little recognition. In the context of the trade imbalances, problems of competitiveness are given prominence, with reference to sectoral imbalances, although the global market positions of US transnational enterprises have remained stable. Political focus on the trade imbalances has resulted in protectionist policy shifts, with some ventures into managed trade.[82]

The trade fundamentals are affected very much by the consequences of prolonged fiscal expansion. Because this raises consumer demand it draws in relatively large flows of products from abroad, including many manufactured at foreign locations by US firms. Heavy government borrowing raises the cost of capital at home for American enterprises, while necessitating high taxation, thus making production abroad a more attractive option. This option also assumes more significance because monetary tightening to lower the inflationary effects of the fiscal deficits is a constant restraint on growth. Meanwhile the welfare costs of relatively high unemployment add to overall tax burdens that are, in effect, heavier for firms exporting from the USA than for those producing abroad.[83]

Because of the political difficulties of achieving fiscal discipline, the US administration seeks opportunities to externalize adjustment costs, through leverage on other states to adopt expansionary policies and allow greater market access. Strong Congressional pressure obligates more emphasis on market-opening measures than on quests for fiscal expansion by major trading partners, and the administration's domestic political interests can be served more effectively by achievements in opening foreign markets. Leverage for this purpose that antagonizes other states and risks provoking retaliation can, however, increase the interests of US international firms in producing within those states instead of exporting to them. These international firms may adopt various political action strategies, opposing protectionist shifts in US trade policy but also supporting them, in order to benefit from whatever outcomes result.

The largest structural interdependencies in the USA's external economic relations are with the European Union, and these have favourable asymmetries, because of the high volume production in Europe by American firms and modest US surpluses in trade with the Union.[84] Because of these asymmetries, and in view of the Union's bargaining strength, US leverage against the Union on trade issues is exerted with restraint. The main US trade concerns are European agricultural protectionism and industrial subsidies, especially for the steel and aerospace sectors. Resorts to pressure on these matters have mainly evidenced the political influence of US steel producers, and have imposed strains on political ties with the Union. These ties have enabled the USA and leading Union states to dominate the international trading system, partly because of Japan's relative political isolation.

Outside the Atlantic context the USA's main trade policy problems are with Japan. The politically prominent issue is Japan's large surplus in bilateral trade, which is being reduced by Japanese production in the USA and gradual increases in American exports to Japan. Market-opening pressure on Japan by US administrations derives support from the popular notion that each bilateral trade relationship should be balanced. US exports to Japan in 1992 totalled $47,764 million, while sales in Japan by majority- and minority-owned affiliates of US firms amounted to $161,732 million, the US direct investment position on an historical cost basis being $26,590 million. US imports from Japan were $99,481 million and the Japanese direct investment position in the USA on an historical cost basis was $96,743 million, resulting in sales within the USA estimated to be about three times greater than the export total. The imbalance in market penetration was increasing, despite reductions in the Japanese trade surplus, because Japanese direct investment in the USA was growing larger relative to US direct investment in Japan.[85] As the overall change in structural interdependence had strategic significance, because of Japanese gains in the US higher technology market, American average has sought matching sectoral market shares in Japan.

The US pressure tends to have alienating effects throughout Japan's intercorporate system. American firms with interests in the Japanese market thus have incentives to avoid association with it and to work independently towards developing and expanding their own links with appropriate Japanese partners. The assimilative potential of the Japanese intercorporate pattern offers opportunities for building such relationships. The planning of US firms, moreover, has to recognize that their administration's trade policy activism has an uncertain future, because of likely shifts in the preferences of succeeding executives.

Japan's trade policy, shaped consensually in a broadly inclusive policy community with a long-term perspective, expresses administrative identification with vigorous outward-oriented entrepreneurship in the integrated national intercorporate system.[86] The preservation of solidarity in that system is tacitly given high priority, because the efficiencies generated are responsible for superior structural competitiveness. The socialization of incoming foreign firms into the system's relational bonds is a further concern, and this has increasing significance as Japan hosts modest numbers of foreign enterprises while its international firms extend their operations in North America and Europe. The system-conserving capacities of the intercorporate pattern are very strong, and ensure the maintenance of stable domestic market positions by Japanese enterprises.

Administrative measures in virtually all other areas of macromanagement support Japan's trade policy, in line with a well-established elite consensus to continue the impressive achievements of export-led growth, with complementary development of industrial capacity at foreign locations. Subsidies for export promotion are not required, because of the resources and dynamism of the outward-oriented firms, and the solidarity which ensures risk-sharing and cost-sharing in the intercorporate system. Strong achievement orientation tends to produce higher levels of overall efficiency than in Germany, where industrial subsidies induce corporate dependence.

The dynamic involvement of relationally linked enterprises in foreign trade and international production results in a widening pattern of market internalization, with increasing influence over structurally linked market processes. This has been evident in the development of the integrated Japanese production and marketing system for North America, and the extent to which participating firms dominate commerce between the USA and Japan.[87] The overall market-internalizing effects of relational bonds in the internationally expanding Japanese intercorporate system give a strategic dimension to Japan's foreign economic relations, posing entry barriers and facilitating concerted penetration of external markets. The competing firms of trading partners, operating individually, are disadvantaged. Governments in these trading partners typically have difficulties in evolving retaliatory strategic trade policies because firms in their generally less cohesive intercorporate systems fail to cooperate with each other and with their administrations, but seek collaboration with the successful Japanese firms.

Emphasis on the penetration of global high technology markets adds to the strategic significance of Japan's international economic involvement. Large-scale global operations are necessary to fund research and development and the commercial applications necessary for increasing competitiveness in world markets. Ties within the Japanese industry groups and networks make possible collaborative global activities that provide funding for high levels of investment in new technology. Moreover, as these ties sustain extensive cost-sharing and risk-sharing, as well as information-sharing, competitive investment by rival American and European firms becomes difficult.[88] Efforts by the US and European governments to protect their high technology markets, while hindered by weak cooperation in their business communities, also tend to be hindered by competitive government bidding for Japanese direct investment.

European Union trade relations are managed under a common commercial policy, implemented under the direction of the European Commission, in line with decisions by the Council of Ministers. The non-tariff barriers of member states that affect commerce with non-Union countries are being harmonized, to facilitate the operation of the Single Market, or are being eliminated as the integration of that market is completed. The common commercial policy maintains formal barriers to market penetration that are set mainly in bargaining with the USA. Most of these barriers are relatively low, reflecting complementary interests based on high volume intraindustry Atlantic trade in manufactured products.[89] Within each member state the degree of market openness is determined very much by its intercorporate pattern, and by links between this pattern and the administration. In Germany strong informal bonds between firms are sources of restraints on imports, and in France strong administrative influence on firms limits the significance of formal market openness.

Export performance under the common commercial policy, determined by efficiencies in the national intercorporate patterns, reflects trade levels within the Single Market. Germany leads, with exports to the USA (the main trading partner of the Union) that are 50 per cent higher than Britain's and double those of France. The Union's total exports to the USA are, however, only slightly higher than Japan's, and these, it must be stressed, have greater strategic significance, because of their concentration in higher technology sectors and the extent to which they are complemented by Japanese manufacturing in the USA.[90] Technological lags by European firms are adversely affecting their prospects for competition in the US market.

Interests in restraining imports from Japan influence Union policy, but the lack of political will which hinders the development of a more active common policy on Japanese direct investment tends to prevent the introduction of strong import restrictions, despite persistently large Japanese surpluses.

Germany and Britain are Japan's main trading partners in the Union, and are the principal European host countries for Japanese direct investment. Rationalizations of European Union operations by Japanese firms tend to be managed from bases in Germany and Britain. The history of the common commercial policy evidences protectionist tendencies, reflecting the influence of French, Italian and Southern European interests, and general elite awareness in the Union that European shares of world markets have been declining over the past few decades because of American and Japanese competition. For increased competitiveness in international markets, it is clear that European firms will have to maximize their use of opportunities in their Union market, where American enterprises already have a strong position.[91] European protectionism, however, attracts foreign direct investment into manufacturing for the Union market, and the competition between member governments to draw such investment entails acceptance of substantial imports by the incoming firms.

Collective management of the common commercial policy involves multiple incentive conflicts for Union governments, because of their rivalries regarding the spread of gains from commerce in the Single Market, their unevenly shared interests in enhancing European competitiveness, and their opportunities to gain advantages at the expense of Union partners through expedient deals with non-European firms. There are general incentives to cooperate for the freer operation of market forces in the Union, but there are more immediately relevant incentives for each government to assist national firms seizing regional opportunities, and informally to protect the domestic market positions of these firms. For deepening integration in the Union the most significant possibilities for resolving incentive conflicts are those in the Franco-German relationship. Strong economic nationalism tends, however, to be reinforced in Germany's elites as their macromanagement achievements remain superior to those of the less integrated French system. The pervasive influence of intense nationalism in that system hinders collaborative efforts to attain more symmetrical structural interdependence with Germany, and accordingly French policy has to recognize options for coalition-building with other European partners, yet their policies can be ambivalent because of their ties with Germany.

CORPORATE STRATEGIES

National policy environments influence corporate strategies first of all through diverse effects on the assimilative capacity of each political economy, which is largely determined by the system-building functions of each pattern of intercorporate relations. Comprehensive macromanagement in the public interest, encouraging trustful cooperation between firms, and between firms and the national administration, can promote a high degree of integration if corporate cultures are oriented towards the building of relational ties in industry groups and networks. National firms then develop strong home country loyalties, which, for example, are expressed in location preferences and collaborative adjustment efforts to prevent dislocations caused by outward direct investment. Incoming foreign firms are drawn into the integrated pattern of cooperation, and can thus develop host country loyalties.

Intensely individualistic business cultures do not encourage the development of relational ties, and administrative responsiveness to aggressive but fragmented representations of corporate interests generally do not inspire trust and cooperation. Political cultures typically express value orientations identical with those in national business cultures. A strongly individualistic political culture tends to be responsible for deficient administrative performance, with much emphasis on support-maximizing allocations. The government failings, and their increasing costs, give managements incentives to implement the highly self-reliant and totally competitive strategies to which they are already inclined by their individualistic business cultures. For these managements, moreover, ventures into international operations that can spread risks, exploit world market opportunities, and reduce regulatory exposure at home, tend to become imperative. Motivations to engage in international operations are also strong for firms benefiting from relational ties in more integrated political economies, but they can undertake extensive foreign production with the advantages of collaborative risk-sharing and cost-sharing.

In the increasing competition associated with the continual linking of world markets, firms belonging to integrated national systems of industry groups and networks, and operating under comprehensively supportive national administrations, are advantaged. Concerted entrepreneurship that in effect internalizes markets on a large scale tends to restrict opportunities for enterprises operating individually out of less integrated business communities under less efficient governments. These enterprises may, however, derive benefits from established positions in large home country markets.

Fiscal expansion in the less effectively managed states that cannot achieve allocative discipline raises internal demand in their economies, drawing imports from the more integrated states. Their products tend to be internationally competitive because of efficiencies generated through all the relational cooperation in their business communities. In the evolution of the current pattern of major Euro-Pacific structural interdependencies, heavy fiscal expansion in the USA and considerable fiscal expansion in most of the European Union states has provided export opportunities for Japanese firms. The American and European deficit financing, while raising costs of government and diverting much investment from productive use, has hindered growth, making it more difficult for national firms to achieve greater international competitiveness, except through undertaking more extensive global operations. These firms have increasing incentives to produce at low cost foreign locations for their home markets, but thereby contribute to the deindustrialization that increases the economic burdens of their governments. Meanwhile the more integrated states, achieving higher growth, tend to draw portfolio investment from the slower growth states under weaker macromanagement.

In the competition for world market shares, transnational enterprises from the integrated and the less integrated states strive to maximize efficiencies through endeavours to rationalize operations at the regional and global levels. Enterprises based in the more integrated states tend to be advantaged, as their higher levels of organizational unity and their industry group and network bonds facilitate rationalized operations at both levels. Firms with individualistic corporate cultures operating out of less integrated states have to contend with organizational problems when attempting rationalized global operations. Centralized management becomes difficult because of diverse forms of organizational manipulation to assert autonomy and advance personal interests. Large middle management layers are necessary to impose central control through bureaucratic discipline. Regional rather than global management can thus be a second-best solution, but it leaves unchallenged the advantages gained by the more integrated firms because of their capacities for organizational performance at the global level.[92]

High levels of integration based on uniform corporate cultures enable Japanese enterprises to achieve superior organizational performance in regional and global operations. In US firms, however, strong individualism and top down management to discipline that individualism, make central coordination of globally dispersed subsidiaries very difficult. Many of these subsidiaries, moreover, having been operating for several decades, have been under managements inclined to assert autonomy because of local experience. Most of the Japanese subsidiaries have been of more recent origin and are under managements closely identified with the perspectives and operating practices of their parent companies.[93]

The strategies of US international firms show strong preferences for European locations. The European Union is the only large integrated regional market outside the North America Free Trade Area (NAFTA), and its growth prospects exert strong attraction, especially because the generally weaker competitiveness of European firms limits their capacities to exploit the opportunities of their Single Market. American transnational enterprises have had a strong presence in Europe over the past four decades, and enjoy high degrees of social acceptability. Moreover, the restrictions of several European governments on Japanese exports and direct investment enable US firms in Europe to operate with relatively weaker Japanese competitive challenges than those encountered in the United States. American corporations in Europe are able to rationalize their regional operations with major advantages over their Japanese rivals because the latter have a smaller presence, and do not benefit from the cultural and ethnic affinities that assist the European activities of American firms.

Within Europe the policy environments tending to draw US direct investment are mainly those in Germany and Britain. The principal British attraction is the liberal foreign direct investment policy, while Germany offers opportunities to function within a more comprehensively managed political economy with stronger centres of innovation. Britain has the main European concentration of US direct investment in financial services, insurance and real estate, while Germany hosts US direct investment in manufacturing at a level similar to Britain's, but rising faster.[94] Production costs are above Britain's, as higher labour productivity is offset by higher wages, but access to the Union market from Germany can be assisted by the extensive involvement of German firms in Union commerce. German exports to the Union are twice as large as Britain's.

Operations in Europe assist US firms to consolidate positions in their home market – where the Japanese presence is larger, more challenging and has more scope for expansion, because of the opportunities provided by US firms operating without industry group ties, and the constraints restricting US administrative measures to curb Japanese market penetration. Within NAFTA, US positions in this integrating market are being strengthened through regional rationalization strategies, with increasing use of opportunities for direct investment in Mexico. NAFTA clauses were designed to limit Japanese market penetration by setting high local content requirements for foreign manufacturing investment in Mexico and Canada. The US direct investment in Mexico involves some diversion of production activities from industrializing East Asian states, in response to mixed advantages.[95] Authoritarian practices by East Asian governments suppress labour union activity, holding down production costs for foreign firms, but production in Mexico, although it can offer less opportunities for the exploitation of labour, is conveniently situated for service of the US market.

Japanese international enterprises strive to consolidate their positions in the American market, giving this the highest priority, as the degree of penetration already achieved is exceptional because of its size and because of the factors limiting the options which the US government can take to promote more balanced structural interdependence. Of these factors Japanese investor confidence in the US economy is the most important. The industrializing East Asian states rank next in the strategies of Japanese international corporations, and market shares in these states are being gained faster than in the USA, through exports and direct investment, supported by large scale official aid.[96]

The size of the Japanese presence and its influence on governments and on national firms in the area has been restricting opportunities for US firms, whose interests in East Asia have become less active in recent years. Japan's trade links with the industrializing East Asian states have become as large as its commercial bonds with the USA.[97]

A Japanese integrated international production system for North America is linked with one in East Asia that is being shaped more actively by Japanese policy and corporate activity. Most of the East Asian industrializing states relate to Japan individually, without mutual or group ties, although several of them are members of the loosely organized Association of South East Asian Nations (ASEAN). Most of these ASEAN members have attempted import-substituting industrialization behind high protectionist barriers, with weak technocratic capabilities, and are endeavouring to shift to export-oriented industrialization. Because of the weaknesses of their sheltered firms they tend to look to Japan for investment in outward-oriented manufacturing. As the Japanese industrial and commercial presence in their area increases, it tends to link them individually more with Japan while limiting their options for diversification of their foreign economic relations.

The links between the North American and East Asian production systems apparently enable Japanese firms to implement regional pricing strategies for increasing market gains. They have been able to engage in strategic price-setting for the separate US, Canadian and Mexican markets, while resorting to similar price-setting that has tended to segregate national markets in East Asia.[98] Their capacities to use discriminatory pricing on a regional scale are very significant, because of the cohesion in their integrated foreign production systems, and because their common objectives are long-term market domination, to be achieved with low profit margins. The home policy environment's comprehensive support facilitates the wide-ranging price competition for multiple market penetration by continuously promoting cohesion in the national intercorporate system.

European Union firms, whose policy environments have been changed by the deepening integration associated with the formation of their Single Market, and by the increasing Europeanization of their home country policy processes, have relatively restricted choices. Their generally weak resources and technological lags obligate concentration on opportunities to increase market shares in the Single Market, and the competitive stresses in that market evidently limit consideration of longer-term prospects for using anticipated market shares to support ventures outside Europe. Within the Union German firms have mostly superior positions, because of the size, resources and cohesion of their intercorporate system, and the administrative support which it receives. The home policy environment enables these firms to extend their operations in the other Union countries very competitively. Weaker enterprises in these countries are being forced into declines which tend to obligate acceptance of mergers and acquisitions by American, German or Japanese corporations.[99] American companies are often favoured because of their greater resources, and apparently also because dealings with them can be on more equal terms. German firms have behind them the influence of their home government in the European Union, while Japanese firms derive collective support from the bonds in their industry groups and networks.

NOTES

1. See John H. Dunning, 'Governments, Economic Organization and International Competitiveness', in Lars-Gunnar Mattsson and Bengt Stymne (eds), *Corporate and Industry Strategies for Europe*, Amsterdam: North-Holland, 1991, 41–74.
2. See *Technology and the Economy: The Key Relationships*, Paris: OECD, 1992.
3. See Michael L. Gerlach, *Alliance Capitalism: The Social Organization of Japanese Business*, Berkeley: University of California Press, 1992.
4. On the competitive pressures influencing governments see John M. Stopford, Susan Strage and John S. Henley, *Rival States, Rival Firms*, Cambridge: Cambridge University Press, 1991.
5. On patterns of intercorporate relations see W. Carl Kester, 'Industrial Groups as Systems of Contractual Governance', *Oxford Review of Economic Policy*, 8 (3), Autumn 1992, 24–44.
6. See observations in Kirsten S. Wever and Christopher S. Allen, 'The Financial System and Corporate Governance in Germany: Institutions and the Diffusion of Innovations', *Journal of Public Policy*, 13 (2), April 1993, 183–202; and Bart Van Ark and Dirk Pilat, 'Productivity Levels in Germany, Japan, and the United States: Differences and Causes', Brookings Papers on Economic Activity, 2, 1993,1–70.
7. See Masaaki Kotabe and K. Scott Swann, 'Offshore Sourcing: Reaction, Maturation and Consolidation of US Multinationals', *Journal of International Business Studies*, 25 (1), First Quarter 1994, 115–140.
8. Record capital outflows increased the US direct investment position abroad on a historical cost basis by 10 per cent in 1993. See *Survey of Current Business*, 74 (6), June 1994, 72–85.
9. See Gerlach, *op. cit.*
10. See *Germany*, Paris: OECD Economic Survey, 1994.
11. On the strategies of US firms engaged in global oligopolistic competition see David B. Yoffie (ed.), *Beyond Free Trade: Firms. Governments, and Global Competition*, Boston: Harvard Business School Press, 1993, Chapter 10.
12. See Alan J. Auerbach, *The US Fiscal Problem: Where We Are, How We Got There, and Where We're Going*, Cambridge: National Bureau of Economic Research, Working Paper 4709, 1994.
13. See Martin Feldstein (ed.), *The Risk of Economic Crisis*, Chicago: University of Chicago Press, 1991.
14. See *Government Securities and Debt Management in the 1990s*, Paris: OECD 1993, 220.
15. See Thomas Mayer (ed.), *The Political Economy of American Monetary Policy*, Cambridge: Cambridge University Press, 1990.
16. See Terry M. Moe, 'Political Institutions: The Neglected Side of the Story', *Journal of Law, Economics and Organization*, 6, Special Issue, 1990, 213–54.
17. On the weaknesses of US banks see Allen B. Frankel and John D. Montgomery, 'Financial Structure: An International Perspective', *Brookings Papers on Economic Activity*, 1, 1991, 257–310. Problems in the US thrift industry are reviewed in Steven M. Fries, 'An Expen-

sive Thrift Industry', in Yusuke Horiguchi and others, *The United States Economy: Performance and Issues*, Washington D.C.: International Monetary Fund, 1992, 373–98.
18. See James R. Crotty and Don Goldstein, 'Do US Financial Markets Allocate Credit Efficiently? The Case of Corporate Restructuring in the 1980s', in Gary A. Dymski, Gerald Epstein and Robert Pollin (eds), *Transforming the US Financial System*, Armonk: M.E. Sharpe, 1993, 253–66.
19. On the fiscal policy process see Heizo Takenaka, *Contemporary Japanese Economy and Economic Policy*, Ann Arbor: University of Michigan Press, 1991, Chapter 11. On the roles of the Ministry of Finance see Frances McCall Rosenbluth, 'Financial Deregulation and Interest Intermediation' in Gary D. Allinson and Yasunori Sone (eds), *Political Dynamics in Contemporary Japan*, Ithaca: Cornell University Press, 1993, 107–29.
20. See Rosenbluth, *op. cit.*, and Stephen K. Vogel, 'The Bureaucratic Approach to the Financial Revolution: Japan's Ministry of Finance and Financial System Reform', *Governance*, **7** (3), July 1994, 219–43.
21. See Wever and Allen, *op. cit.*, and Norbert Kloten, 'Germany' in Joseph A. Pechman (ed.), *The Role of the Economist in Government*, New York: New York University Press, 1989, 47–72.
22. See *Germany*, OECD Economic Survey, *op. cit.*
23. See Paul De Grauwe, 'The Political Economy of Monetary Union in Europe', *The World Economy*, **16** (6), November 1993, 653–62.
24. See Ark and Pilat, *op. cit.*
25. See *Government Securities and Debt Management in the 1990s, op. cit.*, 196.
26. See *France*, Paris: OECD Economic Survey, 1994, especially 53–7.
27. See Olivier Jean Blanchard and Pierre Alain Muet, 'Competitiveness Through Disinflation: An Assessment of the French Macroeconomic Strategy', *Economic Policy*, **16**, April 1993, 11–56.
28. *Direction of Trade Statistics Yearbook*, 1993, Washington D.C.: International Monetary Fund, 1993, 56.
29. See De Grauwe, *op. cit.*
30. See Mark Mason, 'Europe and the Japanese Banking Challenge', *Journal of Public Policy*, **13** (3), July–September 1993, 255–78.
31. See *Oxford Review of Economic Policy*, **9** (3), Autumn 1993 – Symposium on UK Economic Policy.
32. See Willem H. Buiter and David A. Currie, 'Options for UK Fiscal Policy' ibid., 62–8, *Government Securities and Debt Management in the 1990s, op. cit.*, 218.
33. See *Direction of Trade Statistics Yearbook*, 1993, *op. cit.*, 400.
34. For a discussion of institutional factors influencing UK growth see N.F.R. Crafts, 'Institutions and Economic Growth: Recent British Experience in an International Context', *West European Politics*, **15** (4), October 1992, 16–38. See also Michael Hodges and Stephen Woolcock, 'Atlantic Capitalism versus Rhine Capitalism in the European Community', *West European Politics*, **16** (3), July 1993, 329–44.
35. See Maria Papadakis, 'Did (Does) the United States have a Competitiveness Crisis?', *Journal of Policy Analysis and Management*, **13** (1), Winter 1994, 1–20.
36. See Kotabe and Swann, *op. cit.*
37. See Paul M. Romer, 'Implementing a National Technology Strategy with Self-Organizing Investment Boards', *Brookings Papers on Economic Activity*, **2**, 1993, 345–89. See also Roger G. Noll, 'Structural Policies in the United States', in Samuel Kernell (ed.), *Parallel Politics: Economic Policymaking in the United States and Japan*, Washington D.C.: Brookings Institution, 1991, 230–80.
38. See William D. Coleman, 'State Traditions and Comprehensive Business Associations: A Comparative Structural Analysis', *Political Studies*, **XXXVIII** (2), June 1990, 231–52.
39. See David J. Teece, 'Competition and Cooperation: Striking the Right Balance', *California Management Review*, **31** (3), Spring 1989, 25–37.
40. See Edward M. Graham, 'Industrial Policy Issues in the USA' in Gunnar K. Sletmo and Gavin Boyd (eds), *Industrial Policies in the Pacific*, Boulder: Westview Press, 1994.
41. On the rationale for this trade policy activism see Laura D'Andrea Tyson, *Who's Bashing*

Whom? Trade Conflict in High-Technology Industries, Washington D.C.: Institute for International Economics, 1992.

42. See Kotabe, *op. cit.*, and details of the US direct investment position abroad and its operations, *Survey of Current Business*, *op. cit.*, 72–85 and 42–62.

43. See Gerlach, *op. cit.*, and Martin Fransman, *The Market and Beyond: Cooperation and Competition in Information Technology Development In the Japanese System*, Cambridge: Cambridge University Press, 1990. See also Shumpei Kumon and Henry Rosovsky (eds), *The Political Economy of Japan Vol. 3*, Stanford: Stanford University Press, 1992.

44. See concluding comments by Yasunori Sone in *Political Dynamics in Contemporary Japan*, *op. cit.*, 295–306, and Takenaka, *op. cit.*, 167–80.

45. See Toyohiro Kono, *Long Range Planning of Japanese Corporations*, Berlin: Walter de Gruyter, 1992 and Ken-ichi Imai, 'Japan's Corporate Networks' in *The Political Economy of Japan*, *op. cit.*, 198–230.

46. See Allen J. Morrison and Kendall Roth, 'The Regional Solution: An Alternative to Globalization', *Transnational Corporations*, **1** (2), August 1992, 37–56.

47. See Thomas S. Arrison, C. Fred Bergsten, Edward M. Graham and Martha Caldwell Harris (eds), *Japan's Growing Technological Capability: Implications for the US Economy*, Washington D.C.: National Academy Press, 1992.

48. See Ark and Pilat, *op. cit.*

49. See Jeffrey A. Hart, *Rival Capitalists: International Competitiveness in the United States Japan, and Western Europe*, Ithaca: Cornell University Press, 1992, 181–222.

50. See *Survey of Current Business*, **73** (7), July 1993, 67.

51. See Sonia Mazey and Jeremy Richardson (eds), *Lobbying in the European Community*, Oxford: Oxford University Press, 1993.

52. See Margaret Sharp and Keith Pavitt, 'Technology Policy in the 1990s: Old Trends and New Realities', *Journal of Common Market Studies*, **31** (2), June 1993, 130–51.

53. See Hart, *op. cit.*, 87–138; Alastair Cole, 'The Presidential Party and the Fifth Republic', *West European Politics*, **16** (2), April 1993, 49–66; and John T.S. Keeler, 'Executive Power and Policy Making Patterns in France: Gauging the Impact of Fifth Republic Institutions', *West European Politics*, **16** (4), October 1993, 518–44. See also references to French business associations in Coleman, *op. cit.*

54. See *Direction of Trade Statistics Yearbook*, *op. cit.*, 177.

55. See Sharp and Pavitt, *op. cit.*

56. See Coleman, *op. cit.*

57. See *Oxford Review of Economic Policy* – Symposium on UK Economic Policy, *op. cit.*

58. *Ibid.*

59. See Hodges and Woolcock, *op. cit.*

60. See *Survey of Current Business*, **73** (7), July 1993, 67.

61. See Lawrence J. White, 'Competition Policy in the United States: An Overview', *Oxford Review of Economic Policy*, **9** (2), Summer 1993, 133–51; B. Dan Wood and James E. Anderson, 'The Politics of US Antitrust Regulation', *American Journal of Political Science*, **37** (1), February 1993, 1–39; and Marc Allen Eisner, 'Bureaucratic Professionalization and the Limits of the Political Control Thesis: The Case of the Federal Trade Commission', *Governance*, **6** (2), April 1993, 127–53.

62. See Mitsuo Matsushita, *International Trade and Competition Law in Japan*, Oxford: Oxford University Press, 1993, 1–169, and Gerlach, *op. cit.*

63. See Frank Upham, 'Privatizing Regulation: The Implementation of the Large Scale Retail Stores Law', in *Political Dynamics in Contemporary Japan*, *op. cit.*, 264–94.

64. See Andre Sapir, Pierre Buigues and Alexis Jacquemin, 'European Competition Policy in Manufacturing and Services: A Two-Speed Approach?', *Oxford Review of Economic Policy*, **9** (2), Summer 1993, 113–32, and Matthew Bishop and John Kay (eds), *European Mergers and Merger Policy*, Oxford: Oxford University Press, 1993. See also Frederic Jenny, 'Competition and Competition Policy' and Alexis Jacquemin, 'Corporate Strategy and Competition Policy in the Post 1992 Single Market', in William James Adams (ed.), *Singular Europe: Economy and Polity of the European Community after 1992*, Ann Arbor: University of Michigan Press, 1992, 69–96,125–44.

65. See Mazey and Richardson, *op. cit.*
66. See Christel Lane, 'European Business Systems: Britain and Germany Compared', in Richard Whitley (ed.), *European Business Systems: Firms and Markets in their National Contexts*, London: Sage, 1992, 64–97, and Ellen Schneider-Lenne, 'Corporate Control in Germany', *Oxford Review of Economic Policy*, **8** (3), Autumn 1992, 11–23.
67. See 'France' in *Formal and Informal Investment Barriers in the G7 Countries: The Country Chapters*, Ottawa: Industry Canada Occasional Paper 1, Vol. 1, 9–50. See also Hart, *op. cit.*, 87–138, and A.E. Safarian, *Multinational Enterprise and Public Policy*, Cheltenham: Edward Elgar, 1993, 208–35.
68. See Mark E. Williams, 'The Effectiveness of Competition Policy in the United Kingdom', *Oxford Review of Economic Policy*, **9** (2), Summer 1993, 94–112.
69. See Bishop and Key, *op. cit.*, 162–99, 239–77.
70. See Raymond J. Mataloni Jr, 'US Multinational Companies: Operations in 1992', *Survey of Current Business*, **74** (6), June 1994, 42–62.
71. See Dennis J. Encarnation, *Rivals beyond Trade: America Versus Japan in Global Competition*, Ithaca: Cornell University Press, 1992, 97–146. On the liberal orientation of US policy see 'United States', in *Formal and Informal Investment Barriers in the G7 Countries*, *op. cit.*, 193–236, and Safarian, *op. cit.*, 362–402.
72. See David Bailey, George Harte and Roger Sugden, 'US Policy Debate towards Inward Investment', *Journal of World Trade*, **26** (4), August 1992, 65–94.
73. On Japanese foreign direct investment policy see *Formal and Informal Investment Barriers in the G7 Countries*, *op. cit.*, 151–92, and Safarian, *op. cit.*, 236–87.
74. See *Japan's Growing Technological Capability*, *op. cit.*
75. See Mason, *op. cit.*, and Raj Aggarwal, 'An Overview of Japanese Finance: Uniqueness in an Age of Global Integration', in Stanley R. Stansell (ed.), *International Financial Market Integration*, Oxford: Blackwell, 1993, 42–56.
76. See Stephen Young and Neil Hood, 'Inward Investment Policy in the European Community in the 1990s', *Transnational Corporations*, **2** (2), August 1993, 35–62.
77. See Safarian, *op. cit.*, 322–28, and *Formal and Informal Investment Barriers in the G7 Countries*, *op. cit.*, 51–86.
78. See Safarian, *op. cit.*, 208–35, and *Formal and Informal Investment Barriers in G7 Countries*, *op. cit.*, 9–50.
79. See *Formal and Informal Investment Barriers in the G7 Countries*, *op. cit.*, 119–150, and Safarian, *op. cit.*, 339–61.
80. See *Survey of Current Business*, **74** (6), June 1994, 72–8.
81. See Kotabe and Swann, *op. cit.*, and Mataloni, *op. cit.*
82. See Stanley D. Nollen and Dennis P. Quinn, 'Free Trade, Fair Trade, Strategic Trade, and Protectionism in the US Congress, 1987–88', *International Organization*, **48** (3), Summer 1994, 491–525; Douglas Nelson, 'Domestic Political Preconditions of US Trade Policy: Liberal Structure and Protectionist Dynamics', *Journal of Public Policy*, **9** (1), January–March 1989, 83–108; and Alan M. Rugman and Michael V. Gestrin, 'US Trade Laws as Barriers to Globalisation', *The World Economy*, **14** (3), September 1991, 335–52. See also *Trade Policy Review: United States*, Geneva: GATT, 1994, Vols 1&2.
83. See Andrew Lyon and Gerald Silverstein, *The Alternative Minimum Tax and the Behaviour of Multinational Corporations*, Cambridge: National Bureau of Economic Research, Working Paper 4783, 1994; and James R. Hines and Eric M. Rice, 'Fiscal Paradise, Foreign Tax Havens and American Business', *Quarterly Journal of Economics*, **CIX** (1), February 1994, 149–82.
84. See Mataloni, *op. cit.*, and *Direction of Trade Statistics Yearbook 1993*, *op. cit.*, 56.
85. See Encarnation, *op. cit.*, and Mataloni, *op. cit.*
86. See Paul Krugman (ed.), *Trade with Japan: Has the Door Opened Wider?*, Chicago: University of Chicago Press, 1991; Marie Anchordoguy, 'Japanese–American Trade Conflict and Supercomputers', *Political Science Quarterly*, **109** (1), Spring 1994, 35–80; Encarnation, *op. cit.*; and David Arase, 'Public–Private Sector Interest Coordination in Japan's ODA', *Pacific Affairs*, **67** (2), Summer 1994, 171–99. See also Gary R. Saxonhouse,

'Do Japanese Firms Price Discriminate in North America?', *The World Economy*, **17** (1), January 1994, 87–100.

87. See Encarnation, *op. cit.*
88. See Gunter Heiduk and Kozo Yamamura (eds), *Technological Competition and Interdependence: The Search for Policy in the United States, West Germany, and Japan*, Seattle: University of Washington Press, 1990, and *Technology and Productivity: The Challenge for Economic Policy*, Paris: OECD, 1991, Part III, B.
89. See Stephen Woolcock, 'The European Acquis and Multilateral Trade Rules: Are They Compatible?', *Journal of Common Market Studies*, **31** (4), December 1993, 539–58; L. Alan Winters, 'Expanding EC Membership and Association Accords: Recent Experience and Future Prospects', in Kym Anderson and Richard Blackhurst (eds), *Regional Integration and the Global Trading System*, New York: St Martin's Press, 1993, 104–25; and David B. Audretsch, *The Market and the State: Government Policy towards Business in Europe, Japan and the United States*, Hertfordshire: Harvester Wheatsheaf, 1989, 254–74. See also references to Europe in David B. Yoffie (ed.), *Beyond Free Trade: Firms, Governments and Global Competition*, Boston: Harvard Business School Press, 1993.
90. See *Direction of Trade Statistics Yearbook*, 1993, *op. cit.*, 403.
91. See Mataloni, *op. cit.* and Bishop and Kay, *op. cit.*
92. See Morrison and Roth, *op. cit.*
93. *Ibid.*
94. See *Survey of Current Business*, **73** (7), July, 1993, 59–87.
95. See Michael Gestrin and Alan M. Rugman, 'The Strategic Response of MNEs to NAFTA', in Alan M. Rugman (ed.), *Foreign Investment and NAFTA*, Columbia: South Carolina, 1994, 183–99.
96. See Arase, *op. cit.*
97. See *Direction of Trade Statistics Yearbook, op. cit.*, 240.
98. See Saxonhouse, *op. cit.*
99. See comments on intensifying competition in the Union, in Alexis Jacquemin and David Wright, 'Corporate Strategies and European Challenges Post 1992', *Journal of Common Market Studies*, **31** (4), December 1993, 525–38.

3. Comparative contractual governance

Michael Blaine*

As used in the literature, the term 'governance' has two disparate but inter-related meanings. The first involves the governance of the firm and deals with problems arising from the separation of its ownership and control. Of particular interest are the structures and processes which constrain managers' pursuit of self-interest and act to align the interests of managers and share-holders. These issues define the domain of 'agency theory' and are often associated with the pioneering work of Berle and Means (1932) and, more recently, of Jensen and Meckling (1976) and Farma and Jensen (1983). The second meaning involves the governance of economic transactions. Here the focus is on the institutions which coordinate and control the exchange of goods and services between economic actors. These issues form the basis of the 'transaction cost analysis' developed by Oliver Williamson (1975, 1979, 1985). According to Williamson, transaction cost analysis entails, '… an examination of the *comparative costs of planning, adapting, and monitoring task completion under alternative governance structures*' [original emphasis] (1985, p. 2). By examining the costs and benefits of various forms of govern-ance, transaction cost analysis attempts to identify the most efficient means of organizing economic activities. This latter connotation provides impetus for the present chapter.

Following Williamson, Kester distinguishes two types of governance – contractual and corporate – and notes that:

> Systems of contractual governance span a continuum bounded at one end by the writing of explicit, detailed contracts, which may then be enforced by court order in the event of attempted breach by one of the parties. At the other end is reliance on implicit, relational contracting founded on enduring trust relationships and reinforced by largely non-legalistic mechanisms structured to encourage volun-tary compliance with informal agreements (1992, p. 27).

Earlier researchers explored a far more limited range of alternative govern-ance mechanisms. According to Richardson: 'The underlying idea … was the existence of two ways in which economic activity could be co-ordinated, the one, conscious planning, holding sway in firms, the other, the price mechanism, operating spontaneously on the relations between firms ...' (1972, p. 883). Over time, however, the notion that transactions could be neatly placed within a dichotomous framework was increasingly challenged by the emergence of a vast middle-ground of alternatives which fell somewhere between the market and the firm. Various forms of 'relational' contracting – from long-term supplier agreements to technology-sharing arrangements and minority joint ventures – defied the formal logic of transaction cost analysis by displaying patterns of exchange which were often costly and inefficient. Nevertheless, the use of these intermediate governance mechanisms continued to grow and by 1985 Williamson acknowledged that: 'Whereas I was earlier of the view that transactions of the middle kind were very difficult to organize and hence very unstable ... I am now persuaded that transactions in the middle range are much more common' (1985, p. 83).

What the strict dichotomy between markets and firms lacked was a means of explaining economic arrangements that did not rely on formal, legal incentives and safeguards to ensure compliance, but instead relied on various social mechanisms such as trust and goodwill. The widespread use of cooperative arrangements fits awkwardly into the 'orthodox' theory of economic organization. Further, many forms of interfirm cooperation blur the boundaries between individual actors, making the distinction between markets and hierarchies appear increasingly obsolete. As a result of these and other developments, a critical re-evaluation of many long-standing economic and organizational theories is underway.

My own thoughts on the subject have undergone a radical transformation during the preparation of this chapter. After reviewing the conflicting strands of current research, I am persuaded that even a major revision of existing theories will not fully explain the enormous diversity of business practices across countries. Further, I am increasingly convinced that many economic and social phenomena are not even 'intendedly rational' and can only be understood within the specific institutional and cultural context in which they occur. The process of exchange is fundamentally a social concept, and therefore the means used to govern economic exchanges necessarily reflect fundamental assumptions about human and physical nature. These assumptions continue to differ in ways that challenge universal conceptual frameworks.

This chapter considers some of the more serious challenges to the 'orthodox' theory of economic organization. In particular, the effect of socio-cultural factors on the institutional structures that support economic activity will be examined. The motivation for this derives from the growing awareness that many of the assumptions of the neoclassical model and of American business practices are incongruous with the social and cultural institutions of other nations.[1] This is clearly evident in the widely divergent attitudes towards competition and cooperation and the individual and the group seen across countries. Such differences in the assumptions and objectives of social and economic institutions may also explain why Japanese or Swedish industry contrasts structurally with American or British industry.

The introductory section of this chapter briefly reviews Williamson's 'markets–hierarchies' approach and traces its genesis.[2] Particular attention is given to the role of markets and firms as alternative means of governing economic activities. In addition, many of the most commonly cited criticisms of this approach are considered. The next section examines the wide range of alternative governance structures which lie between the market and the firm. An attempt is made to identify forces in the international competitive environment that have encouraged the proliferation of these structures and to survey some of the theoretical explanations for their widespread use. The following section examines the role of institutional structure and culture in shaping the organization of economic activity. The basic premise of this discussion is that both markets and firms are 'embedded' within a cultural and institutional context. By explicitly examining the role of culture in defining the institutional environment in which economic activities occur, a further step may be taken towards generalizing and expanding the transaction cost model.

MARKETS AND HIERARCHIES

One of the most fruitful areas of recent economic and organizational research has been the application of 'transaction cost' principles to the study of the firm, particularly the multinational enterprise (MNE). Williamson (1985) traces the origins of this approach to the work of Frank Knight in the early 1920s, and credits Knight with the recognition that both opportunism and bounded rationality – two of the underlying assumptions of transaction cost analysis – play a major role in determining the method of economic organization. Knight also posed a question that was to play a central role in the theory of the firm, namely: 'What determines how large the firm will grow?'[3]

R.H. Coase explored both of these questions in his classic 1937 article. Attempting to explain why firms emerge in a specialized exchange economy, Coase concluded that there were costs associated with the price mechanism that provided a rationale for the firm. He noted that the cost of discovering relevant prices, costs associated with contracting, and the costs of uncertainty – all of which arise when transactions are conducted in the market-place – could in some cases be great enough to justify the coordination of economic activities within the firm.[4] Using marginal analysis, Coase also reasoned that, given these costs, '... a firm will tend to expand until the costs of organizing an extra transaction within the firm becomes equal to the costs of carrying out the same transaction by means of exchange in the open market ...' (1937, p. 394). Alchian and Demsetz (1972) note that the critical importance of Coase's work was the recognition that markets are not costless; but more importantly, Coase explicitly recognized the firm and the market as *alternative* means of organizing economic activities.

This latter point is explored in great detail in Williamson's (1975) classic study, *Markets and Hierarchies: Analysis and Antitrust Implications*. Unlike Coase, Williamson was interested in explaining the firm's behaviour under various market conditions rather than its *raison d'être*. Following Commons (1934), Williamson adopted the transaction as his basic unit of analysis and developed the 'organizational failures framework' to assess the relative efficiency of markets and hierarchies as competing governance mechanisms.[5] He argued that the interaction of a small group of 'transaction costs' (such as bounded rationality, opportunism, uncertainty and small numbers of market participants) often created serious market failures which encouraged the substitution of the market with the hierarchical structure of the firm. Williamson's basic argument can be summarized as follows:

> (1) Markets and firms are alternative instruments for completing a related set of transactions; (2) whether a set of transactions ought to be executed across markets or within a firm depends on the relative efficiency of each mode; (3) the cost of writing and executing complex contracts across a market *vary with the characteristics of the human decision makers who are involved with the transaction on the one hand, and the objective properties of the market on the other*; and (4) although the human and environmental factors that impede exchanges between firms (across a market) manifest themselves somewhat differently within the firm, the same set of factors apply to both [original emphasis] (Williamson, 1975, p. 8).

The insight that the relative efficiency of markets and firms depends on a specific set of human and environmental 'transactions costs' is of course of paramount importance; but equally significant is the central role that Williamson assigns to contracting in his analysis.[6] In fact, he later observed that: 'Transaction cost economics poses the problem of economic organization as a problem of contracting. A particular task is to be accomplished. It can be organized in any of several alternative ways. Explicit or implicit contract and support apparatus are associated with it. What are the costs?' (1985, p. 20).

Williamson explores this theme in a 1979 article entitled, 'Transaction-Cost Economics: The Governance of Contractual Relations'.[7] Following Macneil (1978), Williamson identifies three approaches to contract law –

classical, neoclassical and relational – and argues that each type of contracting is associated with a unique form of governance. Classical contract law has several distinctive features. First, the identity of the parties is considered irrelevant. Secondly, the terms of the agreement are carefully and formally specified, with formal terms taking precedence over informal terms if disputes arise. Finally, remedies are narrowly prescribed and typically known in advance. Williamson notes: 'The emphasis, thus, is on legal rules, formal documentation, and self-liquidating transactions' (1979, p. 101). Neoclassical contracting, on the other hand, is appropriate for long-term contracts executed under conditions of uncertainty. The outstanding feature of this form of contracting is the use of third party assistance (rather than litigation) in resolving disputes over contract execution and performance. Williamson notes: 'A recognition that the world is complex, that agreements are incomplete, and that some contracts will never be reached unless both parties have confidence in the settlement machinery thus characterizes neoclassical contract law' (1979, p. 102). Finally, relational contracting is a response to ongoing relations of increasing duration and complexity which require governance structures that are more transaction-specific and administrative than those associated with neoclassical contracts. According to Williamson: 'By contrast with the neoclassical system, where the reference point for effecting adaptations remains the original agreement, the reference point under a truly relational approach is the "entire relation as it has developed ... [through] time"' (1979, p. 103).[8] Consequently, relational contracting tends to be highly personal and often reflects the norms of the parties involved.

Williamson then develops a scheme for classifying commercial transactions along two dimensions: transaction frequency and investment characteristics (that is, asset specificity). Transactions are either occasional or recurrent, and are supported by investments of a non-specific, mixed or idiosyncratic variety. The thrust of his argument is that, '... governance structures – the institutional matrix within which transactions are negotiated and executed – vary with the nature of the transaction' (1979, p. 103). He argues that market governance is appropriate for transactions that are non-specific and either recurrent or occasional. Since market-mediated exchange ideally occurs between unrelated parties and involves formal contractual terms which offer legal recourse, it closely resembles classical contracting. 'Trilateral' governance is appropriate for occasional transactions of a mixed and idiosyncratic kind. The specialized investments and large set-up costs that characterize this type of governance provide a strong incentive for parties to honour their contractual obligations; however, classical contracting does not provide suitable relief given the size of these investments. Similarly 'bilateral' governance is too costly for transactions that occur infrequently. As a result, an intermediate form is used which employs arbitration or third party assistance (hence *trilateral* governance) as a means of resolving disputes among parties. Thus trilateral governance is closely allied with neoclassical contracting.

Finally, 'transaction-specific' governance is used when transactions are recurring and supported by either mixed or idiosyncratic investments. The idiosyncratic nature of these transactions makes market mediation risky while their frequency allows the costs of specialized governance mechanisms to be defrayed. Williamson distinguishes two types of transaction-specific governance: bilateral and unified. The former occurs when there is some advantage to using a second party to complete the transaction, as in the outsourcing of specialized components. However, while a moderate level of transaction-specific investment provides a strong incentive for both parties to continue their trading relation, the need continually to adapt agreements to changing conditions makes the writing of contracts difficult and costly, while asset specificity invites opportunism. Consequently, under bilateral governance, two parties agree to resolve their disputes by amending contracts and/or negotiating follow-up agreements through a kind of 'obligational contracting'. On the other hand, unified governance occurs when highly idiosyncratic investments offer large economies of scale to a single party. Under these circumstances, there is a strong incentive not to trade, and vertical integration or internal organization (that is, the firm) becomes the preferred mode. Williamson associates both types of transaction-specific governance with relational contracting.

Several points emerge from this brief overview. First, the various forms of contracting span a continuum from the explicit, formal agreements of classical contracting to the implicit, informal arrangements of relational contracting. Secondly, governance structures can be placed on a continuum based upon the autonomy of the transacting parties. This extends from arm's length, impersonal exchanges in the market-place to internally directed transfers with the firm. Thirdly, Williamson's approach explicitly assumes that exchanges take place under conditions of uncertainty, that (at least some) parties behave opportunistically, that there are bounds on rationality, and that actors behave in ways which are '*intendedly* rational, but only *limitedly* so'.[9] Finally, transaction cost analysis is 'microanalytic' in the sense that it uses the smallest divisible unit of exchange – the single transaction – as its starting point and proceeds to deduce the most efficient means of 'governing' or organizing that transaction given a specific set of external constraints. As Williamson notes: 'The ... hypothesis to which transaction-cost economics owes much of its predictive content holds that transactions, which differ in their attributes, are aligned with governance structures, which differ in their costs and competencies, in a discriminating (mainly, transaction-cost economizing) way' (1991, p. 277).

Criticisms of the Transaction Cost Approach

Numerous writers have taken exception to the notion that economic activity can be neatly divided between markets and hierarchies, while others have criticized specific aspects of the transaction cost perspective. Five broad objections to the markets–hierarchies framework can be identified: 1) the clear distinction between markets and firms fails to explain numerous 'intermediate' and alternative forms of governance; 2) many of the underlying assumptions of the transaction cost model are unrealistic, particularly the emphasis on opportunism; 3) the transaction cost approach is largely static in nature and therefore fails to capture dynamic effects; 4) by focusing on the 'micro' level of the transaction, many important 'macro' level phenomena may be misinterpreted or missed altogether; and 5) the lack of a formal definition and method of measuring specific transaction costs makes the model difficult to test empirically. Each of these objections is briefly explored below.[10]

Even before Williamson's classic study crystallized the theoretical distinction between markets and hierarchies, G.B. Richardson had complained that, '... by looking at industrial reality in terms of the sharp dichotomy between firm and market we obtain a distorted view of the how the system works' (1972, p. 884). More recently, Powell stated that: 'I do not share the belief that the bulk of economic exchange fits comfortably at either of the poles of the market–hierarchy continuum', noting that: 'It fails to capture the complex realities of exchange' (1990, pp. 298–9). Both authors were particularly concerned with the presence of 'intermediate' forms which possess characteristics of both firms and markets. Richardson was interested in the role of cooperation in effecting governance and envisioned a, '... continuum passing from transactions, such as those organized in the commodity markets, where the co-operative element is minimal, through intermediate areas in which there are linkages of traditional connection and goodwill, and finally to those complex and inter-locking clusters, groups and alliances which represent cooperation fully and formally developed' (1972, p. 887). Powell, on the other hand, investigated the 'network' as a discrete form of governance. According to Powell: 'In network modes of resource allocation, transactions occur neither through discrete exchanges nor by administrative fiat, but through networks of individuals engaged in reciprocal, preferential, mutually supportive actions' (1990, p. 303).

Williamson answered this line of criticism in a 1991 article which developed the 'hybrid' as a third form of economic organization with its own unique attributes. The hybrid mode includes, '... various forms of long-term contracting, reciprocal trading, regulation, franchising, and the like ...', and is characterized, '... by semi-strong incentives, an intermediate degree of administrative apparatus, displays semi-strong adaptations of both kinds, and works out of a semi-legalistic [that is, neoclassical] contract law regime' (1991, pp. 280–81). The 'adaptations' Williamson refers to are of the 'A' (autonomy) and 'C' (cooperation) type. The former refers to the need to adapt to external conditions such as a change in the supply and demand of a commodity, the latter involves the need to coordinate the activities of independent actors in order to avoid suboptimization. But not everyone has been persuaded by this development. Powell states that, '... although I was earlier of the view that nonmarket, nonhierarchical forms represented hybrid modes ... I now find that this mixed mode or intermediate notion is not particularly helpful' (1990, p. 298). The problem of intermediate governance structures is discussed in greater detail in the following section.

The second major complaint involves the underlying assumptions of Williamson's framework. Some critics have taken exception to its neoclassical foundations, while others have indicted specific assumptions of the transaction cost model. Lundvall, for example, while acknowledging the important extensions transaction cost analysis has made to the neoclassical model, faults it for maintaining, '... the allocation perspective of neoclassical economics and the concomitant emphasis on the exchange of commodities with given value-utility characteristics' (1993, p. 52). Similarly, Johansson and Mattsson (1987) object to the focus on equilibrium analysis and efficiency considerations implicit in Williamson's analysis. Finally, Williamson has been criticized for not completely abandoning the neoclassical assumption of rationality, although he does temper it somewhat by assuming that rationality is 'bounded'.[11]

In all fairness, Williamson is equally uncomfortable with many of the assumptions of neoclassical economics. For instance, he notes that: 'Given bounded rationality, uncertainty, and idiosyncratic knowledge, I argue that prices often do *not* qualify as sufficient statistics and that a substitution of internal organization (hierarchy) for market-mediated exchange often occurs on this account' (1975, p. 5). But transaction cost economics differs from conventional analysis in at least three additional ways. First, it relies on a different set of assumptions about human behaviour and the decision-making process; secondly, it specifically examines the role of information in effecting exchange and does not assume that information is either perfect or costless; and finally, it removes the assumption of 'frictionless' markets and explicitly examines a set of costs associated with economic exchange.

Much more problematic is the assumption of opportunism which is central to Williamson's thesis. Williamson defines opportunism as 'self-interest seeking with guile' and notes that it includes, '... lying, stealing, cheating, and other more subtle forms of deceit. ... More generally, opportunism refers to the incomplete or distorted disclosure of information, especially to efforts to mislead, distort, disguise, obfuscate, or otherwise confuse' (1985, p. 47). Johansson and Mattsson, however, '... do not regard *opportunism* as a basic characteristic of the actors'. Instead they consider, '... its correlate *trust* ... an important concept ...' (1987, p. 44). Hill (1990) provides perhaps the most serious challenge to the assumption of opportunism by demonstrating that the cost of attenuating such behaviour (either through additional safe-guards or internal governance) often dissipates much of the rent generated by asset-specific investments. Using a game-theoretic approach, Hill shows that the value of the quasi-rent inherent in a given transaction is maximized when the parties to an exchange cooperate and trust one another. As a result, Hill concludes that in many cases opportunistic behaviour is not rational and consequently may be far less widespread than commonly believed.

Hill's analysis anticipates two related problems involving the 'discrete-ness' of economic actors and individual transactions. The former assumption suggests that reputation effects are of minor consequence since trading rela-tionships can be conceptually isolated in time and space. This view is strenu-ously opposed by the emerging 'network' theorists. In summarizing Mark Granovetter's contribution to a collection of essays on the subject, Nohria and Eccles make three observations:

> (1) economic action (like all action) is properly seen as embedded in [an] ongoing network of relationships; (2) economic goals are typically pursued alongside such noneconomic goals as sociability, approval, status, and power; and (3) economic institutions (like all institutions) arise from and are maintained by ongoing proc-esses of social construction' (1992, p. ix).

We return to this topic in a subsequent section, but for now it suffices to say that many forms of trading, particularly those based on long-term contractual arrangements such as licensing, subcontracting or minority joint ventures, contain social as well as economic aspects, and therefore cannot be properly understood without reference to both elements. Williamson acknowledges as much in his discussion of the hybrid form of governance. Nevertheless, to many the unrealistic assumptions about human behaviour – including, but not limited to, opportunism and the relationship between economic actors – and the failure to examine explicitly the social as well as economic role of markets (and hierarchies), are the greatest weaknesses of the transaction cost model.

The assumption that transactions are discrete is challenged in a recent study of the Swedish food industry by Elg and Johansson (1993). These authors conclude that the observed relationships between wholesalers and manufacturers cannot adequately be explained using the transaction as the basic unit of analysis since it ignores the larger system of relationships which comprise the industry's 'value-chain'. Accordingly, they argue that a '*system of transactions'* provides the most appropriate unit of analysis. This follows because, '... each transaction is a part of a pattern of transactions involving interdependent organizations. The governance structure that exists in each transaction affects the costs and the governance structures of other, related transactions' (1993, p. 41). The focus on discrete, individual exchanges that characterizes the transaction cost model, '... neglects the fact that a transaction between two parties is always part of a transactional system. It thus neglects system effects on the choice of a governance form ...' (1993, p. 42). Conversely, by examining a 'set' or 'system' of transactions these system effects can be analysed explicitly.

To a large extent, both problems of 'discreteness' are the result of the static, equilibrium analysis implicit in traditional economic theory. While changes in the preferred means of governance can clearly be examined using transaction cost analysis, movement is assumed to proceed from one discrete state to another with little or no reference to 'transitional' or 'evolutionary' arrangements. Similarly, technological, organizational and legal innovations are seen as random, exogenous shocks which may precipitate changes in governance, but their causes remain outside the general scope of analysis. Consequently, the transaction cost approach not only minimizes the role of total system effects – from reputations to interfirm cooperation – it also neglects the dynamic and longer-term effects associated with the passage of time and the introduction of progress, innovation and random events into the system. In defence of the transaction cost perspective, dynamic effects are extremely difficult to model, as studies by Nelson and Winter (1982), Boskin and Lau (1992), Durlauf (1992) and others clearly illustrate. Thus this problem is perhaps best seen as a general comment on the limited capacity of mankind to explain complex external phenomena than a particular indictment of transaction cost economics.

A similar complaint arises from the 'micro' orientation of transaction cost analysis. As Bradach and Eccles (1989) point out, complex relationships often exist between individual transactions as well as between specific governance structures and the contexts in which they occur. They argue that the microanalytic approach inherent in transaction cost analysis runs the risk of overlooking or misinterpreting important aspects of the macro structure. This problem was forcefully stated by Schumpeter in his observation that: 'A system – any system, economic or other – that at *every* given point of time fully utilizes its possibilities to the best advantage may yet in the long run be inferior to a system that does so at *no* given point in time ...' (1942, p. 83). Applied to the present context this suggests that governance structures which economize on transaction costs for every given transaction, and by so doing maximize economic efficiency, may still prove inferior to structures which economize for *no* individual transaction but are more closely aligned with their external environments. This argument is similar to the one Elg and Johansson advanced above.

One reason for this outcome is the failure of the transaction cost model accurately to assess various economic and social externalities associated with the exchange process; another is its failure to view the larger contextual system in which individual transactions occur. But perhaps even more importantly, transaction cost analysis provides no formal mechanism for evaluating the potential economies of scope associated with hierarchical governance. For example, Boyd points out that in making the decision to organize a particular activity through the firm or market, '... the relative costs and benefits relate not only to the economies of having some important functions performed in house or contracted out, but also to the evolving functions of the firm, and especially to the development of entrepreneurial and technological innovation through processes of synergistic interaction ...'.[12] Thus internal organization may create new 'firm-specific' and strategic advantages above and beyond those arising from the reduction of transaction costs. To a large extent, the latter omission is a direct result of the model's 'microanalytic' orientation.

The final objection raised above is the absence of clearly defined, *measurable*, transaction costs. This is an important limitation since it precludes detailed empirical testing. Casson argues that, '... the main problem with Williamson's presentation is the lack of any formal model which specifies precisely the technical structure of the production process and the nature of the market environment which is assumed' (1987, p. 41). This is important for two reasons: first, these factors govern the decision-making logic of managers, and secondly, the absence of a formal model makes it difficult to derive testable hypotheses. Williamson responds to the latter concern in his 1991 article by formally modelling governance structures as a function of asset specificity. Although Williamson's analysis is an undeniable step in the right direction, it remains highly theoretical and does not successfully resolve the measurement dilemma.

A number of other researchers have developed transaction cost 'models' which attempt to articulate formally the costs associated with various forms of governance. For example, models by Anderson and Gatignon (1986), Clegg (1990), Contractor (1990), Hennart (1988), Hill, Hwang and Kim (1990), Teece (1986) and many others attempt to explain the firm's decision to use a specific governance mechanism (such as a wholly owned subsidiary, licensing or a joint venture) in terms of a small set of transaction-oriented variables. Other writers, such as Hallwood (1990) and Buckley (1989), have successfully employed transaction cost methods to explain the structures of specific industries, in this case the oil and tourism industries, respectively. These efforts – most of which appeared *after* Casson's complaint – have greatly expanded the formal validity of the transaction cost model, although they still give the impression that the model is best suited for the conceptualization of questions of governance rather than the specification and measurement of relevant variables.

In closing, Williamson's own words provide perhaps the most cogent criticism of the transaction cost approach: '[It] is crude, it is given to instrumentalist excesses, and it is incomplete' (1985, p. 390). Such criticisms notwithstanding, the approach offers a powerful analytical tool for exploring alternative means of organizing economic activities under a wide range of external constraints.

BETWEEN MARKETS AND HIERARCHIES

At this point, it is useful to examine a question raised briefly above, namely: 'How do we explain the many 'intermediate' forms of governance which display characteristics of both markets and firms?'. More specifically: 'Can these mechanisms be placed on a continuum of governance structures defined by the market at one end and the firm at the other?'. If these intermediate forms can be comfortably placed on a continuum of governance structures, then transaction cost analysis clearly provides a useful template for their examination. Further, since this continuum is based on the autonomy of the transacting parties (ranging from full autonomy in the market to none in the firm), defining the boundaries of individual actors becomes a non-trivial pursuit, bringing us full-circle to Knight's interest in explaining what determines the limits of the firm and which activities are organized within it. Conversely, if intermediate forms are not part of a market–hierarchy continuum, then transaction cost analysis is not appropriate and could instead generate misleading or erroneous conclusions. In addition, a very different set of research questions is posed, including, what are the underlying attributes of these mechanisms, and should they even be seen as governance structures at all?

Before attempting to answer these questions, it is important to note that the subsequent analysis focuses on the use of intermediate mechanisms to organize the *international* activities of the firm. Many of the unique characteristics of international markets have made intermediate contractual forms extremely popular, and the focus on international business illustrates the many differences that exist in business practices between countries. This in turn raises the interesting question of the role of culture in determining the mechanisms used to govern economic activities.

Explaining the 'New Forms of Investment'

Since World War II, the MNE has become a major vehicle for organizing international economic activities.[13] By the early 1990s, the sales of *Fortune's* 'Global 500' represented over 20 per cent of global GNP, while *The Economist* estimated that the world's 300 largest multinationals owned 25 per cent of the world's productive assets.[14] Further, Encarnation notes that: 'Simply put, intracompany shipments between multinational parents and their foreign subsidiaries control international commerce among industrialized countries ...' (1992, p. xi). However, during the 1980s, a large number of firms in a broad cross-section of industries began replacing the equity control of certain portions of their value-adding chains with more flexible contractual arrangements between independent companies. Following Oman (1984), these contractual arrangements have been called 'new forms of investment'. Hennart notes that these, '... include arrangements that fall short of majority ownership, such as various forms of contracts (licensing, franchising, management contracts, turnkey and product-in-hand contracts, production-sharing contracts, and international subcontracting) as well as joint ventures' (1988, p. 212). Consequently, these mechanisms are quite similar to Williamson's 'hybrid' form and represent various types of 'relational' contracting.

To some extent, the use of these 'new forms' can be explained by recent changes in the international political economy which have eroded many of the advantages traditionally associated with hierarchical governance. For instance, Levitt notes that the growing similarities between national markets coupled with the international diffusion of technology has created, '... global markets for standardized consumer products on a previously unimagined scale ...' (1983, p. 92). This is important because, in a world of standardized products, many 'firm-specific' advantages become obsolete, and with them one of the MNE's most important assets – the ability to earn monopoly rents through product differentiation and market segmentation.

Peter Drucker (1986), identifies three fundamental changes in the international economy that have substantially reduced the importance of many 'location' advantages as well. They are:

1. The 'uncoupling' of the primary products economy from the industrial economy, and its accompanying diminution of the comparative advantages associated with natural resources.
2. The uncoupling of employment and production within the industrial economy itself, due largely to increased productivity gains from technology.
3. The partial uncoupling of trade and economic growth, with capital flows replacing trade as the driving force of the world economy.

Finally, declining barriers to international trade and investment, the declining cost of international transportation, and the global trend towards 'free' markets may have reduced many of the market imperfections and transaction costs that initially favoured internal organization. Robinson (1981) has argued that the costs of using internal markets to transfer capital, skills, technology and goods between countries may actually be *higher* in some cases than the costs associated with exchanges in the open market-place. Further, as one set of factors has improved the efficiency of external markets, another has reduced the benefits of hierarchical governance. As noted above, the diffusion of technologies and management practices and the rapid growth of international competition have substantially eroded the basis of many firm-specific advantages. At the same time, the declining importance of natural resources in the production process has diminished the benefits of vertical integration. In both cases, the traditional justification for organizing international economic activities within the MNE is brought into question.

In a world of standardized products and technologies, and similar consumer tastes, two things become paramount: the ability to create and apply new technologies, and the ability to access major international markets. In both cases, hierarchical governance structures like the MNE may provide an unsuitable vehicle for achieving these goals. According to Dunning, vastly different organizational forms and resource endowments may be necessary to take advantage of the technological advances of the 1980s and 1990s. He notes that: 'It is by no means certain that the ... hierarchical structure of firms evolved through the 1960s and 1970s will be suitable for the remaining years of the twentieth century' (1989, p. 26). Root argues that recent events favour the long-term, contractual control of many activities. Specifically he suggests that, '... firms will move away from "internalization" and toward "externalization". They will more freely transfer nonstrategic production processes to firms, say, in the developing countries under arrangements that are based far more on cooperation than on control by the international firm' (1984, p. 23).[15]

As early as 1981, Contractor noted: 'The generalization that multinational firms will prefer "Internalization" via direct investment over the sale of technology via licensing is a proposition that needs to be more closely examined ...' (1980, p. 81). A later study of US firms conducted by Contractor (1990) confirms this view, finding that licensing agreements and joint ventures outnumbered wholly owned subsidiaries by a four to one margin.[16] Studies by Barley, Freeman and Hybels (1992), Gerlach (1992), Gilroy (1993), Hagedoorn (1993), Kotabe (1992), Mytelka (1991) and many others have found a similar interest in the new forms of investment among European and Japanese companies as well, particularly in biotechnology, computers and information, and other high technology industries.

Although a comprehensive theory of these cooperative and contractual forms of governance (which include international joint ventures, offshore production, licensing, R&D agreements and other forms of relational contracting) has not emerged, a large body of research has attempted to explain their widespread use. Elsewhere (Blaine, 1994), I have suggested that these studies fall into four distinct yet closely related 'schools'. For lack of a better terminology, I have called them the 'contingency' school, the 'transaction cost' school, the 'bargaining power' school and the 'strategic' school. In each case, their names reflect their major theoretical orientation.[17] In terms of the present discussion, the wide range of alternative explanations for the intermediate forms of governance suggests that transaction costs may not provide a sufficient rationale for these arrangements in all cases. In addition, anecdotal information strongly implies that there is an industry-specific and nation-specific component in the use of cooperative and contractual forms of governance. The reasons for this latter proposition are discussed at greater length below.

Competitive and Cooperative 'Micromanagement'

The preceding discussion suggests that, in many cases, the contractual governance of transactions between independent parties provides a more efficient means of organizing economic activities than 'internalizing' them within the firm. Accordingly, Contractor (1990) has suggested that there are now two very different models of the MNE (and firm): the traditional model based on globalization and standardization, in which the need for efficiency mandates the use of hierarchical control and internal markets; and a new model in which a number of unique organizational and environmental factors make the use of contractual control and/or external markets the preferred option. Perlmutter and Heenan note: 'The new global model ... is more flexible about ownership and managerial control. It encourages joint decision making, vertical and horizontal planning, and the fusion of competent allies from around the world despite cultural differences' (1986, p. 152). The growing use of joint ventures, strategic alliances and other new forms strongly supports this view.

Carried to an extreme, this model of the firm yields a large, complex 'network' of independent organizations linked together through joint ventures, strategic alliances and a wide range of contractual agreements. These new arrangements have a number of advantages over traditional hierarchical governance mechanisms. *Inter alia*, they can allow the competitive unit to achieve benefits of scale without increasing corporate size; defray the cost of developing new technologies and cultivating new markets; facilitate technology transfer and organizational learning; and shorten the time from product conception to commercialization. As a result of these and other benefits, Lodge and Walton (1989) conclude that the competitive unit of the future will not be the corporation, but a coalition of rivals cooperating with labour, suppliers and customers.

There are striking similarities between this 'new' model of the firm and the Japanese *keiretsu*. The *keiretsu* is a large industrial complex containing a number of loosely related companies linked together through a network of formal and informal business relationships. Blinder (1991) argues that the *keiretsu* represents a third form of industrial organization lying somewhere between vertical integration and arm's-length exchange in the market-place. Since the *keiretsu* consists of independent firms joined through a web of long-term ties, this structure is capable of simultaneously combining the benefits of internal organization with those of the market-place. However, because the relationships between *keiretsu* members are neither hierarchical nor contractual, it is not clear where this form of organization fits on the traditional continuum of governance.

According to Kester (1991) Japanese contractual governance is defined by four traits: 1) implicit contracting founded on trust; 2) extensive reciprocity in equity ownership and commercial trade; 3) managerial incentives aligned towards overall corporate growth and away from transfers of wealth between stakeholders; and 4) selective intervention by key stakeholders to correct problems. Kester concludes that the Japanese approach to governance generates tremendous efficiencies in the execution of business transactions by promoting long-term business relationships. He notes that: 'These relationships have enabled Japanese companies to function with lower degrees of asset-ownership integration ... despite high degrees of interdependence in the transactions supported by those assets' (1991, p. 54).

In the language of transaction cost analysis, Japanese contractual governance has the effect of reducing many of the costs associated with exchanges between independent entities. Specifically, it serves to limit the threat of opportunism, and with it the need to replace the market mechanism with a hierarchical form of governance. As noted above, Hill (1990) contends that the total rents arising from a transaction based on cooperation between independent parties often exceed those earned from an exchange conducted within the firm; therefore, cooperative behaviour often confers a considerable competitive advantage.

The notion that cooperation and trust can provide an alternative form of economic governance is a central theme in the emerging 'network' theory. In general, it is possible to distinguish two types of network in the literature: industrial and social. According to Hakansson and Johanson: 'In an industrial network a number of more or less interrelated industrial activities are performed. Each activity is to some extent dependent on the performance of other activities, which must either precede or follow it. Every activity is, then, a link in a chain of activities' (1993, p. 36). Thus industrial networks appear quite similar to the 'new' model of the firm described above. These structures range from small groupings of firms in a single industry linked through loose technology-sharing agreements, to large complexes of firms in a number of industries related through formal and informal ties, like the *keiretsu*. Several researchers have attempted to model the flow of information and resources within industrial networks. For example, Hagedoorn and Schakenraad (1990) studied interfirm cooperative agreements in the biotechnology and information technology industries and uncovered a dense system of linkages between firms in the US, Europe and Japan.[18] Janet Lowe (1992) observed similar patterns in her study of joint ventures and shared directorates among 25 of the world's largest MNEs.

In contrast to these globally dispersed, horizontal networks of firms in closely allied industries, other researchers have concentrated on regional, often vertical, networks which combine firms at different stages of the production process. Lazerson, for example, describes a '... sophisticated network link[ing] thousands of highly specialized knitwear suppliers with hundreds of manufacturers to form a sophisticated production system ...' in Moderna, Italy (1993, p. 222). Porter describes similar 'clusters' of interrelated industries often concentrated in specific geographical locations ('industrial regions'). According to Porter: 'A nation's successful industries are usually linked through vertical (buyer/supplier) or horizontal (common customers, technology, channels, etc.) relationships' (1990, p. 149). These relationships – which clearly create a 'network' – help facilitate the flow of knowledge and information and provide sources of goal congruence and compatibility among actors. Porter provides insightful case studies of the development of such clusters in printing presses in Germany, patient monitoring equipment in the US, ceramic tiles in Sassuolo, Italy, and industrial robots in Japan.

In most cases, research on industrial networks remains solidly grounded in traditional economic theory, with special attention given to the unique problems of generating and transferring knowledge and coordinating different stages of the production process. As a result, transaction cost principles have been successfully employed to explain these structures. The same is not true of the social network, which appears to rely on a much different set of organizing principles. According to Johannisson:

A social network is generally made up of a set of interrelated dyadic ties between actors. The interconnectedness implies that the outcome of one relationship is dependent on the outcome of others. An emerging network structure is loosely coupled, nonhierarchical, and open-ended ... Reality is objectified by social interaction, and culture is being built and diffused through social networks' (1987, pp. 9–10).

Johannisson identifies three kinds of social network: communication, exchange and normative, which involve flows of information, products and services, and social expectations respectively. Each of the three networks is characterized by a different type of interdependence between actors (or nodes), with information networks displaying sequential interdependence, exchange networks having reciprocal interdependence, and normative networks exhibiting pooled interdependence.

Exchange networks are perhaps most appropriate for describing economic activities, and Johannisson examines three basic types of exchange network: production, personal and symbolic. Linkages between the nodes of a production network are impersonal and develop from opportunities arising in the market-place. These networks are defined by the flow of transactions between parties, and contracts written under conditions of opportunism and bounded rationality regulate interactions within the network. On the other hand, symbolic networks emerge from communities such as ethnic groups or professions where membership is either inherited or based on specific individual traits. Linkages within these networks are defined by accepted norms, and social control and the pressure to conform regulate the behaviour of individual actors. Finally, personal networks are based on affection and friendship. As a result, each node in these networks is unique, and interactions within the network are based on trust.

The personal network has much in common with Ken-ichi Imai's description of Japanese corporate networks. He notes:

> ... in the network view, the basic unit is not the firm as a legal entity but as an economic actor that can make decisions independently or quasi-independently ... Actors within many companies establish linkages with each other through strong or weak ties according to the needs of business. The boundary of the firm or corporation therefore most often changes continuously rather than sporadically. Such linkages are spontaneously formulated, and this spontaneous linkage is the first meaning of self-organization (1992, p. 223).

Imai's observation that networks are 'self-organizing' and that, as a result, their boundaries are fluid rather than fixed, presents a serious challenge to the traditional concepts of organization and governance developed above. For one thing, contracting becomes impracticable when the boundaries of economic actors are ill-defined and/or constantly changing. This in turn invalidates the legal safeguards associated with classical contracting and may make the kinds of long-term relationship required for successful 'relational' contracting difficult and uncertain. As a result, bounds on rationality increase and, without additional safeguards, the threat of opportunism may increase as well. Under these conditions traditional analysis suggests that hierarchical governance will emerge to lower transaction costs and align the interests of parties to an exchange; but the network pushes exchange in the opposite direction – towards relational transactions between independent agents. The obvious question is why, and what additional rules or safeguards are required to facilitate exchange under these conditions?

Animal or Vegetable?

What distinguishes the *keiretsu* and network from traditional forms of economic organization is the explicit recognition that both markets and hierarchies have a *social* as well as economic function. As a result, they have an alternative set of costs and benefits not recognized in the rationalist perspective implicit in the transaction cost model. To some extent, discussions of the problems of agency briefly mentioned above attempt to redress this omission; however, in most cases, the analysis of these issues continues to ignore the social dimension of economic behaviour. Conversely, the network approach views individual actors as 'human' in the fullest sense, being motivated by a wide range of economic *and* non-economic factors.[19] By incorporating the social dimension, organizations like the *keiretsu* and network face transaction costs that are markedly different from those facing traditional governance structures like the firm or market. Thus exchanges of products and information that would traditionally require expensive hierarchical or contractual governance to restrict opportunism may take place between autonomous actors 'loosely coupled' through a complex system of social or normative ties. Further, since relationships within these systems are often general rather than specific and may continue over long periods of time, these alternative forms of governance may develop their own safeguards and sanctions.

Williamson's 'peer group' and Ouchi's 'clan' represent traditional acknowledgements of the social dimension of economic activity. According to Williamson, peer groups, '... involve collective and usually cooperative activity, provide for some type of other-than-marginal productivity and income-sharing arrangement, but do not entail subordination. Such collective organizations offer prospective advantages in indivisibility, risk-bearing, and associational respects' (1975, p. 42). These groups offer a simple non-market alternative, but are plagued with a number of difficulties, particularly the problem of 'free-riding' and the additional costs of collective decision-making. As a result, Williamson considers the peer group of limited usefulness. Further, his analysis of these and other similar mechanisms remains firmly entrenched in the neoclassical assumptions of (bounded) rationality, economic efficiency and profit maximization.

Ouchi (1980, 1981) appears much more rooted in the social sciences than Williamson, and consequently his conception of the 'clan' reflects a strong social dimension. To some extent, this may account for the sharp distinction

Ouchi draws between clans, markets and hierarchies. According to Ouchi, a clan is an intimate grouping of people connected through a variety of ties. He notes, '... clans succeed when teamwork and change render individual performance almost totally ambiguous' (1981, p. 84). Clans depend on long-term relationships built on trust, and require a strong socialization mechanism which aligns the actions of the individual with those of the clan. As Ouchi (1981) demonstrated in his discussion of the 'Z'-type organization, many of the social attributes of clans can dramatically alter the costs of (hierarchical) governance.

Some of these considerations are behind Hakansson and Johanson's (1993) alternative typology of governance structures. Abandoning the familiar market–hierarchy continuum with its numerous 'intermediate' or 'hybrid' forms, these authors develop a 2×2 matrix which specifies four distinct modes of governance: markets, hierarchies, networks and cultures (or professions). More important than the details of Hakansson and Johanson's typology for our purposes is their statement that: 'The important conclusion from our point of view is that the typology implies that network governance should be viewed not as some intermediate governance mode on a unidimensional scale between markets and hierarchies, but as a unique type' (1993, p. 46). Clearly, if one accepts this general proposition, even without accepting the authors' specific typology, much of the traditional thinking about governance will have to be reconsidered.

CULTURE, INSTITUTIONAL STRUCTURE AND CONTRACTUAL GOVERNANCE

This section explores some of the linkages between culture, institutional structure and the means used to organize economic activities. The basic premise of this discussion is that the range of available governance mechanisms and the criteria used to discriminate among them are functions of the institutional structure in which economic activities occur, and that this structure in turn reflects the specific social and cultural assumptions used to interpret human behaviour and the external environment. This argument is based on the notion that economic institutions – from the legal structures which guarantee property rights or contractual compliance, to the social conventions which define acceptable attitudes towards competition and cooperation – exist within larger socio-cultural systems and as such necessarily differ according to the underlying assumptions and ultimate objectives of those systems. As Gerlach observes: 'Markets, therefore, are best seen less as the reification of an abstract ideal – self-sustaining, self-regulating, self-functioning mechanisms running on an internal logic apart from the remainder of society – and more as social inventions that are embedded in larger institutional structures, both legal and social' (1992, p. 52). The same can, of course, be said of firms and other alternative means of governance.

Implicit in this view is the belief that economic institutions are not ends in themselves, but means for achieving more fundamental social objectives. As a result, they can only be understood within the social and cultural context in which they arise.[20] This 'contextual' view of governance is antithetical to the transaction cost approach in at least three important ways. First, it challenges the assumption that the transaction is a 'neutral' unit of analysis. The logic behind this contention is as follows. As noted above, the process of exchange has both an economic and social dimension; consequently, transactions have a set of social externalities that must also be considered in the analysis of alternative governance mechanisms. This would be a trivial matter if the criteria used to evaluate these costs (and benefits) were the same in all settings. However, since the social costs of exchange are a function of the specific assumptions used to describe human nature and define social relations, they have a strong cultural (and subjective) element. This suggests that both the specification of relevant transaction costs and the decision-making calculus used to evaluate those costs will vary from one setting to another. To the extent that the process of exchange – and hence the definition of the transaction – is contextually determined, the transaction becomes an unreliable unit of analysis.

A simple example may help clarify this point. Consider an identical exchange taking place between two family or 'clan' members and two independent actors in the market-place. In the former case, the process used to evaluate alternative governance mechanisms is guided by largely idiosyncratic, contextual information that is absent in the latter case. As a result, a different form of governance may be chosen in each instance, not because the costs of alternative mechanisms differ, but because the meaning attached to the transaction differs in each setting. Clearly, this problem of specification may also arise when the same transaction occurs in two different societies. Again, it is important to emphasize that the problem is not that the *costs* of the transaction vary between settings, but that the process used to *evaluate* these costs differs.

The second disparity involves the 'modified' neoclassical assumption of rationality (that is, 'intendedly rational, but only limitedly so') implicit in transaction cost analysis. Since 'rationality' is clearly a function of the means used to define appropriate behaviour, it is necessarily 'contextual' in nature. This is readily apparent in social behaviour, but is not as widely recognized in economic behaviour because of the latter's assumed universality and neutrality.[21] If, however, one acknowledges that economic activities have a social dimension, the contextual nature of economic behaviour must also be accepted. As a result, what is rational in one setting may appear *ir*-rational (or at the very least unacceptable) in another. Biggart and Hamilton (1992) clearly illustrate this point in their comparison of Western and Asian economic systems. The authors note that the neoclassical concept of rationality is not particularly useful in explaining Asian economic behaviour because the latter is based on very different assumptions about human nature and social relations. They conclude, '... the successful network structure of Asian capitalism reveals the neoclassical model to be not a general theory of capitalism, but rather an ethnocentric model developed from Western experience and applicable only to Western economies' (1992, p. 472).

This leads to a final, related objection: the use of allocative efficiency and profit maximization as the ultimate objectives for economic behaviour. Once again, a disregard for the social dimension of economic activity has encouraged the neglect of numerous legitimate alternatives. Further, when the social aspects of exchange are included in the actors' decision-making calculus, it is possible to imagine one objective dominating in one setting and a very different objective taking precedence in another. Thus maximizing returns by minimizing transaction costs should be seen as just one of many possible rationales for structuring economic relations. Gerlach (1992) provides an interesting example of this in his study of the Japanese *keiretsu*. Gerlach offers compelling evidence that transactions within these loosely linked networks are often given preferential treatment and, as a result, the profitability of *keiretsu* members is actually *lower* than that of similar unaffiliated companies. Of course, one explanation for this finding is that the *keiretsu* offers additional economic benefits (such as risk reduction) which justify the lower returns, or that the long-term ties between *keiretsu* members allow parties to generate higher returns over the life of their trading relationships. Interestingly, however, comments by Japanese executives generally belie these explanations, stressing instead the importance of non-economic factors in structuring exchange relations.[22]

These propositions have profound implications for the analysis of economic exchange and the governance structures used to effect that exchange. First, they strongly suggest that both the set of alternative governance mechanisms and the method used to select among them is a function of the underlying socio-cultural assumptions under which exchange occurs. As a result, markedly different forms of governance may be chosen to structure an identical exchange in two different settings. Note that this conclusion applies to exchanges in both different *social* settings (such as between friends versus strangers), as well as different *cultural* settings (such as the US versus Japan). Secondly, economic actors may make decisions or act in ways which appear perverse or irrational when viewed from a different socio-cultural perspective. Viewing economic behaviour through the narrow lens of discrete, self-interested, profit-maximizing actors necessarily ignores many important social and cultural characteristics that are essential components in a complete theory of economic behaviour. Finally, and perhaps most importantly, the 'contextual' approach requires a different set of analytical tools to examine economic institutions and behaviour. If markets and hierarchies are best seen through the neoclassical lens, then a transaction-oriented methodology combining elements of economics, organizational theory and law will suffice. However, if markets and firms (and alternative mechanisms) are best viewed as 'embedded' within larger socio-cultural systems, then traditional analysis reveals only one dimension of these mechanisms. A comprehensive theory of economic organization also requires an analysis of the unique socio-cultural context in which economic activities take place. Consequently, sociology, anthropology, philosophy and religion may provide valuable additional insight into the nature of observed economic institutions and behaviour.

Interestingly, Williamson makes a strong argument for adopting a 'contextual' approach in his description of the 'organizational failures framework' (that is, transaction cost analysis). Although quoted earlier, the following statement is worth repeating here. According to Williamson, '... the cost of writing and executing complex contracts across a market *vary with the characteristics of the human decision makers who are involved with the transaction on the one hand, and the objective properties of the market on the other* ...' [original emphasis] (1975, p. 8). Thus the major difference between the 'contextual' and transaction cost perspectives is that the former considers both the characteristics of decision-makers and the properties of markets (and hierarchies) to have a strong social and cultural component which the latter perspective does not recognize.

Describing the Links between Culture and Institutional Structure

It is clearly beyond the scope of this effort to produce a broad-based contextual theory of economic behaviour. Perhaps the greatest obstacle lies in specifying the linkages between a set of basic cultural assumptions and the structure of social, political and economic institutions which define the societies in which economic activities occur. As noted above, the fundamental premise of the contextual view is that the institutional structures that characterize economic behaviour reflect deeper cultural assumptions about human and physical phenomena. As a result, it is possible to hypothesize that the direction of causality runs from basic cultural factors to resulting institutions, although this is clearly a simplification since it ignores the second-order effects these institutions, once established, have on the primary culture. Such higher-order effects suggest quite correctly that culture is not fixed but changing, and therefore that the linkages between culture and institutional structure must be seen as dynamic rather than static in nature. Further, in terms of the subject at hand (that is, governance), the contextual approach contends that the range of alternative governance mechanisms, and the decision-making process used to choose between them, is a function of the institutional structure in which economic activities occur.

Davis (1971) provides a useful framework for analysing the interaction between culture and economic behaviour based on three critical elements: values, relations and structures.[23] Davis notes that: 'Values are sets of interrelated ideas, concepts, and principles to which individuals, groups, and societies attach strong sentiments' (1971, p. 10). As such, values are closely allied with culture and represent the underlying assumptions used to structure and interpret various external and internal phenomena. Numerous schemes have been developed to compare cultural values across countries, including important contributions by Kluckhohn and Strodbeck (1961) and Hofstede (1980).[24] According to Davis: 'Values generate rules of behavior, or "norms" when they are applied to specific situations. When norms are associated with specific social positions ... they are called *roles*. ... Roles are the basic building blocks of social relations' (1971, p. 15). Davis identifies five universal patterns of social relations – kinship, fealty (based on loyalty), status, contract and bureaucracy – and notes that these patterns can be observed on the interpersonal, group and societal levels. Further, one can study both the *process* and *structure* of social (and economic) organization. Structure acts to define the way in which behaviour and activities are organized and coordinated, and also emerges at the personal, group and societal levels. Finally, both processes and structures have a formal and informal dimension.

Over time, basic cultural values become 'embedded' in the patterns of social relations and behaviour, and these in turn become 'institutionalized' through formal and informal structures and processes which organize and coordinate behaviour and activities. This institutional environment is of critical importance in the study of economic organization. According to Davis: 'The *institutional environment* is the set of fundamental political, social and legal ground rules that establishes the basis for production, exchange and distribution' (1971, p. 6). The 'contextual' approach argues that: 1) the institutional environment is instrumental in defining a set of alternative structures and processes through which economic activities are organized; 2) to a large extent, the cost of these alternatives is also a function of the institutional environment; 3) institutional environments (structures) vary from one society to another depending *inter alia* on underlying cultural values, the structure of social relations, and the historical evolution of previous institutions; and 4) therefore, the structures and processes used to organize (effect the governance of) economic activities will also vary from one setting to another.

Finally, although it is well beyond the scope of the present effort, it is possible formally to trace the linkages between a set of fundamental cultural values and the resulting institutional environment.

This discussion has a number of implications. First, since the institutional environment at any point in time is the consequence of a dynamic, evolutionary process, history becomes a useful tool for analysing that environment, and particularly for predicting its future 'trajectory'.[25] In addition, once specific attitudes and patterns become 'embedded' in formal (and informal) institutional structures and processes, they: 1) begin to define and constrain current and future actions and behaviours; and 2) become difficult to change. This does not suggest that once formed, institutional structures become fixed; merely that present institutions are in part a reflection of prior institutions. Finally, as Ogburn (1957) has noted, the pace of cultural and social change is generally far slower than the pace of technological change. Thus altering many patterns of economic (and social) organization may require more than a superficial restructuring of current institutions. Instead, long-term change may only result from a fundamental re-evaluation of the often deep-seated attitudes and assumptions upon which these institutions are based.

Haley (1992) provides an excellent example of this latter problem in his study of the effect of the Allied Occupation's legal and political reforms on Japan's postwar political economy. Haley cites numerous instances where attempts to change the basic structure of the Japanese legal and political systems, particularly by creating 'democratic' institutions, were ineffectual, and instead produced formal institutions which ultimately functioned and displayed characteristics of traditional Japanese structures. The emergence of the *keiretsu* from the remnants of the prewar *zaibatsu* is another example of this, and demonstrates the strength of previous institutional forms to influence the direction of future institutional change despite serious efforts (in this case by the Allied Occupation) to the contrary.

The persistence of institutional structures and processes poses a formidable problem during periods of rapid technological change, since societies may be unable to develop appropriate legal and political institutions quickly enough to capture the full benefits of these new advances. Further, the continued reliance on outmoded governance mechanisms may impose severe additional costs on these newer forms of economic activity. A good example of this is the declining importance of patenting as a safeguard of intellectual property in industries characterized by extremely short product cycles or highly complex and costly technologies. Anecdotal information strongly suggests that in some information technologies and certain types of semiconductor, the time required to receive a patent and the need to disclose sensitive information in the application process render this form of protection costly and inappropriate. In its place, *ad hoc* arrangements which allow former competitors to share technologies and engage in joint R&D have become widespread. Thus it is not surprising that many of the highly idiosyncratic forms of governance discussed earlier (that is, the 'new forms of invest-ment') are most prevalent in industries on the cutting edge of technology, such as biotech, semiconductors, computers and other information technolo-gies. The preceding discussion suggests that the inability of countries to adjust their economic and legal institutions to accommodate the special needs of these new industries has encouraged firms to develop their own forms of governance.

The relationship between technological change and institutional structure suggests a further point. If current institutional structures and processes are sufficiently incompatible with emerging technologies or economic activities, these new developments will either fail to prosper or move to locations with more appropriate institutions. This suggests several corollaries: first, institu-tional change is likely to be accompanied by new forms of economic and/or social activity, much of which is difficult to predict in advance; secondly, some institutional settings will be more appropriate for promoting techno-logical innovation (and commercialization) than others; and finally, certain activities may either begin or over time become concentrated in specific locations because they provide a supportive institutional environment. Taken together, these ideas provide a powerful argument in favour of industrial policies which attempt to develop institutional environments that support important nascent technologies and activities. Further, they suggest that a nation can gain a competitive advantage in specific industries by creating a set of social, economic or political (legal) institutions which either provide an environment conducive to the industry's growth or lower the cost of organiz-ing essential related activities. Accordingly, Casson (1987) has argued that nations provide a bundle of services, including legislation, property protec-tion, adjudication and executive government for the payment of their cor-responding taxes. Thus firms may choose among alternative institutional environments and locate activities in the one(s) that offer the most appropriate setting.

Finally, like social organization, it is possible to view 'governance' in terms of both process and structure. This distinction is important because the act of 'governing' is distinct from the mechanisms used to effect 'govern-ance'. These two aspects are, however, related in much the same way that social processes are related to social structures. Adopting an evolutionary perspective, it is possible to argue that over time the specific processes used to govern economic transactions become 'embedded' or 'institutionalized' in formal structures which ideally produce a desired outcome. But much like social institutions, once established, governance structures begin to affect current and future behaviour and become difficult to change. Further, in periods of rapid change, extant governance structures will often be costly or ill-suited for new activities and technologies, the success of which may ultimately require a radical re-evaluation of both the structures and the decision-making calculus used to organize economic activities. Clearly, the analysis of these and similar issues can proceed only so far within the boundaries of transaction cost analysis.

Comparative Contextual Governance

Many of the aforementioned ideas are useful in the analysis of two important questions: the definition of the firm and attitudes towards cooperation. Answers to each vary widely between countries due to basic differences in the structure of social relations, attitudes towards work, power and ownership, and the importance placed on the individual versus the group.

Jensen and Meckling have noted that, '... most organizations are simply *legal fictions which serve as a nexus for a set of contracting relationships among individuals*' [original emphasis] (1976, p. 309). The authors stress: 'This view of the firm points up the important role which the legal system and the law play in social organization, especially the organization of economic activity' (1976, note 14).[26] Whether the firm is viewed as a 'nexus of contracts' or an important structure in the lives of its employees, the legal definition of the 'firm' and its designated rights and responsibilities, as well as social expectations of acceptable firm behaviour, will be critical determinants of the form of governance used to organize economic activities.

An obvious example of this is the impact host government restrictions on foreign direct investment have had on the MNE's choice between alternative means of organizing local activities. During the 1970s, many developing countries passed legislation which effectively eliminated the option of pure hierarchical governance (that is, the majority ownership of a local subsidiary) and thus dramatically altered the costs of the remaining forms of governance. Many firms concluded that the benefits of these options did not justify their costs and either withdrew or declined further investments in these countries.[27] However, host government restrictions have also been cited as a major factor in the use of the 'new forms of investment'. For example, a study of US MNEs by Blaine (1994) found that host country restrictions on ownership and trade were a major determinant of minority joint venture usage. Thus in many cases the mechanism used to govern a particular economic activity is a function of the legal system in the host (or home) country and similar institutions which both define the range of allowable governance mechanisms and may influence the costs of specific alternatives. Further, to the extent that the firm is a 'nexus of contracts', contract law and the specific remedies available for non-compliance will also play a major role in defining transaction costs and the method used to attenuate these costs.

A second example underscores the importance of social institutions in affecting the cost of various governance mechanisms. Consider a society that has only minimal *legal* sanctions against opportunistic behaviour, but employs a strong *moral* or social sanction such as 'shunning'. In such a society the cost of guarding against opportunism would be quite different than in a society which relied primarily on legal and contractual safeguards. Further, since only non-opportunistic actors would remain members of the former society for any length of time, the risk of opportunism could be roughly gauged by the inverse of a party's longevity. Murakami and Rohlen (1993) use a similar argument to explain the relative lack of opportunistic behaviour in Japan despite the minimal legal safeguards against such behaviour. Since most workers remain with the same firm for long periods of time, and since normative and communication networks both within and between firms are extremely dense, opportunistic behaviour becomes widely known and effectively discredits an actor within the larger social group. Thus specific *social* institutions (in this case the 'network' structure of Japanese society) are also capable of providing protection against opportunism and lowering the costs associated with transactions between largely independent actors.

Finally, nations differ in their social expectations of firm behaviour. It should come as no surprise that the neoclassical model of the firm, while widely accepted in Anglo cultures, is not universally appealing. In many nations the firm is seen not as a 'nexus of contracts', but as an extension of the family, and is largely staffed and run by relatives. Even in the West, this form of economic organization was widespread until the 19th century, and it still characterizes many, even large, firms in South East Asia, Korea and, to a lesser extent, Japan. The concept of the firm as an extended family carries with it unique expectations about the responsibility of the firm to its workers and the communities in which it operates. Specifically, firms are expected both to structure and to provide meaning to the lives of their employees and, as a result, the relationship between the firm and its workers is generally more personal and paternalistic than in Western companies. Gerlach (1992) provides an interesting example of this in his description of a failed merger attempt between Sumitomo Bank and Kansai Sogo Bank in Japan in the mid 1970s. He notes that the takeover was ultimately blocked by a media campaign which focused on the firm's responsibility in, '... maintaining the employees' *ikigai* (their purpose or meaning in life)' (1992, p. 230).

The second issue cited above concerns attitudes towards (interfirm) cooperation and competition. The *Oxford Review of Economic Policy* (Summer 1993 issue) examines the effect of cultural factors and regulatory policies on the competitive behaviour of firms in different countries. Numerous studies of managers also confirm that nations differ in the importance they place on competition as a means of ensuring efficient economic outcomes. For example, a broad-based international study by Hampden-Turner and Trompenaars (1993) asked managers in 12 industrialized nations to choose between two diametrically opposed attitudes towards competition. The first saw competition as an effective means of restraining collusion and price gouging by businesses and thus increasing consumer welfare; the second viewed cooperation as a more effective means of enhancing economic efficiency. Sixty-eight per cent of American managers, 65 per cent of British, 64 per cent of Canadian and 62 per cent of Australian managers agreed with the first statement, compared to only 19 per cent of Singapore, 24 per cent of Japanese, 39 per cent of Swedish and 41 per cent of German managers. Thus even in developed countries, a clear preference for competitive economic environments is evident in Anglo countries.

Not surprisingly, these general attitudes are reflected in specific legislation which limits the ability of firms to cooperate with each other in the US and UK, even in the name of economic efficiency. As a result, many types of interfirm cooperation – particularly among larger firms – common in Japan, Sweden and even Germany are illegal under a strict interpretation of American anti-trust laws. Firms in the former nations can choose from a different set of governance mechanisms and face a different set of transaction cost curves than similar firms in the US. Jorde and Teece (1992) touch upon many of these ideas in their cogent critique of US attitudes towards competition and cooperation. The authors note that America's fear of interfirm cooperation has produced a competitive environment which may actually encourage firms to underinvest in the commercialization of new technologies and certain types of R&D. In addition, outdated anti-trust laws inhibit the 'loose coupling' of independent firms (that is, 'networks') that characterizes the Japanese *keiretsu*, and in some cases encourage mergers instead of more effective cooperative arrangements.[28]

The distrust of interfirm cooperation evident in American anti-trust law and competition policy may stem from the legal status of the firm as an independent economic entity. From a regulatory perspective, the ability to delimit the boundaries and scope of the firm is a necessary prerequisite for granting any rights and protection under the law. Since the kinds of interfirm linkage that characterize the *keiretsu* or network make it difficult to identify both the firm's boundary and its locus of control, these alternative forms of governance violate the theoretical and legal assumption upon which many American institutions are founded. On the other hand, the very different legal status given the firm in countries like Japan or Sweden may explain why network organizations have evolved much further in these nations. It also suggests that the widespread utilization of these alternative forms of governance will proceed only so far in the US and UK without a major re-evaluation of the legal definition of the firm and a restructuring of the institutional framework which grants and enforces the rights of economic actors.

Thus observed differences in the method used to organize economic activities may indeed reflect differences in the costs of alternative governance structures. However, the perception and evaluation of these costs also reflect fundamental differences in economic (and social) institutions and expectations which impose widely divergent total cost curves on a given form of governance in distinct socio-cultural settings. As a result, the analysis of economic institutions and behaviour must take place within the broader contextual setting in which they arise. In fact, it is only within this broader socio-cultural context that differences in economic behaviour acquire meaning.

Before concluding, however, a final point is in order. Recent changes in the international political economy have created the potential for a truly global institutional environment, one which greatly expands the power and reach of current global institutions (such as the IMF, GATT, World Bank, United Nations and so on). To the extent that this becomes a reality, MNEs from all nations will operate under identical legal and regulatory standards. This has three important implications. First, it suggests that the effects of cultural differences on both economic institutions and firm behaviour will diminish over time. Secondly, the ability of individual governments to use industrial policies to promote the interests of their domestic firms and workers will decrease. Thirdly, firms from all nations will increasingly adopt a common set of decision-making criteria and face similar transaction cost curves. In fact, there is already evidence that the strategies and structures of MNEs are converging regardless of their origins, particularly in global industries.

On the other hand, a study by Rosenzweig (1994) suggests that cultural differences are still an important determinant of firm behaviour. Rosenzweig found that many foreign MNEs experienced a number of difficulties managing their US operation due to the differing expectations and behaviours of managers in the home and host countries. *Inter alia*, these problems included: low levels of profitability, communication problems, difficulties in retaining American managers and an unwillingness to give subsidiaries an appropriate degree of independence. Based on the preceding discussion, it should come as no surprise that Swedish and Japanese companies figured prominently in Rosenzweig's discussion. Thus it still appears premature to declare the death of culture.

CONCLUSIONS

Transaction cost economics clearly provides a powerful theoretical framework for studying the problems of governance – both corporate and contractual. However, an analysis of the many 'new forms' of contractual governance strongly suggests that both the methods available to organize economic activities and the decision-making processes used to discriminate among them have a strong socio-cultural basis. Therefore, the problem of governance can only be analysed within a specific environmental context. In short, the study of comparative *contractual* governance leads directly to the study of comparative *contextual* governance.

Economic activities occur within the context of a specific set of social, economic and political institutions which in turn reflect both the cultural and historical evolution of a people and their society. As a result, institutional environments (structures) are not necessarily (and in practice rarely are) rationally constructed solutions to the problems of organizing social, economic and political activities. Instead they reflect the influence of prior structures and processes which often have long-term consequences that are only partially knowable in advance. Thus the environments in which economic (and social) activities take place evolve in a 'path-dependent' way as current decisions continue to exert influence in future periods. But they also contain a 'random' component, as unpredictable shocks and disturbances exert their own influences over the direction of change. It is important to note that the short- and long-term impact of both current institutions and random shocks varies greatly, and that some factors may exert a larger influence in *future* periods than in present ones. From a practical perspective this makes it extremely difficult to predict the impact of many policy decisions, and may explain why inappropriate institutional environments are tolerated, often for long periods, after their failings have been recognized.

The kind of evolutionary process described above can be modelled, as Nelson and Winter (1982) and others have demonstrated. Although predicted outcomes (in terms of institutional structures) will rarely match observed outcomes, the modelling of institutional change can be highly useful in identifying a *range* of potential effects and developing institutional processes and structures that will prove robust under specific conditions. Approaches that rely on universal assumptions about human behaviour, social relations and the ultimate objective of economic activities run a high risk of misinterpreting or, worse still, entirely overlooking many important factors required to understand and explain economic (and social) institutions. It is interesting to note both the vehemence and persistence of the criticisms raised by many Japanese and Swedish scholars about the neoclassical model in general and transaction cost economics in particular. These criticisms suggest that the unique institutional environments observed in both nations do not fit easily into the idealized world of 'orthodox' economic theory. Consequently, scholars from both countries have been instrumental in expanding the transaction cost model and creating new frameworks within which to analyse important alternative forms of economic and social organization.

A somewhat different group of conclusions concerns the role of individuals in effecting governance. Even disregarding the agency problem, the discussion of networks underscores the fact that people really do matter, and that economic processes cannot be divorced from social processes.[29] This has important consequences for the current view of the firm as a 'production function' and in turn for the processes of strategy formulation and implementation. The current wave of downsizing, lay-offs and restructuring that has swept the US and other advanced economies reflects a view of economic activities that is devoid of personal or human characteristics.[30] The network perspective clearly illustrates the fallacy of this view and suggests that as individuals leave their firms they take with them pieces of the networks they composed. The Japanese recognize this fact and have developed governance mechanisms that stress the importance of individual employees and the value of creating dense systems of relationships both within and between individuals and companies. In the US, however, networks serve a very different (and perhaps more personal) purpose since employees must rely on their own contacts rather than the firm to ensure their future security. Ironically, by ignoring the social dimensions of exchange Western governance mechanisms may have made these interpersonal networks even more important (particularly at the upper levels of management), adding further strain to the relationship between a firm's managers and its owners. All of this underscores the importance of examining the informal social structures and processes that are 'embedded' in the formal structures and processes of governance.

At the end of the day, one is left with the impression that a 'sea change' or paradigm shift may be underway. A growing dissatisfaction is evident with the current state of theory in this area. To some extent, the situation resembles the state of the physical science in the first decades of this century, when a host of novel phenomena posed serious challenges to the theories of the past. As in that earlier era, economic and organizational theories have been extended and expanded in an effort to accommodate many of the phenomena that inspired this volume of essays. Over time, however, these addenda may become increasingly inadequate and a new theory may emerge that is capable of explaining the evolution of governance structures and the proliferation of new and ever more complex forms of governance. My own sense is that this new theory will be closely connected to a new socio-economics which acknowledges the realities of global oligopolistic competition, and the close linkages between social, economic and political systems. No doubt the new theory will owe much to the lessons of the emerging and maturing 'Asian miracles' that have increased our understanding of government's role in creating institutions conducive to economic growth.

NOTES

* I would like to thank Lisa Wooles of the Business Library at The Ohio State University for her assistance in accessing some particularly elusive material used in this chapter. I would also like to thank Edward M. Roche, Visiting Professor at the University of California, Berkeley, and Professor Gavin Boyd for their insightful comments on various parts of this manuscript.

1. Examples of recent research that point in this direction include Adler, Campbell and Laurent (1989), Boyacigiller and Adler (1991), and Vance, McClaine, Boje and Stage (1992).

2. Van de Ven and Joyce (1981) and others have used the term 'markets and hierarchies' to describe Williamson's approach. Similarly, this chapter will use the terms 'markets–hierarchies' and 'transaction cost analysis' interchangeably.

3. See Williamson (1985, pp. 2–3) for comments on Knight's recognition of the importance of opportunism and (1985, pp. 132–5) for his contributions on bounded rationality and firm size.

4. See Coase (1937, p. 389).

5. According to Williamson: 'A transaction occurs when a good or service is transferred across a technologically separated interface' (1985, p. 1).

6. A significant portion of *Markets and Hierarchies* is devoted to the topic of organizational structure, and Williamson ultimately concludes that: 'Transaction costs thus explain both the decision to shift transactions from the market into the firm and, within the firm, what organization form will be chosen' (1975, p. 84).

7. A slightly adapted version of this article appears in Barney and Ouchi (1986). Please note that all page numbers refer to the Barney and Ouchi text, *not* the original article.

8. Williamson takes part of this quotation from Macneil (1978, p. 890).

9. The idea of 'intendedly rational, but only limitedly so' can be traced to the work of Herbert Simon in the early 1960s. For its role in Williamson's framework, see 1985, p. 11.

10. Useful criticisms of the transaction cost approach appear in Ouchi (1980), Perrow (1981), Casson (1987), Johanson and Mattsson (1987), Powell (1990), Collin and Larsson (1993), and Elg and Johansson (1993) among others.

11. Eggertsson (1990) notes that one distinction between neoinstitutional economics and the *new* institutional economics of Williamson is that the former approach retains the rational-choice model of neoclassical theory while the latter rejects the optimization assumption and replaces it with Simon's notion of 'satisficing'.

12. I am indebted to Professor Boyd for this observation which is taken from a recent letter to the author on this subject.

13. Explaining the reasons behind the rise of the MNE have become a major preoccupation of international business theory. Major reviews of the theory of the MNE appear in Buckley (1981), Caves (1982), Casson (1983), Clegg (1987), Dunning (1988), Buckley (1989), Doz and Prahalad (1991), and Blaine (1994) among others.

14. See *Fortune* (27 July 1992) and *The Economist* (27 March 1993).

15. The concept of 'internalization' was developed by Buckley and Casson (1976) to explain the phenomena of international production and vertical integration. Simply stated, internalization contends that in a world of imperfect competition, the markets for knowledge and intermediate products are subject to a number of failures. These failures create an incentive for firms to replace external markets with internal ones. Once a firm 'internalizes' a market across national borders it becomes an MNE. The similarities between

'internalization' and transaction cost analysis as rationales for the firm (or MNE) are clear.

16. This is based on a 1982 study that identified over 31,000 independent foreign firms with licensing agreements with US firms; and a 1985 Department of Commerce study that revealed over 16,000 joint ventures or foreign corporations with shared US ownership (roughly 12,000 of which involved 50–50 per cent or minority ownership). These figures compare with a total of only 8 000 foreign wholly owned subsidiaries of US corporations.

17. Studies from the 'contingency' school explain the firm's use of contractual mechanisms in terms of specific characteristics of the firm and/or environment. Studies in the 'transaction cost' school explain these mechanisms by comparing their costs with the costs of alternative forms of governance. The 'bargaining power' school views the firm's decision to use a particular form of governance as the result of a negotiating process between parties, while the 'strategic' school views 'intermediate' forms of governance as a useful tactic in promoting the firm's larger strategic objectives.

18. Studies of the biotechnology industry by Barley, Freeman and Hybels (1992) support the international character of networks in this industry.

19. These include friendship, power, status and quality of life, to mention a few.

20. For an analysis of the relationship between social and economic institutions see Blaine and Lundstedt (1993).

21. A clear example of this is the taking of a human life. Under conditions of war or threat of family or property this act is viewed as rational behaviour and in some cases is even rewarded. However, without such provocation, the same act is considered irrational and subject to severe sanctions.

22. An interesting 'macro' example of the rejection of allocative efficiency is Japan's reluctance to purchase rice from the US despite the strong economic logic of doing so. To some extent this may be explained by the almost sacred position the cultivation of rice holds in Japanese culture. At the very least it represents the perceived social (and political) costs of forsaking an historically powerful political constituency, namely the rural farmers that have traditionally supported the Liberal Democratic Party.

23. Davis is specifically interested in comparing management practices across countries, but the same scheme seems well suited for comparing the broader institutional environments in which management occurs.

24. Using elements of these and other frameworks, Lawrence and Yeh (1994) have identified critical cultural dimensions (values) which are particularly relevant in the analysis of organizational and economic behaviour. They are: hierarchical nature, individualism versus collectivism, attitudes towards work, time orientation, approach to problem-solving, fatalism and view of human nature.

25. Excellent historical overviews of economic and social policies in the 19th and early 20th centuries in Britain, Germany, Japan, Sweden, the US and the USSR appear in Volume VIII of the *Cambridge Economic History of Europe*, Mathias and Pollard (eds) (1989).

26. A slightly adapted version of this article appears in Barney and Ouchi (1986). Please note that all page numbers refer to the Barney and Ouchi text, *not* the original article.

27. Perhaps the classic example of this is Coca Cola's decision to withdraw from the Indian market rather than comply with a law which limited foreign ownership, but there are many other examples as well. See Encarnation and Vachani (1985).

28. Both Kester (1991) and Gerlach (1992) provide clear evidence that the incidence of merger activity is greater in the US than Japan. Both writers note a strong social rationale for this finding.

29. Of course I am not the first to suggest this. A great deal of organizational research is devoted to the examination of the social dimension of organizational (and economic) behaviour. The work of Chris Argyris, Michel Crozier, Henry Mintzberg, Edgar Schein, Eric Trist, Karl Weick and many others provides clear evidence of this.

30. For further development of this theme see Enderwick (1991) and Etzioni (1988).

BIBLIOGRAPHY

Adler, Nancy, Nigel Campbell and Andre Laurent (1989), 'In Search of Appropriate Methodology: From Outside the People's Republic of China Looking In', *Journal of International Business Studies*, Spring, 61–74.

Alchian, Armen and Harold Demsetz (1972), 'Production, Information Costs, and Economic Organization', *American Economic Review*, **62** (5), 777–95, in Jay Barney and William Ouchi (eds) (1986), *Organizational Economics*, San Francisco: Jossey-Bass Publishers.

Anderson, Erin and Hubert Gatignon (1986), 'Modes of Entry: A Transaction Cost Analysis and Propositions', *Journal of International Business Studies*, **17** (3), Fall, 1–26.

Barley, Stephen, John Freeman and Ralph Hybels (1992), 'Strategic Alliances in Commercial Biotechnology', in Nitin Nohria and Robert Eccles (eds), *Networks and Organizations: Structure, Form, and Action*, Boston: Harvard Business School Press.

Barney, Jay and William Ouchi (1986), *Organizational Economics*, San Francisco: Jossey-Bass Publishers.

Bengtsson, Lars (1993), 'Governmental Markets, Regulations, and Hierarchies', *International Studies of Management & Organization*, **23** (1), Spring, 47–68.

Berle, A.A. and G.C. Means (1932), *The Modern Corporation and Private Property*, New York: Macmillan.

Biggart, Nicole and Gary Hamilton (1992), 'On the Limits of a Firm-Based Theory to Explain Business Networks: The Western Bias of Neoclassical Economies', in Nitin Nohria and Robert Eccles (eds), *Networks and Organizations: Structure, Form, and Action*, Boston: Harvard Business School Press.

Blaine, Michael (1994), *Co-operation in International Business: The Use of Limited Equity Arrangements*, Aldershot, England: Avebury.

Blaine, Michael and Sven Lundstedt (1993), 'Government, Economic Growth, and Social Welfare in High Income Economies', *Business and the Contemporary World*, **V** (4), Autumn, 128–39.

Blinder, Alan (1991), 'A Japanese Buddy System That Could Benefit US Business', *Business Week*, 14 Oct., p. 32

Boskin, Michael and Lawrence Lau (1992), 'Capital, Technology, and Economic Growth', in Nathan Rosenberg, Ralph Landau and David Mowery (eds), *Technology and the Wealth of Nations*, Stanford: Stanford University Press.

Boyacigiller, Nakiye and Nancy Adler (1991), 'The Parochial Dinosaur: Organizational Science in a Global Context', *Academy of Management Review*, **16** (2), 262–90.

Bradach, J.L. and R.G. Eccles (1989), 'Price, Authority, and Trust: From Ideal Types to Plural Forms', *Annual Review of Sociology*, **15**, 97–118.

Buckley, Peter (1981), 'A Critical Review of Theories of the Multinational Enterprise', *Assenwritschaft*, **36**, 70–87.

Buckley, Peter (ed.) (1989), *The Multinational Enterprise*, London: Macmillian Press.

Buckley, Peter and Mark Casson (eds) (1976), *The Future of the Multinational Enterprise*, London: Macmillian Press.

Business Week (1975), 'Sumitomo: How the "Keiretsu" Pulls Together to Keep Japan Strong', 31 March, 43–8.

Casson, Mark (ed.) (1983), *The Growth of International Business*, London: Allen and Unwin.

Casson, Mark (1987), *The Firm and the Market: Studies on Multinational Enterprise and the Scope of the Firm*, Oxford: Basil Blackwell.

Caves, Richard (1982), *Multinational Enterprise and Economic Analysis*, Cambridge, England: Cambridge University Press.

Clegg, Jeremy (1987), *Multinational Enterprise and World Competition: A Comparative Study of the USA, Japan, UK, Sweden, and West Germany*, London: Macmillan Press.

Clegg, Jeremy (1990), 'The Determinants of Aggregate International Licensing Behavior: Evidence From Five Countries', *Management International Review*, **30** (3), 231–51.

Coase, R. H. (1937), 'The Nature of the Firm', *Economica*, 386–405.

Collin, Sven-Olof and Rikard Larsson (1993), 'Beyond Markets and Hierarchies: A Swedish Quest for a Tripolar Institutional Framework', *International Studies of Management & Organization*, **23** (1), Spring, 3–13.

Commons, J. R. (1934), *Institutional Economics*, Madison: University of Wisconsin Press.

Contractor, Farok (1980), 'The Composition of Licensing Fees and Arrangements as a Function of Economic Development of Technology Recipient Nations', *Journal of International Business Studies*, **11**, Winter, 47–62.

Contractor, Farok (1990), 'Contractual and Cooperative Forms of International Business: Toward a Unified Theory of Modal Choice', *Management International Review*, **30** (1), 31–54.

Davis, Stanley (1971), *Comparative Management: Organizational and Cultural Perspectives*, Englewood Cliffs: Prentice-Hall Inc.

Doz, Yves and C.K. Prahalad (1991), 'Managing DMNCs: A Search for a New Paradigm', *Strategic Management Journal*, Special Issue on Global Strategy, Summer, 145–64.

Drucker, Peter (1986), 'The Changed World Economy', *The McKinsey Quarterly*, Autumn, 2–26.

Dunning, John (1988), *Explaining International Production*, London: Unwin Hyman.

Dunning, John (1989), *Multinationals, Technology and Competitiveness*, London: Unwin Hyman.

Durlauf, Steven (1992), 'International Differences in Economic Fluctuations', in Nathan Rosenberg, Ralph Landau and David Mowery (eds), *Technology and the Wealth of Nations*, Stanford: Stanford University Press.

Economist (1993), 'Multinationals', 27 March, 5–20.

Eggertsson, Thrainn (1990), *Economic Behavior and Institutions*, Cambridge, England: Cambridge University Press.

Elg, Ulf and Ulf Johansson (1993), 'The Institutions of Industrial Governance', *International Studies of Management & Organization*, **23** (1), Spring, 29–46.

Encarnation, Dennis (1992), *Rivals Beyond Trade: American Versus Japan in Global Competition*, Ithica: Cornell University Press.

Encarnation, Dennis and Sushil Vachani (1985), 'Foreign Ownership When Host Rules Change', *Harvard Business Review*, Sept.–Oct., 152–60.

Enderwick, Peter (1991), 'Patterns of Manufacturing Employment Change', *International Review of Applied Economics*, May, 197–207.

Etzioni, Amitai (1988), *The Moral Dimension: Toward a New Economics*, New York: The Free Press.

Farma, Eugene and Michael Jensen (1983), 'Separation of Ownership and Control',

Journal of Law and Economics, **26**, 301–25, in Jay Barney and William Ouchi (eds) (1986), *Organizational Economics*, San Francisco: Jossey-Bass Publishers.

Fortune (1992), 'The Global 500', 27 July.

Frankel, Jeffrey and Miles Kahler (1993), *Regionalism and Rivalry: Japan and the United States in Pacific Asia*, Chicago: University of Chicago Press.

Gerlach, Michael (1992), *Alliance Capitalism: The Social Organization of Japanese Business*, Berkeley: University of California Press.

Gilroy, Bernard (1993), *Networking in Multinational Enterprises: The Importance of Strategic Alliances*, Columbia, S.C.: University of South Carolina Press.

Grabher, Gernot (ed.) (1993), *The Embedded Firm: On the Socioeconomics of Industrial Networks*, London: Routledge.

Hagedoorn, John (1993), 'Strategic Technology Alliances and Modes of Cooperation in High-Technology Industries', in Gernot Grabher (ed.), *The Embedded Firm: On the Socioeconomics of Industrial Networks*, London: Routledge.

Hagedoorn, John and Jos Schakenraad (1990), 'Strategic Partnering and Technological Co-operation', in B. Dankbaar, J. Groenewegen and H. Schenik (eds), *Perspectives in Industrial Organization*, Boston: Kluwer Academic Publishers.

Hakansson, Hakan and Jan Johanson (1993), 'The Network as a Governance Structure: Interfirm Cooperation Beyond Markets and Hierarchies', in Gernot Grabher (ed.), *The Embedded Firm: On the Socioeconomics of Industrial Networks*, London: Routledge.

Haley, John (1992), 'Consensual Governance: A Study of Law, Culture, and the Political Economy of Postwar Japan', in Shumpei Kumon and Henry Rosovsky (eds), *The Political Economy of Japan, Volume 3: Cultural and Social Dynamics*, Stanford: Stanford University Press.

Hallwood, Paul (1990), *Transaction Costs and Trade Between Multinational Corporations: A Study of Offshore Oil Production*, Boston: Unwin Hyman.

Hampden-Turner, Charles and Alfons Trompenaars (1993), *The Seven Cultures of Capitalism*, New York: Currency Doubleday.

Hennart, Jean-Francois (1988), 'A Transaction Costs Theory of Equity Joint Ventures', *Strategic Management Journal*, **9**, 361–74.

Hill, Charles (1990), 'Cooperation, Opportunism, and the Invisible Hand: Implications for Transaction Cost Theory', *Academy of Management Review*, **15** (3), 500–513.

Hill, Charles, Peter Hwang and W. Chan Kim (1990), 'Searching for a Dynamic Theory of the Multinational Enterprise: A Transaction Cost Model', *Strategic Management Journal*, **9**, 93–104.

Hofstede, Geert (1980), *Culture's Consequences: International Differences in Work Related Values*, Beverly Hills, C.A.: Sage.

Imai, Ken-ichi (1992), 'Japan's Corporate Networks', in Shumpei Kumon and Henry Rosovsky (eds), *The Political Economy of Japan, Volume 3: Cultural and Social Dynamics*, Stanford: Stanford University Press.

Jenkinson, Tim and Colin Mayer (1992), 'The Assessment: Corporate Governance and Corporate Control', *Oxford Review of Economic Policy*, **8** (3), Autumn, 1–10.

Jensen, Michael and William Meckling (1976), 'Theory of the Firm, Managerial Behavior, Agency Costs, and Ownership Structure', *Journal of Financial Economics*, **3** (4), 305–60, in Jay Barney and William Ouchi (1986), *Organizational Economics*, San Francisco: Jossey-Bass Publishers.

Johannisson, Bengt (1987), 'Beyond Process and Structure: Social Exchange Networks', *International Studies of Management & Organization*, **XVII** (1), 3–23.

Johansson, Jan and Lars-Gunnar Mattsson (1987), 'Interorganizational Relations in Industrial Systems: A Network Approach Compared with the Transaction-Cost Approach', *International Studies of Management & Organization*, **XVII** (1), 34–48.

Jorde, Thomas M. and David J. Teece (1992), *Antitrust, Innovation and Competitiveness*, New York: Oxford University Press, p. 163.

Kester, W. Carl (1991), *Japanese Takeovers: The Global Contest for Corporate Control*, Boston: Harvard Business School Press.

Kester, W. Carl (1992), 'Industrial Groups as Systems of Contractual Governance', *Oxford Review of Economic Policy*, **8** (3), Autumn, 24–44.

Kluckhohn, Florence and Fred Strodbeck (1961), *Variations in Value Orientations*, Evanston, IL.: Row, Peterson and Co..

Kotabe, Masaaki (1992) *Global Sourcing Strategy: R&D, Manufacturing, and Marketing Interfaces*, New York: Quorum Books.

Kumon, Shumpei and Henry Rosovsky (eds) (1992), *The Political Economy of Japan, Volume 3: Cultural and Social Dynamics*, Stanford: Stanford University Press.

Lane, Robert (1991), *The Market Experience*, Cambridge, England: Cambridge University Press.

Larsson, Rikard (1993), 'The Handshake between Invisible and Visible Hands: Toward a Tripolar Institutional Framework', *International Studies of Management & Organization*, **23** (1), Spring, 87–106.

Lawrence, John and Ryh-song Yeh (1994), 'The Influence of Mexican Culture on the Use of Japanese Manufacturing Techniques in Mexico', *Management International Review*, **34** (1), 49–66.

Lazerson, Mark (1993), 'Factory or Putting-Out? Knitting Networks in Moderna', in Gernot Grabher (ed.), *The Embedded Firm: On the Socioeconomics of Industrial Networks*, London: Routledge.

Levitt, Theodore (1983), 'The Globalization of Markets', *Harvard Business Review*, May–June, 92–102.

Lodge, George and Richard Walton (1989), 'The American Corporation and Its New Relationships', *California Management Review*, Spring, 9–24.

Lowe, Janet (1992), *The Secret Empire: How 25 Multinationals Rule the World*, Homewood, IL.: Business One Irwin.

Lundvall, Bengt-Ake (1993), 'Explaining Inter-firm Cooperation: Limits of the Transaction-Cost Approach', in Gernot Grabher (ed.), *The Embedded Firm. On the Socioeconomics of Industrial Networks*, London: Routledge, 52–64.

Macneil, Ian (1978), 'Contracts: Adjustment of Long-Term Economic Relations Under Classical, Neoclassical, and Relational Contract Law', *Northwestern University Law Review*, **72**, 854–906.

Mathias, Peter and Sydney Pollard (eds) (1989), *Cambridge Economic History of Europe, Volume VIII*, Cambridge, England: Cambridge University Press.

Murakami, Yasusuke and Thomas Rohlen (1993), 'Social-Exchange Aspects of the Japanese Political Economy: Culture, Efficiency, and Change', in Shumpei Kumon and Henry Rosovsky (eds), *The Political Economy of Japan, Volume 3: Cultural and Social Dynamics*, Stanford: Stanford University Press.

Mytelka, Lynn (ed.) (1991), *Strategic Partnerships: States, Firms and International Competition*, Rutherford, N.J.: Fairleigh Dickinson University Press.

Nelson, Richard and Sidney Winter (1982), *An Evolutionary Theory of Economic Change*, Cambridge, MA.: The Belknap Press of Harvard University Press.

Nohria, Nitin and Robert Eccles (eds) (1992), *Networks and Organizations: Structure, Form and Action*, Boston: Harvard Business School Press.

Ogburn, William (1957), 'Culture Lag as Theory', *Sociology and Social Research*, **XLI** Jan., 167–73.

Oman, Charles (1984), 'New Forms of Investment in Developing Countries', Working Paper, Paris: OECD Development Centre.

Ouchi, William (1980), 'Markets, Bureaucracies, and Clans', *Administrative Science Quarterly*, **25**, 129–41.

Ouchi, William (1981), *Theory Z: How American Business Can Meet the Japanese Challenge*, Reading, MA.: Addison-Wesley Publishing Co.

Perlmutter, Howard and David Heenan (1986), 'Cooperate to Compete Globally', *Harvard Business Review*, March–April, 136–52.

Perrow, Charles (1981), 'Markets, Hierarchies and Hegemony: A Critique of Chandler and Williamson', in Andrew Van de Van and William Joyce (eds), *Perspectives on Organization Design and Behavior*, New York: Wiley.

Porter, Michael (1990), *The Competitive Advantages of Nations*, New York: Free Press.

Powell, Walter (1990), 'Neither Market nor Hierarchy: Network Forms of Organization', in Barry Straw and L. L. Cummings (eds), *Research in Organizational Behavior*, Vol. 12, pp. 295–336, Greenwich, CT.: JAI Press Inc.

Richardson, G.B. (1972), 'The Organisation of Industry', *Economic Journal*, Sept., 883–96.

Robinson, Richard (1981), 'Background Concepts and Philosophy of International Business from World War II to Present', *Journal of International Business Studies*, Spring/Summer, 13–21.

Root, Franklin (1984), 'Some Trends in the World Economy and Their Implications for International Business', *Journal of International Business Studies*, Winter, 19–32.

Rosenberg, Nathan, Ralph Landau and David Mowery (eds) (1992), *Technology and the Wealth of Nations*, Stanford: Stanford University Press.

Rosenzweig, Philip (1994), 'The New "American Challenge": Foreign Multinationals in the United States', *California Management Review*, **36** (3), 107–23.

Sapir, Andre, Pierre Buigues and Alexis Jacquemin (1993), 'European Competition Policy in Manufacturing and Services: A Two-Speed Approach', *Oxford Review of Economic Policy*, **9** (2), Summer, 113–32.

Schumpeter, Joseph (1942), *Capitalism, Socialism, and Democracy*, New York: Harper & Brothers.

Takamiya, Susumu and Keith Thurley (1985), *Japan's Emerging Multinationals: An International Comparison of Policies and Practices*, Tokyo: University of Tokyo Press.

Teece, David (1986), 'Transaction Cost Economics and the Multinational Enterprise: An Assessment', *Journal of Economic Behavior and Organization*, **7**, 21–45.

Van de Ven, Andrew and William Joyce (eds) (1981), *Perspectives on Organization Design and Behavior*, New York: Wiley.

Vance, Charles, Shirley McClaine, David Boje and Daniel Stage (1992), 'An Examination of the Transferability of Traditional Performance Appraisal Principles Across Cultural Boundaries', *Management International Review*, **32** (4), 313–26.

Weick, Karl (1976), 'Educational Organizations as Loosely Coupled Systems', *Administrative Science Quarterly*, **21**, March, 1–19.

White, Lawrence (1993), 'Competition Policy in the United States: An Overview', *Oxford Review of Economic Policy*, **9** (2), Summer, 133–53.

Williamson, Oliver (1975), *Markets and Hierarchies: Analysis and Antitrust Implications*, New York: The Free Press.
Williamson, Oliver (1979), 'Transaction-Cost Economics: The Governance of Contractual Relations', *Journal of Law and Economics*, **22**, 223–61.
Williamson, Oliver (1985), *The Economic Institutions of Capitalism*, New York: The Free Press.
Williamson, Oliver (1991), 'Comparative Economic Organization: The Analysis of Discrete Structural Alternatives', *Administrative Science Quarterly*, **36**, June, 269–96.

4. Internalization and de-internalization: will business networks replace multinationals?

Alan M. Rugman, Alain Verbeke and Joseph R. D'Cruz

The internalization decision of a multinational enterprise (MNE) needs to take into account concepts of business policy and competitive strategy. From the modern theory of the MNE, that is, the theory of internalization, it is recognized that proprietary firm-specific advantages yield potential economic profits when exploited on a world-wide basis. Yet the MNE can find these potential profits dissipated by the internal governance costs of its organizational structure and the difficulty of timing and sustaining its foreign direct investment activities. This leads to de-internalization when the benefits of internalization are outweighed by its costs. The form and type of de-internalization usually occurs within a business network of the type discussed in this chapter. The movement from internalization to business network requires analysis of parent–subsidiary relationships and the governance costs of running an MNE versus managing relationships in a business network.

The first part of this chapter examines the relevance of internalization theory for analysis of the strategic decisions of the MNE, especially foreign direct investment (FDI) decisions. Particular attention will be devoted to the choice of entry mode to penetrate foreign markets. In addition, it will be demonstrated that internalization theory can be extended to deal with the different perspectives of complex parent and affiliate relationships, and the nature of governance costs associated with different institutional arrangements, through which FDI decisions are made.

This work is an extension of Rugman (1980, 1981, 1982, 1986). Rugman has synthesized much of the literature on the theory of the MNE, reviewed here, into the theory of internalization, originally developed by Buckley and Casson (1976). The theory of internalization explains the organizational process by which imperfect markets are internalized by private companies up to the point where the costs of internalization equal its benefits. In this framework, for example, proprietary know-how can be turned into firm-specific competitive advantage on occasions when the market would fail to develop such know-how due to the public goods nature of knowledge. It is shown here that internalization theory constitutes the core theory of the MNE.

From a strategic perspective it can be shown that four conditions need to be fulfilled before an MNE will engage in FDI. These are essentially strategic investment criteria.

First, in spite of the perceived riskiness and 'additional costs' of operating abroad, the MNE must be able to develop production activities that will be competitive in the short or long term compared to the domestic operations of host country companies (for a basic analysis, see Rugman *et al.* (1985), especially Chapter 5). Secondly, the net benefits associated with FDI must be higher than in the case of foreign market penetration through exports, licensing or joint venture activity. Thirdly, one or more optimal locations must be identified for the foreign investment. Finally, the MNE's management must be able to decide upon the optimal timing concerning the execution of the investment project.

Here a theoretical framework is developed which will allow MNE managers to determine when to make a particular FDI decision, based upon judgements regarding the four conditions stated above. The governance costs of management of the organizational structures of MNEs are considered, since these costs offset the perceived benefits of internalization. The literature on the theory of the MNE has focused mainly on the benefits of internalization while ignoring the costs of this type of activity. Consequently, assessment of the firm's decision about FDI is likely to be biased unless the managerial/governance costs of internalization are considered. This work helps to broaden our understanding of strategic investment decisions when the net benefits of internalization may be so limited that alternative structures, such as business networks, need to be considered.

INTERNALIZATION THEORY AND MNE STRATEGIC INVESTMENT DECISIONS

Hymer (1976) was the first scholar to improve on the traditional international trade theory framework, that is, the Heckscher–Ohlin–Samuelson (or HOS) paradigm. In his 1960 dissertation (finally published in 1976) Hymer developed an explanation of the functioning of the MNE which emphasized international production rather than international trade. The HOS paradigm does not explain why companies located in one country are able to transfer intangible assets, such as technological know-how, to other countries, while maintaining property rights and direct control over production activities in these other countries. Such real direct investment contrasts sharply with portfolio investment, where no direct control is exerted by the investors (see Rugman (1987) and Rugman and Yeung (1989) on this issue).

It was apparent to Hymer that FDI decisions could not be explained by differences in financial rates of return in the different countries involved. This is consistent with an interpretation that strategic FDI decisions cannot be compared with portfolio investments. Hymer attempted to explain how MNEs were able to compete with domestic companies in host countries (the first condition for FDI). In his view, competitiveness resulted from the monopolistic advantages of MNEs. Hence FDI would occur primarily in imperfect markets.

This view was elaborated further by Kindleberger (1969) who identified imperfections in markets for finished products and for production factors, together with scale economies and government regulations of output and entry. Caves (1971) investigated why certain MNEs were able to engage successfully in horizontal integration on an international scale. Caves argued, in accordance with Hymer and Kindleberger, that the MNE's ability to achieve product differentiation is the main reason for such investments.

It can be observed that the early work of these three pioneers focused on the first condition for FDI. Unfortunately, this economics-based framework was characterized by an absence of managerial considerations and a neglect of the implications of governance costs for the efficiency aspects of FDI decisions. In short, the Hymer–Kindleberger–Caves approach developed the first condition for internalization of FDI, but it ignored other reasons, as well as the costs of internalization. Both of these issues have been explored in more recent work.

BENEFITS OF INTERNALIZATION

The concept of appropriability implies that individuals and organizations, which possess a unique body of know-how, will attempt to avoid dissipation of this know-how to third parties (see Magee, 1977, 1981). First, the costs required to generate technological know-how can only be recaptured through a stream of benefits flowing to the MNE in the long run. Secondly, technological know-how can become a public good. Once dissipated its use by third parties cannot be prevented by the initial owner, whose ability to singularly exploit it is then severely affected, with a reduction in private benefits. Hence this problem of appropriability explains strategic FDI decisions by MNEs. Internalization is preferred to other entry modes to keep the firm's unique know-how proprietary, a point also recognized by Ethier (1986).

Different prescriptions for managers can be drawn from this analysis. FDI should be preferred to other entry modes when: 1) the reputation or brand name of the firm is considered as important by consumers, so that the MNE must engage in direct quality control; 2) after-sales service is important and cannot be assigned to a domestic firm in a host country through a licensing agreement; 3) complementaries exist among the different products, so that production within the MNE is the most efficient way of operating; 4) products are new and differentiated, leading to an information asymmetry between the buyer and seller, such that internalization through vertical integration may generate large benefits; and 5) diversification of product lines creates learning effects and spreads risks.

Magee's approach therefore mainly deals with the second condition for MNE activity. The benefits of the MNE's know-how can only be fully appropriated through FDI. This framework demonstrates the high complexity of strategic investment decisions in MNEs. Careful assessment of the risks of dissipation of the firm's proprietary knowledge is a key component in the investment process. Buckley and Casson (1976) and Casson (1979) also investigated the issue of control over an MNE's know-how as a major generator of internalization decisions. In their view, imperfections in markets of intermediate outputs are the main rationale for internalization. Such imperfections include: 1) difficulties in developing long term contracts for specific types of intermediate output; 2) the absence of possibilities for price discrimination; 3) the danger of opportunistic behaviour by a contracting party in case of a bilateral concentration of market power; 4) the existence of an 'information asymmetry' between suppliers and buyers, leading the latter to offer an insufficient price for a particular good; and 5) government regulation such as import tariffs and international differences in tax systems. These five elements have a substantial impact on technological know-how and scarce raw materials, often found in limited geographical areas. The creation of an internal market can eliminate problems caused by these market imperfections.

Buckley and Casson recognized that there are, however, governance costs associated with internalization. These include: communication costs among production facilities that are dispersed geographically; administrative and capital costs; and potential political costs (such as when discriminatory measures are taken in favour of domestically owned firms). The costs and benefits of internalization need to be carefully evaluated, and will depend on firm, industry, host country and regional characteristics. This clear statement of condition 2 has been the basis for further work on the theory of the MNE summarized in Buckley and Casson (1985).

THE ECLECTIC APPROACH

Dunning's (1979, 1981) eclectic paradigm explains why MNEs make particular FDI decisions, based on an integrated analysis of the first three conditions for strategic investment. First, the MNE must be competitive with local producers because it possesses ownership advantages, that is, proprietary intangible assets such as patented technology, management know-how and so on. Secondly, FDI must be preferred to contracts with local producers and licensing agreements, when the MNE's core know-how can be protected only through internalization. Thirdly, the best geographical location is typically chosen as the result of careful analysis of different sets of relevant costs, such as costs of production, quality control, transportation and so on. Dunning also recognized that the location element as a major determinant of FDI may differ from one industry to another. In a similar vein, corporate perceptions of environmental factors, such as government regulation of MNE activity, and political stability, are considered important. The key idea developed by Dunning in his eclectic model is the possibility of strong interaction among ownership advantages, internalization advantages and the identification of an optimal geographic location in the FDI process.

In contrast to the Hymer–Kindleberger–Caves approach discussed earlier, some attention has also been devoted by Dunning to managerial issues related to the FDI process. In this context the distinction between structural and transactional advantages of MNEs is essential (see Dunning and Rugman, 1985). The former result from the ownership of distinctive assets which give the MNE a competitive edge in the market, but which are unrelated to the multinational character of the firm. This type of advantage would include scale economies and the use of proprietary assets. In contrast, transactional advantages reflect a comparatively greater efficiency of the foreign investment process in MNEs as compared to uninational firms.

The greater efficiency of MNEs results from four elements. First, a larger set of investment opportunities is available to MNEs. Secondly, they have better access to (and processing of) information on the inputs (cost elements) and outputs (benefits) of particular investment decisions. Thirdly, the possibility of risk reduction through international diversification exists (see Rugman, 1979). Finally, the possibility of exploiting international differences in market imperfections is present (for example, pricing of factors of production). The implications of these four elements for strategy are of major importance, as they help the strategic positioning of the MNE in comparison to domestic companies in host countries.

THE OPTIMAL TIMING OF STRATEGIC INVESTMENT DECISIONS

Buckley and Casson (1980) have also conducted an analysis of the optimal timing for FDI decisions (the fourth condition for FDI). They assume that exports, licensing and FDI are alternatives characterized by a particular mix of fixed and variable costs. Fixed costs would be highest for FDI and lowest for exports, whereas the opposite situation would be characteristic of the variable costs. In cases where each entry mode would constitute an efficient means to serve foreign markets, exports, licensing and FDI will be chosen in a sequential fashion. If the foreign market is large, or if one of the modes is inefficient, such sequences may not be observed. Furthermore, if an MNE already has production facilities abroad and fixed costs to manufacture a new product are low (a case of incremental investment), then FDI may occur immediately. A slightly different model on the timing issue was developed by Giddy and Rugman and is summarized in Rugman (1981).

Furthermore, according to Rugman (1981), the choice of timing (as well as location) constitutes merely a part of the decision to internalize. This means that the third and fourth conditions for FDI are interrelated. Rugman (1986) has demonstrated that the specification of additional parameters such as entry and exit barriers, the risk of dissipation of technological know-how and the level of tariff and non-tariff barriers, determines when a switch occurs among modes of entry. Hill and Chan Kim (1988) have also designed a model aimed at identifying changes in the choice of entry modes in a dynamic perspective. Most MNEs now use modern strategic management techniques which indeed determine these switching points.

In Rugman's view, the investment process in MNEs is characterized by the increasing importance of firm-specific strategic management considerations. These are replacing traditional financial or portfolio capital elements, especially under the pressures of multinational global competition. This is consistent with the findings of a substantial body of empirical studies on multinational finance, summarized in Eiteman and Stonehill (1989).

TRANSACTION COSTS AND ORGANIZATIONAL STRUCTURE

Williamson (1981, 1985) and Teece (1985) view the existence of an efficient organizational structure capable of implementing investment decisions as a major explanatory element in the growth of MNEs in world trade and investment. An example of such an organizational structure is the so-called multidivisional structure (M-form).

An M-form would reduce governance costs associated with the functioning of MNEs as compared to a unitary, or functional, structure (U-form). The main reason is that corporate management would be able to devote most of its time to strategic management decisions including investment decisions. Conversely, management at the divisional level would be concerned mainly with operational decisions and the achievement of profitability for their respective divisions. This view on the functioning of larger corporations is in accordance with the framework developed by Simon (1957) and empirical research by Chandler (1962).

The investment process in unitary or functionally organized MNEs would be less efficient. A functional structure could stimulate opportunistic behaviour by functional managers, even at the corporate level. Furthermore, it would be more difficult to separate strategic decisions such as capital budgeting and operational decisions. Finally, effective control and sanction systems aimed at monitoring the outcomes of the investment process would have a much higher complexity.

Related to such organizational aspects are problems associated with the transfer of technology abroad, such as the problem of 'disclosure' and the problem of 'team organization'. Disclosure concerns the so called 'fundamental paradox', a refinement of the public goods externality as described by Arrow (1971). The value of information, in this case technological know-how, is not known by its potential buyer until it has been disclosed, but through such disclosure the buyer acquires the information at no cost. Team organization implies that technological know-how of a firm is often spread among a number of individuals, each of whom masters only part of this know-how. In such a case a technology transfer contract is excluded. If technological know-how needs to be transferred on a continuous basis, FDI will occur.

In terms of the multinational investment process, Williamson's main contribution is his emphasis on the importance of organizational elements as a major determining factor in strategic investment decisions. His work confirms that the financial, or portfolio, aspects of foreign investment projects are secondary to the issue of control. Teece (1982), (1983) and (1985) has expanded Williamson's analysis by developing a contingency theory which explains the choice of FDI as the preferred entry mode, taking into account governance costs. He distinguishes between investments generating vertical integration and those for horizontal integration.

Vertical integration occurs whenever the presence of specific assets leads to strong mutual interdependence between two economic agents and when the opportunistic behaviour of one party creates high costs for the other. Vertical integration thus eliminates high contractual costs (especially control costs related to the enforcement of contracts). Horizontal integration occurs if two conditions are fulfilled. First, the organization must have assets which are not entirely 'used', such as technological know-how in the form of a patent or brand name. Secondly, the direct investment abroad must lead to higher net benefits than in the case of exports or a licensing agreement.

Teece's work demonstrates that the multinational investment process cannot be reduced to a simple process of choice among different investment projects. The choice of an optimal mode of entry for each individual project considered is, in itself, a decision problem which, at least from a conceptual perspective, needs to occur prior to the choice among FDI projects. Thus the strategic nature of the FDI decision will govern and constrain the investment decision of MNEs.

INTERNALIZATION THEORY AND PARENT–SUBSIDIARY RELATIONSHIPS

It has been argued in the previous section that the main contribution of internalization theory to the multinational investment process is related to its focus on: 1) the choice of entry mode to penetrate foreign markets; and 2) the necessity to control proprietary know-how. The main weakness of the theory, except for the Williamson–Teece approach, is the assumption that the MNE's 'administrative heritage' in investment decisions will not affect the investment process.

Yet the issue of administrative heritage is critical. It is especially critical for ongoing foreign investment decisions (as opposed to the initial choice of FDI as an entry mode by a firm). Exports, licensing, FDI and joint ventures as modes of entry simply cannot be compared without taking into account the administrative and organizational characteristics of the firm involved. In fact, the governance costs associated with FDI will depend largely upon the efficiency of the MNE's organizational structure.

This explains why firms facing similar environmental conditions and having similar characteristics in terms of proprietary assets may still choose a different entry mode. For example, firms that do not have an organizational structure allowing the separation of strategic and operational decisions may prefer not to engage in FDI because of the costs of operating a large hierarchy. According to Williamson (1985), the early availability of the M-form in US corporations provided them with an internal management capability which only became available about a decade later to non-US corporations. This would explain Tsurumi's (1977) observation that FDI by US firms increased rapidly after 1953, while FDI by non-US MNEs only became prevalent in the 1960s.

Moreover, even when leaving aside the issue of choice of entry mode, we should recognize that the outcomes of the investment process itself will be strongly influenced by the firm's administrative heritage. In particular, the structure of parent–subsidiary interactions may substantially affect the outcomes of the investment process.

In other words, the main decision problem in the multinational investment process is not the 'objective' evaluation of the costs and benefits associated with particular internalization decisions. Rather, it is the design of a decision process which allows an objective assessment of: 1) the costs and benefits associated with the different entry modes for each project; and 2) the relative net benefits associated with the optimal entry mode for all projects under consideration.

The next section develops a simple framework to illustrate these points. It should be emphasized that this framework is designed for top management, that is, the strategic planners responsible for the FDI decision. Once the strategic decisions about FDI, or other modes, are made then a centralized finance function is normal. However, at a strategic level, the decision-making can be centralized or decentralized. It depends upon the optimal method of exploiting the proprietary assets of the MNE.

A FRAMEWORK FOR THE STRATEGIC INVESTMENT PROCESS

Using a transaction cost perspective, a conceptual framework can be developed which allows us to determine whether or not the strategic investment process in an MNE can be considered efficient. Only if this is the case can objective assessments be made of the costs and benefits of specific investment projects. This model constitutes an extension of internalization theory since it specifies the conditions to be fulfilled by the investment process in an MNE in order to guarantee optimal resource allocation decisions.

There are four generic types of the investment to be distinguished, as represented in Figure 4.1.

The vertical axis of Figure 4.1 measures the degree of centralization of the strategic investment process. This process includes the design, evaluation and choice of investment projects. It can be either centralized or decentralized. In the former case, all investment activities are executed at the corporate management level. The latter case reflects the execution of specific activities in the investment process by different levels in the hierarchy of the MNE, including the level of subsidiary management.

The centralization of the strategic investment process at the corporate management level will lead to severe problems of 'bounded rationality'. The information-processing capabilities of a decentralized decision structure are, however, much lower than those of a centralized system, as demonstrated by

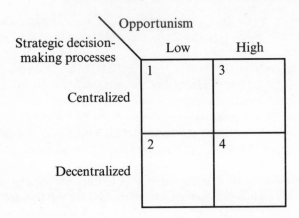

Figure 4.1   Strategic decision processes and opportunism

Simon (1961) and Aguilar (1979). This issue is especially important when the MNE is faced with a rapidly changing and complex environment.

The horizontal axis of Figure 4.1 deals with the transaction cost concept of 'opportunism'. It captures the presence or absence of safeguards in the structural and cultural context of the organization. Such safeguards are necessary to protect the investment process against the impact of local rationality, that is, subgoal pursuit. For an overview of the research on the choice between structural (formal) and cultural (informal) coordination and control systems in MNEs, see Baliga and Jaeger (1984).

The issue of safeguards in the investment process reflects the existence of control costs in a hierarchical mode of organization. The main reason for this problem of control is that managers of the different subsidiaries (in the case of a decentralized system), and even the functional managers at the corporate level, have weak incentives to maximize the total output of the global organization. In the case of a decentralized system aiming at the achievement of high national responsiveness, the knowledge of subsidiary managers as to the expected costs and benefits of particular investment projects is superior to that of corporate managers. The reasons for this include the information asymmetry between subsidiary managers and corporate managers concerning the market characteristics of the foreign environment and the geographic distance between corporate headquarters and the host country environment. These factors make it difficult for corporate headquarters to exert direct control on subsidiary managers. Especially in cases where such projects will affect the functioning and the profitability of other subsidiaries, it is difficult to design appropriate incentives to eliminate the problem of opportunism (see Hennart, 1986). Then, through cultural safeguards such as extensive socialization and training, the goals of subsidiary managers can be made consistent with the goals of corporate management.

GENERIC STRATEGIES AND THE FDI DECISION

Within this framework four generic types of the FDI decision processes can now be distinguished. It should be noted that, conceptually, within each quadrant the normal financially based net present value calculations about FDI can be made. That is, all the usual investment considerations about taxes, exchange rates, cost of capital and so on, are secondary to the prior critical strategic decision as to which quadrant is relevant for the top managers to choose in order to exploit the proprietary assets of the MNE.

The first quadrant of Figure 4.1 refers to the case where the locus of strategic decision-making is centralized and safeguards are introduced against the danger of opportunistic behaviour. Multinational investment processes positioned in this quadrant allow the development of a global strategy aimed at reaping the benefits of integration. An example of such a process would be the one found in an M-form. Hout, Porter and Rudden (1982) have argued in favour of such centralization of strategic decision-making, which allows the integration of a firm's strategies across several domestic markets.

Unfortunately, multinational investment often requires some degree of national responsiveness. In this case realistic investment projects may well have to be initiated at the subsidiary (host country) level. The second quadrant reflects the fact that only 'induced' investment projects are being generated, that is, projects which are in accordance with the MNE's dominating concept of strategy and which fit into the firm's existing product-market domain. In this case, an optimal balance can be found between the requirements of integration and national responsiveness in the investment process. It should be recognized, however, that the decentralization of strategic investment activities towards the subsidiary level may initiate problems of fragmentation if structural and cultural safeguards are not carefully designed.

The issue of cultural safeguards in quadrant 2 is especially important if regional or world product mandates have been assigned (see Rugman, 1983; D'Cruz, 1986; Rugman and Douglas, 1986). In this case, resource allocation decisions taken at the corporate level result from an extensive strategic confrontation between the views of subsidiary managers and corporate-level managers. Elements such as the reputation of subsidiary managers and their ability to initiate commitment at the corporate level become of prime importance. Ghertman (1981, 1988) has investigated the role of 'go-betweens' in investment and divestment decisions of MNEs. Go-betweens include both outsiders (such as consultants) and insiders (such as managers) who understand the divergence between parent and subsidiary views on investment projects. The occurrence of conflicts between the different levels of management in MNEs has been observed by several authors, such as Doz and Prahalad (1981, 1984, 1987) and Globerman (1986). Corporate management should be careful to avoid the introduction of false safeguards in the investment process. These would include short-run profitability requirements of new investment projects, leading to a neglect of valuable long-run investment opportunities by subsidiary managers.

The third and fourth quadrants of Figure 4.1 are characteristic of processes where opportunistic behaviour strongly influences investment decisions. An example of the former (quadrant 3) is the U-form, whereby functional managers at the highest level of the MNE attempt to generate investment decisions in favour of their own functional units. The latter (quadrant 4) includes cases whereby subsidiary managers actually dominate the company and no central coordination at all is performed by the corporate headquarters.

The conclusion of this analysis is that only the investment processes in the second quadrant are efficient. In an environment of global competition, each MNE needs to be responsive to the needs of both integration and national responsiveness. Indeed, it is only in the case of efficient safeguards against opportunistic behaviour that objective assessments can be made of the costs and benefits of different entry modes. Only then can the net benefits of the different investment projects under consideration be found. The basis for such efficient strategic investment decisions by MNEs is the theory of internalization. Neglect of this analytical tool will lead to inefficient investment behaviour by MNEs.

From this analysis it is apparent that neither the conventional centralized, hierarchical, M-form structure of the MNE (in quadrant 1) nor the U-form (in quadrant 3) is really suitable for efficient strategic FDI decision-making. Instead, the managers of an MNE need to cope with a decentralized structure which incorporates critical elements of national responsiveness. Only a few MNEs are good at doing this – see the analysis of ABB by Bartlett and Ghoshal (1993), building upon their concept of the 'transnational solution' in Bartlett and Ghoshal (1989). In terms of this analysis the transnational solution is in quadrant 2. Given the tremendous difficulty facing MNEs in adopting the decentralized and non-opportunistic transnational solution of quadrant 2 it is necessary to consider alternative methods of organization. One of these of great relevance today is a new type of business network, discussed in the next section.

THE FIVE PARTNERS BUSINESS NETWORK MODEL

The five partners model of a business network organizes economic exchange among partner organizations through cooperative, non-equity relationships. It has been developed by D'Cruz and Rugman (1992a, 1992b, 1993, 1994). Specifically, the partners include: a leading 'flagship firm' which is a multinational corporation; key suppliers; key customers; selected competitors; and the non-business infrastructure (see Figure 4.2).

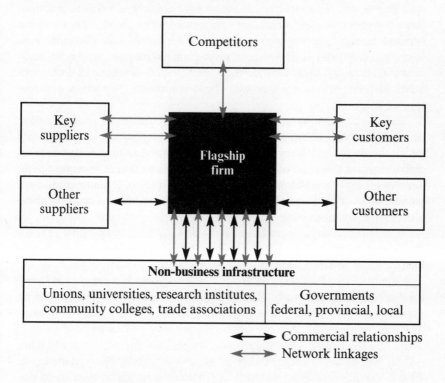

Figure 4.2   The five partners business network

The non-business infrastructure comprises government, the non-traded service sectors, educational institutions, social services, unions, trade associations and non-profit cultural organizations. The business network's governance structure depends upon: 1) asymmetric control of the network's strategic purpose by the flagship firm; and 2) a restructuring of aspects of the partners' business systems (value-chains) to create a network business system.

The flagship firm's resources and global perspective enable it to develop global strategies which can capitalize on the capabilities and knowledge of all partners. Because partners may compete in business systems not related to that of the business network, it should be emphasized that the flagship firm's asymmetric strategic control extends only to those aspects of its partners' business systems committed to the network. Through the adoption of a paradigm of cooperation predicated on long-term association, the business network benefits from the development of trust among network partners. The trust that is developed within the cooperative context of network relationships decreases the need to establish elaborate internal MNE structures and systems to guard against opportunism. That is, relationship stability and longevity, coupled with shared inter-organizational purpose (of the business network), help to decrease inefficiencies similar to those found in traditional MNE M-form governance structures built around the protection of firm-specific assets (FSAs).

The business network's structure of cooperative relationships reduces the amount of asset-specific investments for any given partner. Organizations which choose to participate in a business network realize that the demands of global markets may preclude the ability of any given firm to be competitive in every aspect of their current business. The rapid pace of technology change, product obsolescence and market growth place heavy burdens on companies if they wish to remain competitive.

Many corporations now understand that they are competing against global business systems as opposed to within broadly defined industry groupings. Restructuring and outsourcing those activities in which the partner has no core competence (Prahalad and Hamel, 1990) lessens investments in 'non-core' assets, and particularly those in which the partner has less knowledge. Consequently, the likelihood of investment in assets which quickly become 'non-performing' is decreased. When partners focus on investment in core assets and the exploitation of their core capabilities they are better able to follow, predict and adapt to market changes which affect their operations. If all network partners assume similar approaches, then the boundaries of the business network can shift more easily to accommodate changes in the global market. The network's business system, therefore, benefits from the permeability of its boundaries and its shared strategic purpose.

The five partners business network developed here has many of the attributes of a Japanese interfirm network *keiretsu* system. However, the major difference is that our business network does not have a major bank or a general trading company as a partner, whereas these are deeply involved in the *keiretsus*. For a discussion of the complexities of the Japanese enterprise system, of which vertical (and horizontal) groupings in *keiretsus* are but one form, see Fruin (1992).

STRATEGY AND THE BUSINESS NETWORK'S FIVE PARTNERS

The strategic direction and purpose of the business network is led by an MNE which has the resources and industry perspective to develop and coordinate the execution of global business strategies. This flagship firm's experience in international markets is vital for the business network's determination of which markets to serve and which products/services to produce. Essentially, the flagship firm's strategic hand guides its partners towards a vision of global competitiveness for the network as a whole.

The business network's global strategies will draw from the MNE's experience in market entry; whether it be through international trade, licensing, joint venture or FDI (Rugman, 1981). However, the execution of strategies will differ from past practice because the MNE will not depend on internalization as the sole means by which to protect FSAs and gain competitive advantage. As shown earlier, typically internalization meant vertical and/or horizontal integration in order to monitor, meter and regulate the use of proprietary knowledge (Rugman, 1981). Instead of internalization to protect its knowledge-based FSAs, the flagship firm focuses on sharing knowledge among network partners in order to facilitate inter-organizational learning. This business network strategy reflects the difficulty of gaining competitive advantage via protecting knowledge through internalization: 1) in an environment where ease of communication negates protection from national borders, language differences, physical geography and so on; and 2) in markets characterized by rapid change and innovation (for example, leading to product obsolescence).

The business network as a governance structure operationalizes Kogut and Zander's (1992, 1993) thesis that knowledge-sharing is a determining factor of organizational form and boundary. Specifically, they argue that the boundaries of a firm, and by extension a network of firms, are defined by how well current capabilities (or a recombination of them) generate knowledge. We argue that the business network structure facilitates knowledge generation and inter-organization learning. In particular, we propose that strategic asymmetry assists the development of a 'common language' by which partners can communicate. It follows, therefore, that intra-network learning and knowledge generation are important processes which enable the business network to be flexible and responsive to changes in the external market environment. We argue that this responsiveness outweighs concerns over losing FSAs and in fact obviates the need to protect them through internalization.

The flagship firm's asymmetric strategic leadership is manifested in the following important areas:

1. Adopting and promulgating a long-term relationship-based, cooperation paradigm for network activities.
2. Relocating and restructuring the loci of production and service provision for value-added activities through the network.
3. Benchmarking and measuring network partners' activities and processes to global standards of competitiveness.
4. Encouraging the development of a 'common language' to facilitate knowledge generation and intra-network learning.

It is evident that network partners determine that strategic leadership by a flagship firm offers rewards that could not otherwise be obtained. As with all partners who voluntarily join the business network, *key suppliers* expect that participation in the network will be beneficial to them. These suppliers should receive increased order volumes when the flagship firm undertakes a supplier reduction programme as it converts to a network procurement style. Moreover, the key suppliers can expect to enter multi-year supply contracts. The reduction of risk which accompanies open-ended, multi-year contracts (Fama, 1980) is enhanced by risk-sharing with the flagship firm related to technology and capital expenditures. The second significant benefit of network participation for key suppliers is capturing a higher proportion of value-added activities deintegrated from the flagship firm. Thirdly, through benchmarking to the global standards required by the network, the key suppliers' processes, technologies and systems will reflect standards of competitiveness which may ensure their continued survival and prosperity. Moreover, if a key supplier owns other businesses outside of the network, it may be able to transfer knowledge and learning garnered from network participation to these operations.

Key customers yield to the strategic leadership of the flagship firm for several reasons. First, there may be structural and contractual obligations which tie the key customer to the flagship firm. Automobile manufacturers and their dealers are an example of this type of relationship. Secondly, there may be strategic reasons which compel the key customer to follow the expertise of the flagship firm. Typically, this scenario will be encountered when the network's business system organizes economic activity more efficiently, at a lower cost or with better technological capability than can the key customer. If these activities are integral to the key customer's operations, then it may be willing to cede a measure of control to the flagship firm. While it may seem counterintuitive to follow such a strategy, the logic flows from the inability of the key customer to 'maintain' these activities due to the pace of change in the operational environment. For example, if telecommunications services are integral to a brokerage firm's operations, it may wish to engage the expert services of a third party contractor to oversee its telecommunications needs. This type of arrangement is fairly common and often takes the form of an on-site contract worker or mini-department at the key customer's premises. Therefore, the leap to ceding strategic control to the flagship firm is not so high as might be thought. Beyond being a market for the flagship firm, key customers serve as a market feedback mechanism for the business network as a whole.

The business network model explicitly incorporates the *non-business infrastructure* (NBI) into its partnering relationships. Moreover, it departs from traditional approaches which tend to view that infrastructure as frictional bodies, rather than integral members of economic production. Relationships with the NBI focus on those aspects of the partner's organization which contribute to the strategic purpose of the network. Research ties between the flagship firm and educational institutions are an obvious example of mutually beneficial relationships. The flagship firm, and potentially other network partners, mobilizes financial resources to assist the NBI's efforts. In return, the NBI will agree to pursue activities which exploit resources and competencies in a manner beneficial to the network's purpose. Also, the NBI partners may provide other non-financial resources such as facilities, equipment, human resources or other institutional arrangements.

One of the most important roles for NBI partners, and particularly government and educational institutions, is to provide a forum for cooperative exchange – a non-adversarial venue where organizations can foster relationships. Ouchi (1984, p. 29) makes this point in his research on Japanese trade associations, government ministry 'discussion councils' and public–private economic institutes: these bodies, 'in the end, serve the sole purpose of creating a setting in which competitors can arrange non-adversarial relationships for the common good. It is these institutions that are the loci of social memory'. We argue that government and other NBI organizations can fulfil this role in the context of business networks. To date, North American business has ignored these non-market forums for exchange and has limited its participation in such bodies. The result is that proficiency in contributing to (and accessing) commonly built pools of knowledge is limited; and that inter-organizational partnering remains unsophisticated. However, business network relationships predicated on long-term association will eventually create loci of social/economic memory which network partners can access.

Relationships with *selected competitors* comprise the fifth element of the business network partnerships. The perspective brought to this shared relationship differs from past inter-organizational relationships. Because business network partners understand that internalization may fail structurally to position the firm for competitiveness, they are willing to engage in more open-ended relationships based on knowledge-sharing, not knowledge-protection. Such firms organize their structures to change with the market. The form of relationship, on the surface, appears to be traditional: joint ventures, supplier development, market-sharing arrangements, technology transfers and so on. However, the method of implementation through managerial interaction and joint working teams, rather than static contractual arrangements, is devised to encourage cooperation and knowledge development. Obviously, such relationships generate benefits associated with economies of scope and scale, but such advantages are insufficiently compelling to bind organizations together. Selected competitors commit to a business network because they: 1) understand the learning benefits of the cooperative relationships and the guiding strategic purpose; and 2) wish to 'restructure' their firm boundaries, capabilities and culture to meet the demands of the global competitive environment.

DE-INTERNALIZATION OF THE MNE

The implication of this new analysis of business networks is that such a structure can be a substitute for internalization outside core processes by the MNE. Thus, a well-functioning five partners business network will be consistent with selective de-internalization. An illustration of this is depicted in Figure 4.3.

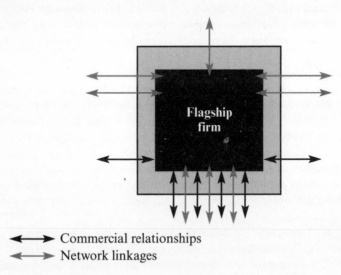

◄────► Commercial relationships
◄────► Network linkages

Figure 4.3   MNE de-internalization in a business network

In Figure 4.3 the five partners business network will shrink the size of the MNE as the need for internalization is retained only for the core activities of the MNE (the black area). The grey area indicates activities previously internalized by the MNE which can now be undertaken by its partners in the business network. The grey area represents newly peripheral activities to the MNE, but these offer considerable value-added to the business network as a whole. The grey area activities are now undertaken by independent companies (that is, there is no equity control of them by the MNE) although, as discussed earlier, the partners have developed long-term relationships with the MNE and there is considerable interdependence between them and the MNE.

While this chapter has its focus on the theory of business networks and the internalization/de-internalization decision of the MNE, it is apparent that these ideas need to be tested by further research on the actual existence of such business networks, and the trends towards de-internalization by MNEs. But that is in the scope for future research.

BIBLIOGRAPHY

Aguilar, F. (1979), *Scanning the Business Environment*, New York: Macmillan.

Arrow, Kenneth (1971), *Essays in the Theory of Risk-Bearing*, Chicago: Markham.

Baliga, B. and A. Jaeger (1984), 'Multinational Corporations: Control Systems and Delegation Issues', *Journal of International Business Studies*, **15**.

Bartlett, Christopher A. (1986), 'Building and Managing the Transnational: The New Organization Challenge', in Michael E. Porter (ed.), *Competition in Global Industries*, Boston: Harvard Business School Press.

Bartlett, Christopher A. and Sumantra Ghoshal (1989), *Managing Across Borders: The Transnational Solution*, Boston: Harvard Business School Press.

Bartlett, Christopher A. and Sumantra Ghoshal (1993), 'Beyond the M-Form Toward a Managerial Theory of the Firm', *Strategic Management Journal*, **14**, Special Issue, Winter.

Buckley, Peter J. and Mark Casson (1976), *The Future of the Multinational Enterprise*, Basingstoke and London: Macmillan.

Buckley, Peter J. and Mark Casson (1980), 'The Optimal Timing of a Foreign Direct Investment', *The Economic Journal*, **91**, March.

Buckley, Peter J. and Mark Casson (1985), *The Economic Theory of the Multinational Enterprise*, London and Basingstoke: Macmillan.

Casson, Mark (1979), *Alternatives to the Multinational Enterprise*, London: Macmillan.

Caves, Richard E. (1971), 'International Corporations: The Industrial Economics of Foreign Investment', *Economica*, **38**, 1–27.

Chandler, Alfred J. (1962), *Strategy and Structure: Chapters in the History of the American Industrial Enterprise*, Cambridge, Mass.: MIT Press.

D'Cruz, Joseph R. (1986), 'Strategic Management of Subsidiaries', in Hamid Etemad and Louise Seguin Dulude (eds), *Managing the Multinational Subsidiary*, Kent: Croom Helm.

D'Cruz, Joseph R. and Alan M. Rugman (1992a), *New Compacts for Canadian Competitiveness*, Toronto: Kodak Canada Inc.

D'Cruz, Joseph R. and Alan M. Rugman (1992b), 'Business Networks for International Competitiveness', *Business Quarterly*, **56** (4).

D'Cruz, Joseph R. and Alan M. Rugman (1993), 'Developing International Competitiveness: The Five Partners Model', *Business Quarterly*, **58** (2).

D'Cruz, Joseph R. and Alan M. Rugman (1994), 'The Five Partners Model: France Telecom, Alcatel, and the Global Telecommunications Industry', *European Management Journal*, March.

Doz, Yves and C.K. Prahalad (1981), 'Headquarters Influence and Strategic Control in MNC's', *Sloan Management Review*, **23**.

Doz, Yves and C.K. Prahalad (1984), 'Patterns of Strategic Control Within Multinational Corporations', *Journal of International Business Studies*, **15**.

Doz, Yves and C.K. Prahalad (1987), *The Multinational Mission: Balancing Local Demands and Global Vision*, New York: Macmillan.

Dunning, John H. (1979), 'Explaining Changing Patterns of International Production: In Defence of the Eclectic Theory', *Oxford Bulletin of Economics and Statistics*, **41**, November.

Dunning, John H. (1981), *International Production and the Multinational Enterprise*, London: George Allen and Unwin.

Dunning, John H. and Alan M. Rugman (1985), 'The Influence of Hymer's Dissertation on the Theory of Foreign Direct Investment', *American Economic Review*, **75**, May.

Eiteman, David K. and Arthur I. Stonehill, (1989), *Multinational Business Finance*, Englewood Cliffs: Prentice Hall.

Ethier, Wilfred J. (1986), 'The Multinational Firm', *The Quarterly Journal of Economics*, November.

Fama, Eugene (1980), 'Agency Problems and the Theory of the Firm', *Journal of Political Economy*, **88**.

Fruin, W. Mark. (1992), *The Japanese Enterprise System: Competitive Strategies with Cooperative Structures*, Oxford: Oxford University Press.

Ghertman, Michel, (1981), *La Prise de Decision*, Paris: PUF.

Ghertman, Michel (1988), 'Foreign Subsidiary and Parents' Roles During Strategic Investment and Investment Decisions', *Journal of International Business Studies*, Spring.

Globerman, Steven (1986), *Fundamentals of International Business Management*, Englewood Cliffs: Prentice-Hall.

Hennart, Jean-Francois (1986), 'What is Internalization?', *Weltwirtschaftliches Archiv*, **122** (4), Winter.

Hill, Charles W.L. and W. Chan Kim (1988), 'Searching for a Dynamic Theory of the Multinational Enterprise: A Transaction Cost Model', *Strategic Management Journal*, Summer.

Hout, Thomas, Michael E. Porter and Eileen Rudden (1982), 'How Global Companies Win Out', *Harvard Business Review*, September–October.

Hymer, Stephen H. (1976), *The International Operations of National Firms: A Study of Direct Investments*, Cambridge, Mass.: MIT Press.

Kindleberger, Charles P. (1969), *American Business Abroad: Six Lectures on Direct Investment*, New Haven: Yale University Press.

Kogut, Bruce and Udo Zander (1992), 'Knowledge of the Firm, Combinative Capabilities, and the Replication of Technology', *Organization Science*, **3** (3).

Kogut, Bruce and Udo Zander (1993), 'Knowledge of the Firm and the Evolutionary Theory of the Multinational Corporation', *Journal of International Business Studies*, **24** (4).

Magee, Stephen P. (1977), 'Multinational Corporations, the Industry Technology Cycle and Development', *Journal of World Trade Law*, **11**, July–August.

Magee, Stephen P. (1981), 'The Appropriability Theory of the Multinational Corporation', *Annals of the American Academy of Political and Social Science*, November.

Ouchi, William G. (1984), 'Political and Economic Teamwork: The Development of the Microelectronics Industry in Japan', *California Management Review*, **26** (4).

Prahalad, C.K. and Gary Hamel (1990), 'The Core Competence of the Corporation', *Harvard Business Review*, **90** (3).

Rugman, Alan M. (1979), *International Diversification and the Multinational Enterprise*, Lexington: D.C. Heath.

Rugman, Alan M. (1980), 'Internalization as a General Theory of Foreign Direct Investment: A Re-appraisal of the Literature', *Weltwirtschaftliches Archiv*, **116**.

Rugman, Alan M. (1981), *Inside the Multinationals: The Economics of Internal Markets*, New York: Columbia University Press.

Rugman, Alan M. (ed.) (1982), *New Theories of the Multinational Enterprise*, New York: St Martin's Press.

Rugman, Alan M. (ed.) (1983), 'Multinational Enterprises and World Product Mandates', in *Multinationals and Technology Transfer: The Canadian Experience*, New York: Praeger.

Rugman, Alan M. (1986), 'New Theories of the Multinational Enterprise: An Assessment of Internalization Theory', *Bulletin of Economic Research*, May.

Rugman, Alan M. (1987), 'Multinationals and Trade in Services: A Transaction Cost Approach', *Weltwirtschaftliches Archiv*, **123** (4), 651–67.

Rugman, Alan M. and Sheila Douglas (1986), 'The Strategic Management of Multinationals and World Product Mandating', in Hamid Etemad and Louise Seguin Dulude (eds), *Managing the Multinational Subsidiary*, Kent: Croom Helm.

Rugman, Alan M. and Bernard Yeung (1989), 'Trade in Services and Returns on Multinational Activity', *Weltwirtschaftliches Archiv*, **125** (2), 386–91.

Rugman, Alan M., Donald J. Lecraw and Laurence D. Booth (1985), *International Business: Firm and Environment*, New York: McGraw Hill.

Simon, Herbert A. (1957), *Models of Man*, New York: John Wiley and Sons.

Simon, Herbert A. (1961), *Administrative Behaviour*, 2nd edition, New York: Macmillan.

Teece, David J. (1982), 'Towards an Economic Theory of the Multiproduct Firm', *Journal of Economic Behaviour and Organization*, March.

Teece, David J. (1983), 'Technological and Organizational Factors in the Theory of the Multinational Enterprise', in Mark Casson (ed.), *The Growth of International Business*, London: George Allen.

Teece, David J. (1985), 'Transactions Cost Economics and the Multinational Enterprise: An Assessment', *Berkeley Business School International Business Working Paper Series*, No. IB-3.

Tsurumi, Yoshihiro (1977), *Multinational Management*, Cambridge: Ballinger.

Williamson, Oliver E. (1981), 'The Modern Corporation: Origins, Evolution, Attributes', *Journal of Economic Literature* (19), 1537–68.
Williamson, Oliver E. (1985), *The Economic Institutions of Capitalism*, New York: Macmillan.

5. Japanese culture and the performance of the Japanese firm*

Edward M. Graham

In 1989, Japanese firms seemed ready to conquer the planet. The 'Japanese challenge' to European and North American firms had been mounting for years, but until the late 1970s it had been largely limited to the low to medium technology industries. By the early 1980s, however, Japanese firms were rapidly gaining global market share in high technology industries such as computers, telecommunications and (especially) semiconductors. Japanese firms were not, however, simultaneously abandoning ground gained in medium technology sectors such as autos. Rather, in the auto sector the major Japanese firms were continuing to expand their market share in the United States and were poised to do likewise in Europe.

Indeed, the auto industry gave rise to the term 'Toyotism', coined to describe new and putatively superior ways of Japanese organization and management. The opposite of Toyotism was held to be 'Fordism', the old Western approach to mass production. Toyotism came to imply lean and flexible production, non-hierarchical organizations in which decision-making is based on consensus, cooperative and harmonious relations between workers and management, and stable long-term relations between large firms and their upstream suppliers. Fordism came to imply repetitive assembly line production, hierarchical decision-making, confrontational industrial relations, and short-termist managerial outlooks.

In the management and economic organization literature, by 1990 articles by Japanese and Western scholars suggested that Western – and especially American – firms were likely to be consigned to the scrap heap of history, victims of their own shortcomings and of the cohesive, efficient and inventive nature of the Japanese organization. One issue which was hotly debated was whether the attributes that made Japanese firms such formidable competitors were so embedded in Japanese culture and tradition as to be inaccessible to non-Japanese organizations. This issue notwithstanding, practitioner-oriented authors spewed forth articles urging Western firms to adopt Japanese management practices, most of them with scant reference to the cultural context in which Japanese management takes place.[1]

Closely tied to the success of Japanese firms is the success of Japan as an economy, and one issue that has challenged economic historians has been the identification of factors that have made Japan grow at extraordinarily high rates. Most historians have focused on economic aggregates, such as high gross and net savings rates, high rates of capital formation, and the role of technology and human capital. Recently, a new literature has been developing on the role of the Japanese business organization in fostering growth (for a review, see Aoki, 1990).

1989 was an especially interesting year for a Westerner to visit Japan, as this author did. This was the height of the 'bubble economy', and although some analysts in 1989 were already seeing an overheated economy driven by excess and speculation,[2] others saw the skyrocketing prices of Japanese securities and land prices as the beginning of a new Japanese millennium. One highly respected senior Japanese government economist indeed extrapolated that within a decade, gross annual Japanese domestic investment would exceed that of the United States, in spite of the fact that Japan and the United States at that time had roughly equal *per capita* incomes and the United States had over twice Japan's population.

Interestingly, while articles in US and European journals extolled the virtues of Japanese organization, there was beginning to appear within Japan a stream of what might be termed 'angst' literature: works that questioned whether either the newly found wealth of Japan or the competitive might of its industrial enterprise was really bringing any net improvement to its people. One of the most widely read of these works was former Ministry of International Trade and Industry (MITI) official Taichi Sakaiya's *What is Japan* (Sakaiya, 1993[3]), which viewed the Japanese post-World War II economic 'miracle' from the perspective of long history.

Sakaiya's work was a cool-headed appraisal of what have been the historic strengths and weaknesses of Japan and what are their historical and cultural bases. Sakaiya pointed out that Japan's industrial strengths continue to be concentrated in the manufacture of mass produced, standardized products. By the early 1990s, these included an impressive array of items ranging from ball bearings for household door hinges (which, Sakaiya observed with obvious pride, are manufactured to the same exacting tolerances as the bearings used in precision machinery) to advanced semiconductor microchips. However, Sakaiya also noted that Japanese firms still were not very good at producing highly complex products or systems in relatively small lots (for example, large commercial aircraft, nuclear power plants), or do not entail manufacturing at all (such as computer software and other advanced service activities). He also noted that the vast majority of products produced so well by Japanese firms were originally invented in the West. The Japanese contribution to these products had been cost reduction – implying in most cases superior production technology and management – coupled with product improvement. In many cases the product improvement had been so radical that the product has been virtually transformed.

Beginning in 1991 but only becoming fully apparent in 1992, a major recession hit Japan. The root causes of the recession will long be debated, but the main factors appear to be, first, difficulties in the financial sector brought about by falls in the prices of securities and land and, second, collapse of demand in the consumer durables sectors. The latter includes most notably both electronics and automobiles, the two sectors where the virtues of Japanese management have been held to be strongest. Japanese firms in these industries have been facing lean times.

The recession has been marked by falling gross domestic investment which, coupled with rising household and public sector savings, has brought on a sharp increase in the balance-of-payments surplus on current account. At the same time, many Japanese have experienced liquidity problems domestically and hence have repatriated funds from abroad. The combined effect of increases in the balance-of-payments surplus and repatriation of funds has been a significant appreciation of the yen, reducing price competitiveness of Japanese exports.[4] As a consequence of the high yen (*endaka*), Japan's trade surplus in manufactured goods actually fell from ¥31 trillion in 1985 to ¥25 trillion in 1993; but this was more than offset by a fall in the deficit in non-manufactured goods, from over ¥20 trillion to under ¥12 trillion, so that the overall trade surplus rose by about ¥2.5 trillion. The rise in the trade surplus has, in turn, intensified pressure on Japan to reform the ways in which it conducts its affairs with foreign nations. But, ironically, concern in Japan itself has swung towards fears of domestic deindustrialization as the result of loss of manufacturing competitiveness, especially relative to surging economies elsewhere in Asia (see, for example, Nakamae, 1994).

US-based firms have thus found their fortunes rising. During the 1990s they recouped a portion of that share of world market lost to Japanese in high technology sectors during the 1980s, for example, semiconductors, computers and telecommunications. Even US auto-makers have found themselves on new and firmer footing relative to their Japanese rivals. In 1993 and 1994, for the first time in over a decade, the domestic US market share held by the Detroit 'Big 3' began to rise.

Some of this newly found success has resulted from the combination of US recovery, Japanese recession and the high yen. But it is also undeniably true that many US firms have substantially transformed themselves and have entered the 1990s with new product lines, reduced costs and higher product quality levels. Many of these firms have borrowed management techniques from the Japanese, although it would be an exaggeration to say that these firms have adopted the 'Japanese model'.

It remains to be seen whether this reversal of the early 1990s will endure. Rivalry among firms is, after all, a dynamic process, and it is entirely possible that after the Japanese economy comes out of recession, as it surely will, there will be a renewal of the 'Japanese challenge'. But it is also possible that the strength of this challenge was exaggerated during the 1980s, just as the 'American challenge' was exaggerated during the 1960s, only 20 years before.

Whichever of these two scenarios turns out to be the case, it seems appropriate to have a fresh look at the Japanese organization and to re-evaluate its management practices. This chapter is meant as a starting point (and no more than that) for such a re-evaluation. The main goal is to look at some of the historic and cultural underpinnings of the Japanese organization with a view to understanding why it has developed as it has.

THE CULTURAL WELLSPRING OF THE JAPANESE ORGANIZATION

In Japanese society, there is an emphasis on cooperation and harmony within the community that is carried out with a fervour lacking in most other societies. The role of the individual is subordinated to community goals to an extent that would be seen as downright oppressive in the Western democracies. Most Japanese accept this subordination with equanimity and resignation: to work hard while foregoing one's own comforts for the good of the community is seen as proper and noble behaviour. During the height of the 'bubble economy', to be sure, conspicuous consumption was the rage. But many Japanese in 1994 regard the recession as some sort of a punishment for the excesses of the 1980s, and there has been in Japan during the early 1990s something of a reversion to the traditional values of self-sacrifice and hard work.

Japanese communitarianism embodies many qualities that many Westerners would recognize as desirable, if not noble, when measured against their own values. Among these qualities is a certain equalitarian spirit, one that manifests itself in a universal educational system that produces the world's best educated body public, a relatively level distribution of income, and low rates of crime and other socially deviant behaviour.

Other aspects of Japanese communitarianism, however, are less in tune with Western values. Westerners, for example, are quite comfortable with hierarchical organizations wherein the most important decisions are made by a small group of individuals (or even one person) at the top of the organizational pyramid. The archetype (and, simultaneously, the ancestor) of the Western hierarchical organization is the Catholic Church, where decisions regarding doctrine are made by one person (acting with the advice and guidance of the College of Cardinals). Within Japanese organizations, by contrast, decision-making itself tends to be much more communitarian. Relative to their Western counterparts, Japanese firms are typified by fewer hierarchical managerial levels, and most decisions are made on the basis of a 'bottom-up' consensus rather than orders from the 'top-down'.

Within a Japanese firm, for example, key decisions regarding product design can be more influenced by the views of a salesperson who is close to the customer than by the views of the company president. It is assumed that the salesperson is in a position better to know the detailed needs of the customer than is the senior executive, whose job is more to guide the decision-making process than actually to make decisions. It thus should come as no surprise that Japanese organizations have innovated such 'total quality control' concepts as the 'stop button', whereby any worker on a production line can stop the whole process if he or she detects something going wrong (see, for example, Aoki, 1990).

It is important, however, not to overstress (or oversimplify) the differences between Japanese and Western organizations in this regard. There is variance in the degree of hierarchical divisions among both Western and Japanese organizations. Some Western organizational forms are highly communitarian and, in some Japanese organizations, decisions are made on a more 'top-down' basis than most academic descriptions of the decision-making process would lead one to believe.[5] Even so, it is a safe statement that Japanese organizations typically are less hierarchical and more communitarian in their decision-making than are their Western counterparts.

Japanese society is permeated with a sense of social order that baffles most Westerners and leaves them feeling vaguely uncomfortable. Everyone in Japan, it would seem, knows his or her place and, perhaps more importantly, accepts it. This order is by no means static, and social mobility is taken almost for granted – a son or daughter born into a lowly working class family can reasonably expect to attend Japan's best universities, if that son or daughter can pass the entrance exams, and from there enter into Japan's elite. Nonetheless, at any given moment the social order is understood and respected in Japan, and a Japanese knows his or her place in it. Those that aspire to move up are well advised not to let their ambitions show too much, and to respect their social superiors even as they advance up the ladder.

For all of the strengths of Japan there are readily apparent flaws that affect the performance of organizations based there.[6] Some of these are evident in the vaunted educational system. Japanese schools emphasize hard work and achievement, but they also require very high levels of conformity. Accordingly, Japanese critics frequently complain that their educational system stifles creativity. Students' energies are devoted to passing standardized examinations after passing through a highly standardized curriculum. The examinations determine who can gain admission to universities and, for most Japanese, this admission (or its lack) determines what one is going to do for the rest of one's life. It is also widely acknowledged that Japanese universities are not, even at the elite level, of the same calibre as the best Western institutions.[7]

These shortcomings notwithstanding, there can be little question that Japan's educational system produces a work-force that is motivated and prepared for work in the Japanese corporation. Indeed, both the strength and the weakness of Japanese education is that it compresses both ends of the distribution towards the mean. Students of lower aptitude tend to come out of the Japanese system better educated than comparable students elsewhere, but students of higher aptitude may not have had their abilities developed as well as they might have been elsewhere. The latter is probably most evident if a student has special talents combined with special weaknesses. The Japanese system will do a marvellous job at correcting the weaknesses, but it may develop (and, indeed, often does not even recognize) the special talents. Japanese society places great value on uniformity and conformity, and Japanese schools reflect this value. As Sakaiya (1993) notes, in Japan it is better to receive all 'Bs' in school than three 'As' and two 'Cs'.

Thus Japan cultivates all of its students to high levels of achievement, but provides a relatively poor environment for those who would be truly superb achievers. The system provides a large supply of young persons well suited for working in a large but communitarian organization. But few of these persons can be counted upon to exercise much creativity or to come up with radically new ideas.

The present Japanese educational system, one might note, is the product largely of post-World War II 'administrative guidance', and in earlier periods Japanese education was neither as equalitarian nor as demanding of conformity as is the present system. Even so, Japan has long valued education, and even at the time of the Meiji Restoration of 1867, the literacy rate among Japanese was higher than in most other countries.

GEOGRAPHY AND HISTORY

Apart from the educational system, from whence do Japanese values come? One answer is in Japan's geography. Japan is an island nation separated from the Asian mainland, and there have been very few efforts by mainlanders to invade Japan. The only really serious efforts until the 20th century were by the Mongols during the 13th century. These were defeated not so much by the Japanese themselves as by nature; the two major offensives by the Mongols were broken up by typhoons, which have entered into Japanese mythology as the *kamikaze* or 'divine winds'. Also, and again in contrast to much popular belief in the West, Japan has rarely been expansionist. Rather, military activities by Japanese outside of Japan have been isolated events and, until the last 100 years or so, were largely limited to the Korean Peninsula.[8] The effort to establish a 'Greater Asian Co-prosperity Sphere' earlier in this century is, of course, a very major exception to this pattern, and the defeat of Japan reinforced the isolationist beliefs held by many Japanese.[9]

Over the centuries, however, Japanese isolation has been far from total. For at least 2 000 years, Japan has experienced periods of regular exchange with the Asian mainland. These have occurred during periods of high civilization in China and Korea, during which Japan imported various artefacts of culture, religion and technology. When transplanted these artefacts have, however, undergone substantial adaptation, whether one is speaking of importation of Buddhism during the fifth and sixth centuries from Korea or of copper casting technology from China during the eighth century. This last importation may be the first recorded case where Japan imported a foreign technology and subsequently substantially improved upon it: construction of the Great Buddha at Nara, it is widely acknowledged, required mastery of copper casting techniques that clearly originated in China, but it is doubtful that Chinese craftsmen of the era could have successfully constructed a statue as large or complex as the one at Nara.[10]

If some periods of Japanese history have been marked by cultural and technological exchanges with the Asian mainland, other periods – some lasting centuries – have been characterized by nearly total isolation. The most recent of these, the Tokugawa period, lasted for more than two centuries and ended only during the 1860s (about which more later). Thus it is no surprise that Japan has developed a culture that is to a large extent *sui generis*.

The rugged terrain of Japan, plus a lack of indigenous animals suitable for domestication, made a society based on either nomadic hunting or animal husbandry impractical.[11] Rather, agriculture and fishing became the basis for Japanese subsistence. Japanese mythology links the growing of rice to the spirituality of the nation, and the simple pragmatics of rice-growing suggest that this sowed the seeds of the communitarian approach to organization that characterizes Japan to this day.[12] Japan has for millennia cultivated rice by wet growing techniques, and these in a preindustrial society required that the work be done communally. This was because wet rice-growing requires the construction of dikes, terraces and irrigation channels on a scale that could not be accomplished by a single family.

Civil wars, however, were rife over at least the thousand years or so from 550 AD to 1650. Some were religious conflicts, and Buddhism became a state religion (alongside Shinto) because Buddhists largely prevailed during these wars. In 609 AD Buddhism was formally proclaimed by the Emperor to be the religion of Japan alongside the traditional Shinto religion. The two religions could hardly be more different, Buddhism being a monotheistic religion emphasizing self-restraint and Shinto a polytheistic religion emphasizing fertility. However, ever since the proclamation of them both as state religions, the Japanese have accepted their coexistence complete with the sometimes contradictory values embedded in each.[13] The visitor to Japan who wonders why the fleshpots of Kabukicho can coexist so easily with the asceticism of Zen might indeed want to keep this religious coexistence in mind.

Japan was more or less united as a nation under the imperial family during the Nara and Heian periods (645 to 794 AD and 794 to about 1100 AD, respectively; these are broken into two periods by historians because the imperial capital was transferred to Nara to what is now Kyoto in 794 AD). Today, the whole epoch is looked upon as a 'golden age' by Japanese. Art, literature, architecture and other cultural activities thrived, particularly so during the Heian period. Many of the temples and shrines of Nara and Kyoto to which modern-day tourists flock were built during these periods.

The Heian period ended with a large civil war around 1150 between two powerful aristocratic families, the Tairas and the Minamotos. The Minamoto family prevailed and briefly established its leader, Minamoto Yoritomo, as *sei taishogun* (essentially Chief of the Lords), only to be thrown out of power in the early 13th century and replaced by the Hojo family. The combined reigns of the Minamoto and Hojos are referred to in Japanese history as the *Kamakura bakufu*. *Bakufu* literally means 'tent government', but it was in effect something of a supreme council of the feudal lords who controlled regions of the country.

The failed Mongol invasions occurred during the 13th century and doubtlessly had some unifying effect on the Japanese islands, but towards the end of the century Japan re-entered a period of civil war following a failed *coup d'état* by the Emperor. Following the failed coup, the imperial house divided and, for about 60 years, a northern and southern branch of the family each contested the other. The division ended when the northern branch established the Muromachi *bakufu* under the Ashikaga family in 1338, and the two branches of the imperial family were forcibly reunited in 1392 under this second *bakufu*.

The years 1560 to 1603 are commonly called the 'Warring Countries' period, and during this period one *daimyo*, Toyotomi Hideyoshi, was able to unify Japan briefly beginning in 1583. Toyotomi invaded Korea in 1592. The Korean campaign went badly, however, and after eight years the Japanese invaders withdrew. With the death of Toyotomi in 1598, civil war broke out anew, ending with the victory of Tokugawa Ieyasu in 1603.

Tokugawa established the third and most stable period of *bakufu*. He proceeded to attack even those *daimyo* who had been loyal to him, if these exhibited too much personal power. There would ensue about two and a half centuries of relative stability under what is now known as the Tokugawa shogunate. During this period, the basic political structure of Japan remained feudal in the sense that *daimyo* still retained control of civil power in their regions, but this power was subordinate to that of the *shogun*.

The long periods of civil strife in Japan did not break down the communitarian nature of Japanese society. *Samurai* warriors followed a code of behaviour (*bushido*) that was relatively benign towards civilians. The *samurai* never attempted a 'scorched earth' approach to defeating their enemies. *Bushido* in fact stresses the concept of *ie*, a Japanese word that can be translated as 'family' but also could be translated as 'resident social group'. To the Japanese, *ie* implies a reciprocal loyalty – one is loyal to one's servants as well as to one's masters, and master and servant are expected to look out for each other's interests.

Following the establishment of the Tokugawa shogunate and the crushing of the military power of the *daimyo*, most *daimyo* and the *samurai* employed by them were disarmed. But Tokugawa did not attempt to eliminate either the *daimyo* or the *bushi* as social classes. The *daimyo* were allowed to remain wealthy. Much of the arable land in Japan was thus owned by the *daimyo*, who were allowed to extract rents and/or taxes from tenant farmers who worked the land.[14] The *samurai*, by contrast, remained an elite but propertyless class whose allegiance was shifted from the *daimyo* to the *shogun*. Many of the *samurai* became regional administrators, and the military nature of the class became increasingly symbolic. The *samurai* warrior was expected to work hard. Scholarship and asceticism were encouraged, as was a strict code of honourable behaviour. As administrators, the *samurai* had to enforce the *ritsu-ryo* system of law, requiring often that they had to make decisions outside the letter of the law. This meant that the administrator had to be both respected and trusted. To many Japanese today, the way of life of the *samurai* is seen as an ideal.

The *samurai* ideal did not wither with the *bushi* class, but spread to the common citizenry and, as interpreted by philosophers such as Ishida Baigan, formed the basis for the Japanese work ethic. Ishida taught that in order to have character, a person must be diligent, frugal and hard-working. His ideas, which embodied the Zen Buddhist philosophy of the *samurai* and altered it, swept through Japan during the late 18th century. The key difference between pre-Ishida and post-Ishida Zen was that the former emphasized asceticism and spirituality whereas the latter raised work to the level of a virtue. Pre-Ishida Zen put great weight on meditating but did not consider working in the fields to be a honourable activity; post-Ishida Zen required that one start the day not by meditating but by sweeping the floor, and follow this with a day of hard work. Both versions of Zen consider frugality and poverty to be virtues but, in the case of Ishida-school Zen, one could be wealthy and still be virtuous if one maintained a simple lifestyle.

Given the rather hard existence of the Japanese rice farmer or fisherman, it is rather easy to see the appeal of the Ishida school, which could transform the average Japanese person into the spiritual equivalent of a *samurai* without requiring much change of actual lifestyle. Likewise, the Ishida school appealed to those former *bushi* who forsook honour and poverty in the pursuit of material wealth. But the Ishida school went somewhat beyond this; it emphasized scholarship, even among the agrarian and working classes. It emphasized attention to detail and to quality of output. To this day, Japanese demand that products be of superb quality down to details that do not affect the functioning of the product, a trait which has caused many imported products to be rejected as being of inferior quality.

The Tokugawa period shaped Japanese character in other ways as well. Popular attitudes regarding conformity and conflict resolution took their modern shape during this period. The Tokugawa shogunate was ruthless in its suppression of anyone that even looked like a challenge to its power. But the shogunate also recognized that public uprising usually reflected legitimate complaints. Accordingly, public discord was dealt with in a manner that was simultaneously harsh and fair. The harsh side was that persons identified as leaders of any popular disorder were dealt with severely. The fair side was that legitimate grievances were redressed. Under this system both public officials and those subject to their administration learned to settle their disputes amicably. Likewise, persons of ambition learned not to allow their ambitions to become too evident.

Many of the characteristics of modern Japan – attention to quality and detail, a ferocious work ethic, a respect for education, humility – can be traced to the Tokugawa era. But these characteristics were laid on an earlier foundation, the communitarianism that the very geography of Japan moulded and which survived long periods of political instability and transformation.

THE MAKING OF MODERN JAPAN AND THE BIRTH OF THE LARGE JAPANESE INDUSTRIAL FIRM

The Tokugawa period was one of strong centralized government but one where the *daimyo* continued to hold sway even though they were disarmed and closely watched. Towards the end of the period, in the mid 19th century, the hold of the Edo-based *shogun* over the *daimyo* began to relax. At about the same time, heavily armed foreigners, first from the United States and then from Europe, were able to force the *bakufu* to end the commercial isolation of Japan and to enter into limited trading relationships with Western powers.[15] The ease with which these powers were able to win concessions, by the demonstration of overwhelmingly superior weaponry, convinced many in Japan (including senior civil servants from the *samurai* class, influential merchants and certain major *daimyo*) that Japan would have to strengthen its military capabilities, modernize its economy and end its isolation. Meanwhile the ease with which the foreigners won concessions from a supposedly all-powerful *shogun* convinced many that the *shogun* had become weak.

The shogunate was overthrown in 1867 in what amounted to a *coup d'état*. To legitimize this *coup*, the emperor was formally moved from Kyoto to Edo (the latter then being renamed Tokyo, or 'East Capital City', with the last syllable gradually falling into disuse) and nominally 'restored' to full power. This nominal change (termed the 'Meiji Restoration', after the Emperor Meiji) led to major transformations.

At the time of the Meiji Restoration, Japan was not particularly backward except in terms of industrial technology. It had a working national government, complete with an effective judicial system and other administrative functions. Educational levels were high; probably half or more of all adult males were literate in 1867, a figure unmatched in most other countries at the time. The country was relatively urbanized. Roads were, by the standards of Europe at the time, excellent. Indeed, as Patrick and Rosovsky (1976) note, in 1868 Japan was already an advanced country even if a backward one by most economic measures.[16]

This backwardness was largely limited to the manufactured goods sector. At the time of the Meiji Restoration, most manufacturing was on a cottage industry basis. Although the quality of gods produced was often high, productivity was low and high prices prohibited any but the wealthiest people from acquiring these goods. Agriculture, in contrast to manufacturing, was quite productive, and the agricultural sector by 1867 was producing substantial surpluses.

Between the Meiji Restoration and the outbreak of World War II Japan's economy, in real terms on a *per capita* basis, grew at about 2 per cent a year, making it one of the fastest growing economies in the world through the entire time.[17] Nonetheless, Japan didn't really achieve advanced nation status until the 1930s.

During the final three decades of the 19th century and the first decade of this century, the growth rate was high – but in fact no greater than that of other newly industrializing economies, the United States and Germany. Central to Japanese growth was a sharp increase in agricultural productivity, enabling Japan both to export agricultural goods and to transfer labour and savings from the agricultural sector to other activities.[18] Figuring in this transformation was forfeiture of most large landholdings by the *shogun* (who in 1867 owned perhaps a quarter of the arable land) and by most of the *daimyo*, who were compensated via the issuing of state bonds. Importantly, increased agricultural productivity raised the incomes of individual farmers. As the Japanese economy began to grow during the final decades of the 19th century, funds from wealthy farmers and *daimyo* often financed new industrial enterprise.

Motivated largely by military concerns, the Meiji Government encouraged infrastructure development, including especially the building of railroads and ports. The government resorted to heavy deficit spending to finance these large-scale infrastructure projects. Industrial development encouraged by the government centred on the cotton textile and metallurgical industries, as well as the development of military goods. Efforts were also made by the government to upgrade the extractive industries.

In all these industries priority was given to acquiring technology by sending thousands of Japanese students to study abroad and by bringing to Japan upwards of 4,000 trained engineers and other technical personnel to help develop indigenous enterprises. (See, for example, Kawasaki (1985) for an account of the role of foreign engineers in the building of the iron and steel industries in Japan during the late 19th century.)

Importation of industrial technology did not proceed without problems; studies of early Japanese industrial development are filled with stories of locomotives that blew up because Western designs were not copied well, or because metallurgy was deficient, or because of other problems (Macpherson, 1987). By most accounts, Japanese engineers and technicians during this period tended to copy imported technologies without trying to improve them. What is critical is the rapidity with which Japan developed the capability to absorb foreign technology, a rapidity doubtless made possible by traditional Japanese values with respect to learning.

During this time, however, xenophobic tendencies ran high. The sending of Japanese abroad and the importation of foreign technicians were seen by the Meiji Government as temporary measures, to be employed only until Japan was able to generate from within technically qualified people to reduce dependence upon foreigners. To help achieve self-reliance, the Ministry of Education was created in 1871, and under its guidance compulsory primary education was gradually introduced. A series of state secondary schools, vocational and technical institutes, and universities were subsequently established. However, vocational and technical education became concentrated in business enterprises, which provided extensive 'on-the-job' training for technical personnel, while state schools concentrated on providing primary, secondary and university education.[19]

Japanese commercial and banking law were reworked along Western lines (according to Macpherson (1987), commercial law was largely borrowed from the United Kingdom and Germany, while banking law was modelled on that of the United States). A system of national banks was created in 1872, but these proved unstable, and the Japanese government began to implement a central bank system beginning in 1881. In that year the Bank of Japan (*Nihon Ginko*) was created as a European-style central bank, while the national banks were privatized, so that commercial banking was almost entirely in private hands by 1885. These moves created the foundation for a stable monetary system. In 1900 the Industrial Bank of Japan was set up as a state-owned institution to intermediate funds into long-term investments, a role that the private banking system failed to develop. The decision to do this reflected a pragmatic attitude that where private enterprise failed to meet a need, the government should step in to do the job.

During the first 10 to 15 years following the Meiji Restoration, efforts were made to launch industrialization through the creation of state-owned enterprises. Also, foreign interests were allowed to acquire control over a number of important enterprises, for example, in railroads, mining and metallurgy. However, after a period of tumult, the authorities encouraged private enterprises to carry out new industrial activities, albeit often under governmental guidance (see Johnson, 1982). Also, beginning in the 1880s, foreign ownership of important commercial concerns was discouraged (see Mason, 1992). After 1880, most state-owned enterprises were sold to the private sector, and especially to the emergent *zaibatsu*, although the government continued to maintain official monopolies in the tobacco, salt and camphor industries, to control a large part of the railway system, to operate dockyards and munitions facilities, and to operate the nation's largest iron and steel facility, the Yawata works (Allen, 1981). During the late 19th century, the industrial groups known as the *zaibatsu* came into existence (Nakamura, 1983).

One characteristic of the late 19th century Japanese economy was the simultaneous development of modern industry (for example, introduction of factories to spin cotton yarns and weave fabrics) and traditional industry (for example, the silk spinning and weaving industry). 'Traditional' in this case does not necessarily imply that the relevant enterprises clung to traditional technologies, but rather that enterprises operating in these industries had existed prior to the Meiji Restoration. Silk spinners and weavers did adopt new technologies, even though the industry largely remained one of small enterprises.[20] Much of this adoption involved simultaneous adaptation of imported technologies to meet the specific needs of the Japanese enterprises: indeed, Nakamura (1983) describes this industry as one that the Japanese transformed from modern to traditional. Interlinkages developed between these traditional firms and newer industrial organizations, for example, traditional weavers absorbed much of the output of the newly established cotton spinning mills during the 1870s. The industrial sector thus took on a 'dual structure', where newly established factories operated alongside traditional crafts-based enterprises, but where the latter did absorb modern technologies. Overall, industrial production rose at rates about equal to those of the United States and Germany (Ohkawa, 1957).

Firms in the traditional industries were the first Japanese manufacturers to export in significant quantities, beginning in the 1880s. Exported products included silk goods, ceramic ware and handicraft items such as oiled paper umbrellas.[21]

Noteworthy of this period also was the rise of a professional entrepreneurial and managerial class. Early in the Meiji period, the emergent members of this class were largely from the former *bushi* class, but by the end of the century the managerial class was augmented by well-off farmers-turned-businessperson, merchants and even former *daimyo*. The cotton textile industry, for example, was dominated at upper management levels by former merchants. Indeed, until well into the 20th century, top management of most Japanese firms tended to consist of individuals who were simultaneously managers and large shareholders in the firms.

However, not all members of the managerial class were founders (or members of the families of founders) of their firms; persons who rose to the top tended to use their high incomes to buy into the common stock of the firms for which they worked. Some of these persons then moved on to found and manage banks and other enterprises. Members of the nascent managerial class shared a number of attributes, including (importantly) that they were all well educated by the standards of the period. By the early 20th century, an increasing percentage of the managerial class consisted of university graduates.

Most Japanese enterprises – modern and traditional – respected the concept of *ie* (see previous section), so that the management expected loyalty from, and exhibited loyalty towards, its employees. However, some firms grew so large that top managers could not get to know their workers individually and, in at least some of these firms, practices were implemented that essentially institutionalized the standards of *ie*. These practices did not, however, become widespread until the 1920s. In spite of *ie*, during the 19th century working conditions in many Japanese factories were deplorable, hours were long, and wages of Japanese workers were low in comparison to their counterparts in the Western nations.

In spite of the rapid growth of industry, in 1900 modern factories accounted for only about 6 per cent of domestic output in Japan and traditional industries about 7.5 per cent whereas agriculture accounted for upwards of two-thirds of output (Ohkawa *et al.*, 1974, cited in Nakamura, 1983). The bulk of the remainder was in the extractive industries.

The next phase of industrial development, as identified by Patrick and Rosovsky (1976), lasted roughly from the Russo-Japanese War to the beginning of the Great Depression. A boom coinciding with World War I was followed by major recessions in 1921 and 1927, the second leading to instability that culminated when the military effectively took control of the government during the 1930s. During the first half of this period, agricultural productivity stagnated and rural incomes declined relative to urban ones. In the 1920s, wages of workers in the traditional industries stagnated, while wages in the modern industries rose faster than during earlier decades, and wages rose especially quickly for workers employed by the *zaibatsu*. Thus wages of workers employed in the traditional industries fell relative to those employed in the modern ones. In spite of the uneven economic performance during this period, overall growth in the economy was positive, and Japanese-manufactured goods in the modern industries, especially cotton textiles, became competitive on world markets. By the end of the period, agriculture accounted for less than 50 per cent of the work-force, and factory output of modern industries had risen to 19 per cent of domestic output. Throughout the period, but especially during the 1920s, there was significant capital deepening in the modern industries.

A major recession hit Japan shortly after the end of World War I, the effects of which were magnified by the Kanto earthquake of 1923 that destroyed much of Tokyo. The ownership of many of Japan's largest firms was transferred as the result of bankruptcy proceedings from entrepreneurs and top management into the hands of the *zaibatsu* and the large banks and other financial institutions they controlled; these latter themselves became more concentrated.[22] This trend accelerated after the 1927 recession.

During this period the *zaibatsu* grew to reach the zenith of their influence. During the 1920s, there were four major *zaibatsu*, Mitsui, Mitsubishi, Sumitomo and Yasuda. These organizations had their roots in business families that had been prominent even before the Meiji Restoration (the Mitsui families in particular had been prominent for centuries[23]) whose members had close political ties with the movements that had supported (or with *daimyo* that had supported) the Meiji Restoration. Ties between these families and senior members of the government continued after the Meiji Restoration, and the *zaibatsu* were first created to carry out the economic development sought by the new government. These organizations throughout the 19th century were favoured with preferential government contracts and, in some cases, were allowed to acquire state-owned properties at favourable prices. They also managed much of Japan's foreign trade, helped to finance wars against China and Russia, and developed economic activities in Korea, Formosa and areas of China under Japanese control. During and following the recession of the early 1920s, the *zaibatsu* greatly expanded their activities by acquiring banks, insurance companies and industrial firms that had fallen on hard times. By 1928, a year when these organizations were at the peak of their power,[24] they held extensive interests in the mining, metals, machinery, electrical, textile, paper, cement, glass, chemicals and shipbuilding industries, as well as in banking, insurance, shipping and commerce, including international trade. In all of the four *zaibatsu*, these last activities (banking, insurance, shipping and commerce) were considered the most important and, indeed, control of finance and commerce (including distribution systems) was a much more important source of their earnings than control of manufacturing activities.

The *zaibatsu* were not the only large business groups in Japan at this time – others included Asano in cement, Okura in trade, mining and textiles, and Furukawa in metals and electricity generation, and there existed large Japanese firms not controlled by any group – but the *zaibatsu* held a special place in terms of their size, diversity and political clout.

The *zaibatsu* extended their influence during the 1920s into categories of business activity that were the historic province of small producers, via financial, technical and subcontracting links. The beginnings of what is now known as 'alliance capitalism' were born in these giant organizations, albeit that the alliances were most unequal.

In most activities, the *zaibatsu* were quite strong rivals. Indeed, one source of strength was that these organizations did compete with one another over a wide range of activities, and thus many of the benefits of competition were preserved even though many industries became heavily concentrated as once-independent firms fell under the control of the *zaibatsu*. The *zaibatsu* did not, however, compete in all spheres. On political issues – of increasing importance as the government of Japan became increasingly militaristic during the 1930s – the four big groups tended to present a united front. (In spite of Western perceptions to the contrary, the *zaibatsu* were not heavily in favour with the militarists, albeit that the latter were dependent upon the former.) And in certain commercial areas, the *zaibatsu* cooperated rather than competed. For example, in the development of the electrical grid of Japan, where their role was mostly to finance (jointly with the Industrial Bank of Japan, then a state-owned enterprise) the troubled electrical utility firms, the *zaibatsu* tended to act jointly rather than in competition.

The internal organizations of the *zaibatsu* reflected a curious blend of modern and feudal characteristics. Ownership of each of these groups ultimately resided in a family or a group of families, and control over the groups ultimately was vested in a council of family members. In the case of Mitsui, the decisions of the council were made in the context of a code that was centuries old and was based on principles governing relationships between *daimyo* and persons under the control of the *daimyo* (*bushi* as well as common persons). This code emphasized two-way loyalty between the firm and its employees; its implementation marked the origin of the practices of lifelong employment and the basing of wages on education and seniority that many Japanese companies extended to their employees after World War II. During the 1920s, these practices were limited to the *zaibatsu*.

The council in turn controlled a holding company (*honsha*), which held ownership of the constituent firms. According to Allen (1981), the extent to which family members exercised managerial control over the day-by-day activities of the firms varied from *zaibatsu* to *zaibatsu*. In the case of Mitsubishi, members of the dominant Iwasaki family filled most major roles in operating management up until the beginning of World War II, whereas in Mitsui (Roberts, 1973) an elite of professional, non-family managers that had evolved in the 19th century handled most operating decisions during the interwar years.

A third phase of the pre-World War II development as identified by Patrick and Rosovsky (1976), occurred during the Great Depression of the 1930s. In contrast to the United States or most of Europe, Japan did not suffer a depression during the 1930s; rather, overall economic growth during the 1930s was, in real terms, over 5 per cent per annum, faster than during any of the previous five decades. But part of the growth of the 1930s was recovery from an earlier recession. Later growth during the 1930s was the result of expansion of heavy industry in response to orders for militarily related goods placed by a government increasingly controlled by the army. This expansion entailed a large-scale programme for modernizing heavy industries. Cotton textiles, the only modern manufacturing industry in which Japanese firms were internationally competitive during the 1920s, began to lose its place as the major export sector, and Japanese firms began to export goods originating in the heavy industries on a large scale.

This was not an unmixed blessing, however. During the 1930s, Japan experienced worsening terms of trade, and had to expand exports rapidly to meet growing demand for imported goods, especially raw materials and intermediate goods. The deterioration in the terms of trade was caused by the Great Depression, which suppressed world demand – and hence output and prices – for many products and commodities (especially agricultural ones) that Japan exported, and unemployment in the sectors producing these goods rose. At the same time, there was widespread international ill-feeling towards Japan because Japanese products were seen as being 'dumped' on world markets.

These developments all fuelled already extant sentiment against the government and against the *zaibatsu*. The early 1930s were thus a period of considerable political turmoil. The government was unstable, and Japan experienced a rapid succession of prime ministers. In 1931 there was an aborted attempt at a *coup* by the military (the 'March incident') and a failed effort to detonate a bomb at a meeting of the Cabinet (the 'October incident'). In between these, a skirmish provoked the Japanese army into occupying southern Manchuria. In early 1932 young military officers assassinated former Finance Minister, Junnosuke Inouai and Mitsui's General Manager, Takuma Dan. A competent but fiscally conservative minister, Inouai had resisted pressure from the military to reflate Japan's stagnant economy. Dan was assassinated because Mitsui was believed to have speculated against the yen at the time of the devaluation. Some months later in 1932 Prime Minister Tsuyoshi Inukai was assassinated, also by disaffected military officers, following which even nominal parliamentary democracy ended and a Cabinet largely beholden to the military was installed.

From 1931 to 1936, Inouai's successor as Finance Minister, Korekiyo Takahashi, increased government expenditure to bring unemployed resources back into use and to meet increasing demands by the military for more armaments.[25] Spurred by government deficit spending, the output of capital goods (especially non-electrical machinery) and chemicals (including synthetic textile fibres) rose sharply, as did the efficiency of these industries and the quality of output.[26] Increased efficiency coupled with a devalued yen enabled these sectors for the first time in Japanese history to begin to export in substantial quantities. Other new economic activities grew rapidly, including production of aircraft, automobiles and electrical machinery, although none of these were exported. Much of the increased output came from firms not part of the traditional *zaibatsu*, and the role of the *zaibatsu* in the Japanese economy during the 1930s shrank measurably. Some of the new, non-*zaibatsu* firms were Nissan, Toyota, Showa Denko, Japan Soda, Japan Nitrogen and Nakajima Aircraft; also, older non-*zaibatsu* firms such as Hitachi and Yasukawa (both in the electrical machinery industry) began to expand.

Although Takahashi had successfully brought Japan out of recession and back to something like full employment, two problems ensued. Japan experienced chronic deficits in its balance of payments, and full employment (with continued government deficit spending monetized by the central bank) brought on inflation. Takahashi was determined not to create inflationary pressures, and in 1936 he attempted to reduce the fiscal deficit by cutting military expenditure. He was assassinated by young military officers[27] and, subsequently, the military assumed effective control of the government.

In spite of continuing balance-of-payments and inflation problems, the new Finance Minister, Eiichi Baba, agreed to raise military expenditure and to try to finance this by tax increases and new bonds. A near crisis ensued; financial leaders, centred in the *zaibatsu* and the central bank, objected and the Governor of the Bank of Japan, Eigo Fukai, resigned in protest. In 1937,

Japan began moving towards a system of direct government control over the economy in what amounted to full-scale military mobilization.

A government planning office was established in May of that year, and its efforts to plan general mobilization quickly became constrained by Japan's large and growing balance-of-payments deficit, which required that imports be allocated among competing sources of demand. The effectiveness of the planning efforts is subject to considerable question. Nakamura (1983) suggests that it was mostly a grand failure. Although growth was high, Nakamura believes that its imbalanced and artificial nature would have led to major problems even if war had been averted. Allen (1981) notes that economic growth spurted and that very high investment added greatly to the capital stock of the nation; he nonetheless condemns the whole period for being driven by an aggressive military that led Japan down the road to disaster. Sakaiya (1993) sees this planning as the beginning of 'administrative guidance' which (in his view) was employed by the Japanese MITI successfully to guide first Japan's reconstruction following the disaster of World War II and then her rise to industrial superpower status. Sakaiya's views are generally shared by Johnson (1982) except that Johnson sees the beginnings of a successful Japanese industrial policy in the middle 1920s.

Japan emerged from World War II an almost totally devastated nation. The rapidity of its comeback was facilitated by government guidance, high savings and investment rates, and the characteristics of Japanese culture that have already been described. It will doubtlessly never be resolved how critical was the first element (government guidance); Johnson (1982) sees it as absolutely central, but there is a growing school that tends to downplay its importance or effectiveness (for example, see Okuno-Fujiwara, 1991).

The *zaibatsu* and certain other large groups of firms were formally split apart by the Occupation authorities but they partially recreated themselves as the so-called 'financial *keiretsu*' after the end of the Occupation. The term *keiretsu*, it should be noted, is used to denote not simply these partially recreated groupings but also vertical groupings for firms (for example, the suppliers and distributors associated with Toyota). The organizational structures of Japanese firms became more complex and more diverse with management by a professional managerial elite. The bedrock values that drove management, however, were those derived from an earlier era.

JAPANESE CULTURE AND THE MODERN JAPANESE ORGANIZATION

Japan of the Tokugawa period, modified during the pre-World War II period, is the foundation upon which the modern Japanese economy, including its business institutions, is built. Virtually all of the elements that make the Japanese business organization different from its Western rivals can be traced to this foundation. Take, for example, the close vertical linkages of firms within the Toyota family of firms (or other large firm groupings), including such aspects as just-in-time inventory, cooperative approaches to product design and production management, and mutual loyalty between upstream and downstream firms in the vertical chain. To explain why these linkages work, one might recall *bushido* and its embodiment of the concept of *ie*, and especially the *ie* notion of reciprocal loyalty and responsibility between master and servant. *Bushido* was the code of behaviour of a class that became Japan's managerial elite, both within the *zaibatsu and* the civil service. Even if not every member of the modern managerial elites can trace his or her ancestry to the *bushi* class, the ideals of this class were adopted widely through Japanese society during the middle Tokugawa years. *Bushido* goes a long way towards explaining the lifelong employment system that functioned in Japan's blue chip business organizations throughout the post-World War II era. If one seeks to explain the consistent and meticulous high quality that characterizes so many Japanese products, one might recall the Ishida interpretation of Zen, with its emphasis on hard work, self-discipline and attention to detail. The Ishida notion that everyone should be a master pervades Japan to this day and serves as one independent factor behind the dynamism of the Japanese economy that is probably underrated.

The cultural foundations have created a Japanese form of organization that is different from the Western form and, indeed, superior in terms of performance along many dimensions. These dimensions include – in addition to product quality – manufacturing efficiency, industrial relations and rate of product and process improvement. On this latter, Japanese firms have proven themselves without parallel by implementing incremental but continuous improvement; much of this comes as the result of contributions by production line workers and other individuals whose direct responsibilities would not, in Western eyes at least, include product or process improvement. This would seem to be another example of the outcome of extended communitarian values. Thus, favourable industrial relations and an impressive track record of product and process improvement within Japanese organizations seem to walk hand-in-hand, in the sense that common communitarian values enable both.

Japanese organizations do not surpass their Western counterparts in all dimensions, however. The most glaring case is that identified by Sakaiya (1993) and noted earlier: while Japanese firms since the early post-Meiji period have been remarkably adept at absorbing Western technology and, since World War II, substantially improving upon it, they have rarely (if ever) been the source of an entirely new technology. This continues to be the case in some important areas. For example, having captured an early lead in the development of high definition television (HDTV) using refined versions of the old analogue technology, the major Japanese electronics groups have found themselves unprepared for the possibility that HDTV will be based on digital technology, where the lead currently resides in the West.

Thus this author finds somewhat incredulous the statements by Cantwell (1992) and Kodama (1992) to the effect that Japanese firms are significantly better placed than their Western counterparts to capture the benefits of what they both term the 'new technological paradigm' brought about by the biological and information revolutions of the last years of the 20th century. Indeed, many Japanese interviewed by this author are self-critical of Japanese failures fully to internalize information technology; Japanese organizations have typically been slow to use personal computers, local area networks and so on. More importantly, while Japan is perhaps the leading producer of computer hardware, software development lags considerably.

The point here is not to predict a bleak future for Japan but, rather, simply to note: 1) that the Japanese mode of organization has been highly effective along certain dimensions but less so along others; and 2) that both the strengths and weaknesses of Japanese organizations to a large extent are rooted in Japanese culture. On the latter point, the experiences of large Japanese firms in replicating their structures in foreign cultures have been mixed; some aspects appear to be successfully adaptable but others less so. Thus before management specialists in the West decide that Western modes of organization should be replaced with structures modelled on the Japanese, it is worth taking a closer look at what aspects of the Japanese organization depend upon characteristics that are *sui generis* to Japan. Equally, it is worth taking a closer look not just at the strengths of Japanese organization, but also at the weaknesses. The 1980s proved to thoughtful Westerners that there was much to be said for the Japanese organization. But the 1990s are showing that there are limits as well.

NOTES

1.   One is tempted to note that the publication of Jean Jacques Servan-Schreiber's *Le Défi Americain* (1966), which sent blood pressures among Europeans skyrocketing for a number of years, occurred just when, with retrospect, the 'American challenge' was waning.
2.   See, for example, Emmott (1990).
3.   1993 is the date of the English Language version; the Japanese language version appeared several years earlier.
4.   A balance-of-payments surplus puts foreign currencies into the hands of Japanese enterprises. The need to convert these into yen, rather than investing them abroad, *ceteris paribus* places upward pressure on the yen.

5. The author makes this statement on the basis of interviews conducted while in Japan. Japanese business firms that are relatively 'top-down' would seem to include the very successful firm Kyocera and a number of other successful firms that are entrepreneurial in nature, that is, which are owned and managed by their founders.
6. See Sakaiya (1993) and Emmott (1990).
7. Thus US elementary and high school students, who on average do poorly in international comparisons relative to their Japanese counterparts, gain back some of the ground lost if they are lucky enough to attend the better US institutions of higher learning.
8. And even these were quite infrequent. The only major Japanese military incursions into Korea occurred in the third, 16th and the late 19th to early 20th centuries. The first two were largely unsuccessful and, indeed (as described later in the text), the 16th century incursion was disastrous. In contrast, Korea was conquered by the Japanese in 1910 and remained under Japanese occupation from that year until 1945.
9. This is not to downplay the severity of Japanese militarism or the brutality of the Japanese towards conquered peoples during the 1930s and 1940s. Numerous episodes in Japanese history indeed demonstrate that the Japanese, like all peoples, can be brutally aggressive in their treatment of their fellow human beings. The point is rather that the Japanese have rarely sought to conquer peoples outside the Japanese islands.
10. See Sakaiya (1993).
11. This is reflected in the fact that almost uniquely among all of the peoples of the world, the Japanese people have subsisted without eating red meat. Meat did not enter the Japanese diet on any significant scale until the 1970s.
12. Many of the same observations would apply to fishing, where the construction and operation of ocean-going vessels, nets and other apparatus needed to harvest large numbers of fish require a communal approach.
13. In this regard, it is important to realize that this coexistence does not imply that some Japanese practise Buddhism whereas other practise Shinto, and that the two communities get along with each other. Rather, individual Japanese simultaneously are practitioners of both religions! (Today, however, it must be noted that the percentage of Japanese who practise any religion on a regular basis is quite small, although many Japanese will occasionally visit a Buddhist or Shinto temple or shrine and perhaps even pray there, and most Japanese get married or buried in a Shinto ritual.)
14. A significant amount of the arable land not owned by the *daimyo* was owned by the *shogun*, and rents and taxes from this land financed the *shogun's* army and the central government.
15. As noted in the text, commercial isolation of Japan under the Tokugawa governments had never been total, and in particular a Dutch-controlled port had operated all through the period. But this port had been located near Nagasaki on the southern island of Kyushu, far from the centre of Japan and, indeed, in territory not fully under the control of the *shogun*. In contrast, following the visit to Japan by Admiral Perry, a large commercial enclave was opened in Yokohama only a few dozen kilometres from Edo Castle. Even so, in the early days of this enclave, foreigners were not permitted into the interior of Japan.
16. On this, see also Macpherson (1987).
17. National income and product accounts were not kept in Japan, and hence growth rates must be estimated. There is some disagreement over exactly how fast Japan did grow during the period 1867–1940. Nakamura (1983) discussed various credible estimates that have been made.
18. Exactly how much agricultural productivity rose is, however, subject to some controversy. Nakamura (1983, based on research first published by him in 1966) argues that agricultural productivity in the Tokugawa period was higher than generally appreciated, largely because official records of rice production reflect the propensity of farmers to understate their harvests in order to avoid the payment of taxes. There is no doubt, however, that agricultural productivity did rise significantly following the Meiji Restoration, largely because of the introduction of fertilizers.
19. According to some scholars of the period, the state schools also fomented nationalist and xenophobic attitudes among young Japanese, including a doctrine of emperor-worship.

20. Although not entirely so; by the late 1890s, larger spinning mills were beginning to replace smaller operations. Some details are provided in Allen (1981).
21. The author owns a number of heirloom ceramic pieces that found their way to the United States as exports from Japan during the 1890s, and the quality of these pieces is almost dazzlingly high.
22. Because large banks were central institutions in the *zaibatsu*, the statement that the ownership of large business enterprises fell increasingly into the hands of banks and *zaibatsu* is partly redundant.
23. A comprehensive history of the Mitsui organization and the associated families is provided in Roberts (1973). Most of the *zaibatsu* were controlled by several families; Mitsubishi, however, was under the control of just one family.
24. Exactly how much of activity was in fact under *zaibatsu* control is hard to determine, but in 1928 the paid-up capital of firms under the control of the *zaibatsu* was slightly over 15 per cent of the total net paid-up capital of all Japanese firms. Following 1928, this figure began to decline (Nakamura, 1983). The 15 per cent figure only includes those firms directly under control of the *zaibatsu*; because they exercised indirect control over other firms, the *zaibatsu* almost surely had a longer 'reach' than the figure would suggest.
25. Takahashi remains a controversial figure to this day in Japanese history, because his policies represent both a successful application of Keynesian-style use of government spending to stimulate aggregate demand (an application that was made before Keynes had published his *General Theory!*) and an accession to military demands for increased expenditure on armaments.
26. Many histories of Japan credit military expenditures with bringing the Japanese economy out of recession during the Takahashi years. However, exactly how much of the stimulus came from the military and how much from other *demandeurs* is open to some controversy; while there was much demand for militarily related goods, most investment during these years was in non-military sectors. See Nakamura (1983) for details.
27. Prime Minister Okada barely survived the same attack.

BIBLIOGRAPHY

Allen, G.C. (1981), *A Short Economic History of Modern Japan*, 4th edition, New York: St Martin's Press.
Aoki, Masahiko (1990), 'Toward an Economic Model of the Japanese Firm', *Journal of Economic Literature*, **28** (1), 1–27.
Cantwell, John (1992), 'Japan's Industrial Competitiveness and the Technological Capabilities of Japan's Leading Firms', in Thomas S. Arrison, C. Fred Bergsten, Edward M. Graham and Martha C. Harris (eds), *Japan's Growing Technological Capability: Implications for the US Economy*, Washington, D.C.: The National Research Council.
Emmott, Bill (1990), *The Sun Also Sets: The Limits to Japan's Economic Power*, New York: Times Books.
Johnson, Chalmers (1982), *MITI and the Japanese Miracle: The Growth of Industrial Policy, 1925–1975*, Stanford, CA.: The Stanford University Press.
Kawasaki, Tsutomu (1985), *Japan's Steel Industry*, Tokyo: Tekko Shimbun Sha.
Kodama, Fumio (1992), 'Japan's Unique Capability to Innovate: Technology Fusion and its International Implications', in Arrison *et al.*, *Japan's Growing Technological Capability*, supra.
Macpherson, W.J. (1987), *The Economic Development of Japan c. 1868–1941*, Houndsmills, UK: Macmillan Education.
Mason, Mark (1992), *American Multinationals and Japan: The Political Economy of*

Japanese Capital Controls, 1899–1980, Cambridge, MA.: The Harvard University Press.

Nakamae, Tadashi (1994), 'Japan's Secret Decline as a Manufacturing Power', paper presented at American Enterprise Institute (AEI) conference, Kyoto, Japan, 9–10 April.

Nakamura, Takafusa (1983), *Economic Growth in Prewar Japan*, New Haven, CT. and London: Yale University Press; translated and updated from Nakamura, *Senzeki Nihon Seicho no Bunseki,* Tokyo: Iwanami Shoten, 1971.

Ohkawa, Kazushi (1957), *The Growth Rate of the Japanese Economy Since 1878*, Tokyo: Kinokuniya Bookstore Ltd.

Ohkawa, Kazushi, Nobuyiko Takamatsu and Yuzo Yamamoto (1974), *Kokumin Shotoku* ['National Income'], Tokyo: Toyo Keizai Shimpo Sha.

Okuno-Fujiwara, Masahiro (1991), 'Industrial Policy in Japan: A Political Economy View', in Paul R. Krugman (ed.), *Trade with Japan: Has the Door Opened Wider?* Chicago: University of Chicago Press for the National Bureau of Economic Research.

Patrick, Hugh and Henry Rosovsky (1976), 'Japan's Economic Performance: An Overview', in Patrick and Rosovsky (eds), *Asia's New Giant: How the Japanese Economy Operates*, Washington, D.C.: The Brookings Institution.

Roberts, John G. (1973), *Mitsui: Three Centuries of Business*, New York and Tokyo: John Weatherhill.

Sakaiya, Taichi (1993), *What is Japan? Contradictions and Transformations*, Tokyo: Kodansha International; originally published in Japanese as *Nihon to wa Nani ka?* in 1991 by Kodansha Ltd.

Servan-Schreiber, Jean Jacques (1966), *Le Défi Americain*, Paris: Editions Noël.

6. International production networks and alliances

Hamid Etemad

The idea of joining forces to take advantage of relative strengths, complementarities and synergies that partnerships offer can be traced to the early stages of international commerce. Informal networks and/or alliances (NOAs), as social organizations, to structure production and distribution, are neither new nor particular to any region or historical era. They have functioned across time and state boundaries.

Even a cursory examination of early trade and commerce documents reveals not only the prevalence of NOAs: more importantly, it uncovers a rich tradition containing concepts which are now being rediscovered and discussed. They cover the full spectrum of activities. Artisan production leading to trade in Phoenicia, Assyria, Sumeria, Persia and even in much of the Roman Empire, for example, was not then based on international contracts or current means of enforcing performance. It was mostly based on social sanctions and a chain of symbiotic relationships between many specialized agents who transformed resources for subsequent requirements on the chain.

Grain production in many of the villages in Asia Minor still functions informally. Most of the activities, spanning a year, are based only on confirmations of past verbal promises, simple requests or the traditional ways of doing things: farmers count on the landlord or money lenders for their financing of seeds and equipment up to harvest time; odd jobbers show up at harvest to buy relatively small amounts to consolidate for shipping to local distribution warehouses; and distributors consolidate, grade, package and enter the harvest into the distribution pipeline, which in itself is a large coalition of informally linked small merchants, local traders and other intermediaries. Other ancillary informal networks produce goods and services which are necessary for production, distribution and the full use of grains. Surprisingly, not much money or contractual papers change hands, and the system works with a reasonable predictability. The main uncertainties are, indeed, the climatic elements.

The roots of current concepts of NOAs are readily observable in the older systems. Bilateral and multilateral experiences over the years have led to an observable level of trust and predictability between individuals, and only the degree of informality varies across individuals and professions. Interdependence, survival needs and personal relationships conditioned by time-honoured experience have sorted things out and perfected them to the extent that participants take part in some chains of activities, but not in others.

In much of Asia, especially on the low side of commercial activities, similar patterns are observable. A small army of people participate in a chain of production and the movement of goods and services. Though much of the activity remains informal, it is supported by structured social networks. On the high-commerce side, where trade and investment agents deal with complexities, changing conditions, inherent uncertainties and must interface with formal systems, there is a much higher level of formalization. In response, formal NOAs are set up. In between, however, the degree of formalization, as expected, varies tremendously.

In international commerce and investment, one would expect to see higher formalization, to avoid potential misunderstandings and misinterpretations (because of cross-cultural, non-verbal and other complexities of commercial communications). As complications are always costly, formal systems have gradually evolved, to settle responsibilities before firm understandings are arrived at to establish a level of trust and allow relations to become routinized.

A fundamental question is what accounts for the dormancy, revival and prevalence of NOAs, with various degrees of formality, in the past two or three decades, across sectors and countries? Different parallel approaches will be utilized in this chapter. Part I covers the broad forces of change in the latter part of the century which have been conducive to the formation of NOAs and have greatly contributed to restructuring production and distribution world-wide. Through an examination of current examples, Part II presents the business logic for production NOAs. Part III proposes a taxonomical framework to distinguish the various profiles and the inner dynamics of such arrangements. A theoretical exploration and conclusion follow.

PART I: FORCES OF CHANGE AND THEIR IMPACT

The world of international production, trade and commerce has experienced unprecedented change in the past two to three decades. The magnitude of change has been so great that not many people will accept a scenario for 2025 constructed on similarly paced change over the next three decades. The main thesis of this section is that four sets of forces have been causing change: three are very broadly based, fully encompassing and dynamically evolving macro forces, while the other is equally fundamental but regionally based. These forces have played significant roles in re-engineering industrial structures across all nations, especially in internationally oriented production. They will be referred to as altered policy environments, rapid technological advancement, fixed costs dominance and structural differentials. Combined, they necessitate a new economic paradigm.

Altered Policy Environments

The shift in policy environments has been unprecedented in magnitude and impact. Consider some of the more tangible manifestations:

Trading blocs

Europe has set aside its nationalistic and policy differences, constructed a Single Internal Market and advanced towards economic union. The change will embrace most European nations in the next two decades. There are indications that the pace of change could accelerate. Sweden, Norway and Austria have started the process in the last two years and are expected to join shortly. Eastern European nations are now pushing to join the European Community (EC) and other Western institutions at the fastest possible speed.

Transformation in North America has also been impressive. Three highly protective nations have formed the North America Free Trade Area (NAFTA) to build the largest borderless trading bloc over the next decade. Other nations of Latin and South America are eager to join. NAFTA and the European Union are harmonizing trade and investment policies to create an expanded sphere of economic activity, although the NAFTA members are not committed to deepening integration like that in Europe.

East and South East Asian nations, isolated in the past, have combined with the USA and Canada in the Asia Pacific Economic Cooperation forum. The Association of South East Asian Nations provided the initial nucleus for this cooperation and is forming its own free trade area. The People's Republic of China, Hong Kong and the Republic of China (Taiwan) are constituting a Greater China trading area. After a half century of closed market operations, India (with the second largest population in the world) has opened her doors and is indeed a trading bloc of her own.

The policy shifts towards regional economic integration have been profound, reflecting incentives which have influenced all governments. The genesis of the shift can be traced to policy learning influenced by awareness that economic growth results from increases in gains from trade that are facilitated by large-scale market integration.

Deregulation and privatization

A wave of deregulation and privatization – reducing micromanagement of free enterprise systems – was engineered by US President Reagan and the

British Prime Minister Lady Thatcher. Despite strong socio-political pressures they provided more scope for market forces and succeeded in exhibiting the merits of their positions. Their ideological stance, understood as progressively less government interference, is now widely viewed as the preferred basis for economic management. It has charted the general direction of change to limited government, without setting clear demarcations of administrative responsibilities. Some governments rely totally on competitive market forces (for example, in the US, UK and Canada) and others keep or impose certain structures and policy guidelines in order to shield and control their firms, however partially. Through cooperative arrangements within and between private and public sectors, the latter governments have tried to moderate potentially destructive market pressures and create additional strengths for their enterprises (for example, in Germany, Japan and Korea).

The collapse of central planning – in the former Soviet bloc – could be viewed as the failure of that extreme polar case, tending to validate the value system and principles on which the free market economies are based. But this should not be viewed as all-around 'winning' of the 'game'. Some market economies have grown much faster than others (for example, Japan and the Asian newly industrializing countries (NICS)). It could indeed be argued that the unevenness is mainly due to structural differentials[1] that are tending to become more significant.

Rapid Technological Advancement

The past three decades have also witnessed rapid technological change, not limited to any product or industry. This has already affected, and will continue to impact on, many aspects of international trade, commerce and investment. Two broad trends which have had a pervasive impact are highlighted below.

The shortening of technological cycles: a supply push

The shortening of technological cycles cannot be attributed to any single factor or simple process; it has come about because of a plethora of complex processes. The cost of R&D to introduce new products or upgrade previous technologies has greatly increased. Even incremental improvements come at increasingly higher costs and greater uncertainties. The risks have increased tremendously due to constantly rising numbers of participants, and proliferating technologies in widening and intensely competitive markets.

The market for new products, processes and technologies has grown continuously beyond borders. Although general barriers to the international movement of goods and services have been falling dramatically over the past several decades, markets for R&D, technology and their derivatives have led the way and surpassed most others. They are now among the freest international markets. In these markets technology moves freely through many international channels, including scientific and industrial journals, learned conferences, corporate correspondence or documents, and especially through interactions in scientific communities.

The first to succeed in commercializing technological fruits reap all the 'first-mover advantages' and capture all the 'leader's' privileges. The second and the third best may be recognized as followers. Of the other market participants those who need new technologies for economic survival are always under time pressure and will tend to go with the sure winners, not the second, not the third, or others.

Consumers instinctively support the winners (that is, the first). Consequently there is a sequence of push–pull processes. There are pressures on suppliers to achieve results at the lowest cost and in the shortest time, and to keep ahead even at higher costs (Peterson, 1993). But not many firms can absorb several losses. Technologically oriented producers are introducing newer product generations in record times to stay ahead. To recoup the increasing cost, as the useful life of each current generation decreases rapidly, ever larger markets have to be exploited in the shortest time possible. Trade liberalization has made reaching larger markets increasingly more feasible; and a double-edged strategy – time and market coverage on each side – has become the only viable choice for many firms in the technological race. As technology becomes obsolete at a faster pace, the length of time for serving the *largest* market possible has become shorter. The super-imposition of time pressure has transformed the process (technology push) into a high stake and high speed race.

Increased value and deferral: a demand pull?

There is an equally complex phenomenon on the demand side. Although the desire to receive the highest value possible has been a rational expectation of the corporate and the consuming publics for a long time, the supply-stimulated push has intensified quests for utility maximization.

The marginal interest of a common consumer is stimulated by reviews, exhibits, advertising and 'demonstrative effects'. A typical response is curiosity, followed by a more active search, leading to the stark discovery: that there is a tremendous diversity of choice; that various producers package different combinations of goods with much differentiation; and that there is a wide array of competing technologies of which several generations are available at the same time. This may at first be very confusing. But our consumer soon learns that products and technologies are indeed comparable in that they perform similar functions and possess similar attributes. They are presented differently so that they can capture the highest perceived degree of leadership and competitiveness which a market can offer. Comparative shopping can lead to the realization that the most recent generation, not necessarily the best or the most useful, commands the highest current price and that the previous model is sold at a considerable discount. Even to a mildly rational buyer, this suggests a high premium for the technological cutting-edge and high discount rate for elapsed time or technological age, regardless of true functionality.

A mildly logical consumer is likely either to buy the previous generation at a discount or wait to get the current product at a lower price (for example, 60 to 70 per cent discount in approximately a year or two). The experience is bound to suggest that a purchase deferral has no risk and would result in obtaining better value. Typical customers, for whom time has less urgency than others, begin to demand higher value for increasingly shorter elapsed times; and hence deferral soon begins to dominate the criteria for current purchases. The experience of the past two decades with technologically derived or technologically based products does indeed confirm the above behaviour. Customers have begun to demand the highest competitive value; or else they use deferral to obtain increasing value at no additional cost. Repeated experiences can easily translate into accumulated expectation and result in a firmly established pattern of behaviour. The demand pull for increasingly higher value (that is, a better, more sophisticated, improved, newer generation product) at a fair price indirectly supports the ongoing technological race at the producers' level. Suppliers are forced to deal with deferral. They face two choices: either to push forward with R&D to bring to market the cutting-edge technology before others in order to preserve whatever technological edge they possess regardless of the cost; or resign to share the market with, and compete intensely with, many others while perfectly functioning products lose their value. Neither policy is pleasant or avoidable. The end result is likely to be a faster introduction of cutting-edge generations at decreasing prices.

This interaction of supply push and market pull has slowly forced technology-related markets to the highest gear, and there is no abatement in sight. Consequently, R&D costs are increasing, time cycles are shrinking, total delivered value is rising, product quality is improving, variety is proliferating and, in short, the risks and total costs are skyrocketing. Thus participation in such markets for many enterprises is becoming intolerable to bear alone. Non-participation is voluntary suicide. The obvious solution is based on sharing core competencies. This limits the risks of participation and involvement by forming alliances and networks. Interestingly, they are facilitated, and at times stimulated, by the new policy environment.

Fixed Costs Dominance

The combination of shortened technological cycles and increasing value expectation and deferral on the demand side, have produced an unusual operating environment. This is characterized by increasing and unavoidable fixed costs and shrinking variable costs. This evolutionary change is affecting the basis of most decisions and operations. The traditional rule for creating value was to increase productivity, decrease costs (mostly variable) and improve quality. In the new environment and on the consumption side, quality is given: customers demand top quality and top value. They are otherwise willing to wait. On the supply side, production and marketing is characterized by: 1) expensive R&D and equally expensive and risky commercialization; 2) bursts of high marketing expenditure to introduce products and reduce hostile competitive reactions; and (above all) 3) investment in reducing variable costs to take advantage of higher scale economies. All of these high expenditures are necessary, unavoidable and more or less fixed. Quality is also increasingly correlated with high technology and precision manufacturing through computer-assisted design (CAD), -engineering (CAE), -manufacturing (CAM) and industrial robots (Musich, 1988). All these technologies have high price tags and short lives (Ophisanwo and Dasiewicz, 1987). In short, there has been a trend towards computer-assisted and -controlled manufacturing, with very high fixed costs – and away from variable operating costs (for example, labour).

Once a firm is committed, the fixed cost regime reduces flexibilities with variable costs. The only sensible operating rule, given consumers' pattern of behaviour, is to maximize sale and production in order to minimize per unit fixed cost contribution margins. This requires access to large and diverse international markets (which the shift in policy environments has made possible); but it depends on flexible manufacturing enhanced by fast cycles and low costs (supported by a shift from variable to fixed costs). High fixed cost operations (requiring high outlays) need wide open global markets. The globalization of markets and industries is therefore the logical consequence of preceding causes and processes.

The massive amount of effort required to succeed in active global markets to support high fixed costs requires access to large, highly productive resources. These resources cannot be allocated in a concentrated fashion to *any* given task or function (such as distribution, manufacturing, procurement or management) alone; for a weakness anywhere could be fatal. There is a need for a well-connected chain of activities. With constrained resources, not many single entities can independently mount and manage the entire process. Global competitors can neither ignore any source of weakness, nor discount any potential source of strength. A weakness would need to be overcome by pooling the most competitive resources and most effective capabilities. Ideally, they would then function as if they were parts of a single entity. Such a degree of cooperation can develop in multicountry and multifunctional coalitions.

Structural Differentials

Some countries have developed structures for superior competitiveness based on *structural differentials*. These are mainly Eastern countries whose family and societal value systems and work ethics have influenced corporate behaviour and societal–corporate–government relations. Competitive edges, gained from coordination and cooperation, have enabled them to accelerate ahead of others, while influencing the other systems with which they have interacted. Confucianism, Buddhism and Shintoism as major religions of the region have personified individuals more in terms of group identity and membership, group harmony and work for the common good, and much less with reference to individual goals on which Western societies are structured.

In Japan, Korea and China, the family tradition of patriarchal mentoring gradually extended to corporate sectors, causing similar patterns of behaviour and value systems in corporate families and their practices. Similar to families, cooperative units (or industrial complexes) have traditionally included the weak and the strong, and small and medium sized, as well as the large (and even conglomerate) members. The long-term common good of the collective would always prevail over an individual corporate member's wishes. From a Japanese perspective, the *keiretsu's* unwritten rules of cooperation and sanctions against deviants are viewed as normal extensions[2] of the social norms by which Japanese have governed themselves over decades, if not centuries.

This cooperation has now proven to be superior, in the absence of comparable Western structures. This is the structural difference to which this chapter attributes a differential advantage.[3] For survival, Western corporate players had to find a competing strategy. NOAs, especially with firms possessing such differentials, were the obvious choice.

This chapter will later return to the subject of structural differentials as a partial basis for coalitions, alliances and networks with Asian-based entities. The discussions in the following sections will deal with policy shifts and rapid technological change as factors causing transitions from variable cost minimization to fixed cost absorbtion. These forces have changed self-contained and independent entities into interdependent, fragmented, yet specialized, productive chains. Hence they have necessitated and accommodated the explosive multiplication of 'alliances' and 'networks' in many industries and across nations. Both alliances and networks are bound to expand further and will restructure international production, together with other business functions, nationally and internationally.

PART II: REASONS AND JUSTIFICATIONS FOR PRODUCTION NETWORKS AND ALLIANCES

The combination of circumstances which attract any given partner to form mutually acceptable arrangements depends on unique conditions and circumstances at that time. Abstracting from these conditions, the received literature arrives at some generalizations. But the power, the richness and the flexibility associated with NOAs are generally lost. Although a taxonomical structure will be presented at the end of this chapter, documented cases of NOAs will be studied below to capture their efficiencies and to examine reasons for their formation. Before doing so, however, it is necessary to state that both networks and alliances share many similarities and belong to the family of efficient and flexible inter-organizational structures which enable a firm to organize activities and resources more productively (Gadde, 1993).[4] Gadde states that NOAs are much more conducive to such optimization than any other given form because of their extreme flexibility (*ibid.* pp. 49–60).

Bridging Gaps and Discontinuities

Many NOA cases involve discontinuities which partners find difficult to bridge independently. Production discontinuity, for example, leads to an NOA responding to the production inadequacies of at least one of the partners (Bloom, 1992). Similarly, technological gaps and discontinuities dictate an NOA for many of the reasons outlined in Part I (Eckerson and Wallace, 1991; Harrison, 1994; Sylla and Arinze, 1991). Once one NOA becomes active, some experience is gained and a degree of confidence is obtained; other complementary NOAs may be added; and parallel ones may follow (Back and Jackson, 1993). A product-induced need (for example, a discontinuity in a firm's product line) may serve as an impetus for pooling R&D or sharing technology in order to arrive at more efficient production arrangements (Hackney, 1994; Oleson, 1993). The limited capabilities or constrained resources of one partner can then easily be bridged by the under-utilized capabilities (or resources) of the other partner or a network of partners (Burns, 1994).[5] These are mostly short-term options for long-term survival (Back and Jackson, 1993; Cottril, 1993; Dornheim, 1994; Smith, 1994).

Technological discontinuity occurs when products, processes or technologies are pushed to obsolescence beyond expectations. Glasmeier reports on such disasters in the Swiss and American watch industries (Glasmeier, 1991).

Digital technology replaced Swiss and US time pieces. Although the Swiss watch industry lost its leading position and world dominance, it revived by restructuring however, the US industry did not recover. Both US and Swiss firms possessed a degree of expertise in the previous analogue technology and yet found themselves in need of deploying the new technology quickly.

In other cases, the complete lack of a technological base combined with a strategic desire to have a presence in a sector has led to NOAs. Consider the commercial and fighter jet industry: Sino-Pakistani co-production of Saab MF1-17 Safari with Teledyne Continental TS10-360MB turbocharged engines and avionics; the alliance for a twin turbo regional transport plane (Avion Transport Regionale-ATR) between the French Aerospatiale, the Italian Alenia and a Chinese Aircraft Manufacturing Company (*Aviation Week*, 21 February 1994); Japan's co-production of F-18 fighter jets; Korea's production and co-production of parts of jet engines and fuselage (Bond, 1990; Morrocco, 1989); and China's love affair with McDonnell Douglas's MD-82 and MD-11 (Rosenthal, 1989; Smith, 1994) are just a few examples. F-18s are manufactured under strict licence, due to US 'national security' concerns and fear of technology transfers to Japan, but Korean and Chinese arrangements are reported to be much looser. In Europe, the consortium of Air Bus Industries, sponsored by seven European governments, has begun to break Boeing's commercial dominance. Meanwhile, an alliance of seven aircraft engine manufacturers, International Aero Engines draws on the technical and technological expertise of its seven allied parents for assembling its team of engineers, designers and experts. They meet on a bi-monthly basis at one of the seven head offices to increase their interaction, reduce their psychological distances, and build a solid basis of trust and cooperation (Wolf, 1994).

Wolf quotes David Jones of the Engineering Construction Division of Raytheon Co. that, 'no alliance can survive without trust and companies tend to undervalue personal relationships' (Wolf, 1994, p. 13). A lack of trust is reported to account for differences in aerospace alliances, especially when governments are involved.

In the commercial aircraft industry, Golich sees two sets of complex forces – centripetal and centrifugal – which interactively propel and impede corporations entering into international arrangements, thus affecting the degree of looseness or control exercised or desired (Golich, 1992). Based on the perceived policy environment and corporate strategic objectives, three prototypical structures of international production are outlined and their implications and examples examined, but no particular structure stands out. In a similar study Mayere and Vinot looked at the interaction of firm structures in production networks and found that the informal structure of networks allowed both formal and informal organizations to function side-by-side and create a hybrid form (Mayere and Vinot, 1993). Other studies show that gaps in policy environments in at least two of the home countries lead to various restrictions and controls.[6] Such restrictions manifest themselves in regulations covering transfers of technology, minimum industrial spin-offs, offsets, employment, use of foreign exchange and trade balances, as well as immediate commercial and security factors. Combined, they also influence government subsidies (or sanctions) in affected industries.

Farsighted corporate executives or government officials may act on perceived gaps or discontinuities, and may not wait for a real discontinuity to threaten. A perceived future strategic advantage (or disadvantage) can be sufficient to activate an NOA with a partner who seeks the mirror image advantage. Cunningham and Ford report that a perceived strategic advantage realizable in an NOA is likely to be used as a major competitive source. Such advantages propel potential candidates to conclude cooperative arrangements (such as NOAs) which in turn enable them to *cooperate* and *compete* at the same time (Cunningham and Ford, 1993).[7]

As the range and diversity of technological needs expands, the useful life of any given proprietary technology declines, while the cost of R&D, commercialization and production escalates, newer markets emerge and older ones fragment. Because of time pressures and constrained resources, the need for simultaneous cooperation in some areas in order to compete in others increases proportionally. NOAs can respond to these needs if lines of demarcation between cooperative and competitive spheres can be clearly identified and the corresponding executives can manage them accordingly. Bridging discontinuities appropriately may not be an easy task or of concern to the corporate sector alone; governments usually get involved. Some of those discontinuities are policy-induced, yet government authorities press their concerns. Some of these concerns reflect directly those of the corporate sectors. High definition television (HDTV) standards is a case in point.

Although there is a universal consensus that the US's telecommunications regulating agency, the FCC's selected standards are bound to dominate the market, EC officials have supported a European HDTV alliance and have pressed for adoption of independent European-wide HDTV standards. The backdrop for this policy is (and has been) an expectation that the US sponsored standards will eventually have to be licensed and produced by Europeans to give them a chance to survive.[8] Naturally, European producers will have to adopt the standards later as they arise (Spangler, 1993) and subsequently write off their prior investments. In the absence of government support or a conducive policy environment, it should be fairly obvious that with several strong US- and Japanese-dominated coalitions in highly advanced states, the European alliance of Thomson SA and Philips Electronics for HDTV would not have been pursued at all (Levine, 1992). A study of 14 strategic alliances between high technology partners concluded that successful alliances had to insulate their activities from the vagaries of international politics (Farr and Fischer, 1992). Alliances are at times formed to minimize the impact of government regulations (Little, 1987; St Pierre, 1993). This appears to be a part of the telecommunications industry's emerging strategy.[9] Let us examine it closely.

The interaction between the two powerful telecommunications regulating agencies in the US and Canada, namely the FCC and CRTC, respectively, each pursuing its own regulatory and oversight actions, has created different operating environments. The development of telecommunications as the prelude to the formation of the 'information highway' industry is likely to diverge in the two countries.

In the US, several prototypical combinations of expertise from potentially complementary industries are pulled together. They include firms from telecommunications (for example, US West, one of the Baby Bells), entertainment (for example, movie production and music, such as Times Warner Inc.), technical hardware (Apple Computer Inc.) and cable–telecom–software (such as Via Com International Inc.). A range of their capabilities are networked or aligned (that is, allied in a formal alliance) to resolve both the technological and environmental challenges of this emerging industry (Chan and Heide, 1993; Del Nibletto, 192; Mason, 1992; Pesmen, 1993; Pinnington, 1992; Spangler, 1993; Teece, 1992). In the smaller Canadian market, with interprovincial barriers and a different regulatory environment, telecommunications firms (or entertainment firms) are far from establishing a network for bridging the technological gap of the emerging 'information highway' industry. Yet against the CRTCs centrifugal forces, US pressure may have served as a centripetal force to bring the Canadian firms together and *force* a regulatory change in recent years: Canadian Stentor Network Management, the alliance between Stentor Telecom Policy Inc. and Telecom Canada, is indeed a formal alliance between two companies which were each owned by the nine Canadian telecommunications companies (St Pierre, 1993).

Many similar patterns are evident in the aerospace and information highway industries. They are entering a new phase which will be affected by the interaction of all previously identified forces (that is, induced by policy, technology change and structural differentials). The bridging discontinuity has served as a motivation for an NOA; and it continues to offer a wide and rich spectrum for research and discussion. NOAs cope with location problems (Gandy, 1993); escalating needs to become more competitive than one's resources permit in terms of cost of performance (Hagedoorn and Schakenraad, 1993; Weiss, 1993); lack of resources for penetration into wider markets (Weiss, 1993); customer–vendor or supplier–vendor distances (Gladkowski, 1993); unequal risk-sharing (Magee, 1992); the deflection of competitive pressures (Fitzgerald and Daly, 1993; Teece, 1992); and needs to exploit advantages of infrastructure facilities (Hagedoorn and Schakenraad, 1993; Larson, 1994; Malincoe, 1992; O'Leary, 1993). All the above topics have been documented as primary justifications for NOA formations.[10]

Competitive and Logistic Concerns

NOAs have become the most favoured quick responses to immediate-, short- and medium-term competitive concerns, as well as mechanisms for attaining longer-range strategic objectives. Competitive concerns cover a wide spectrum:

Fast response
A rival's advance, either in an isolated field or on a broad basis, needs a quick response. Left unbridled, the attacker is bound to penetrate as rapidly and deeply as possible, in order to consolidate its market position and overwhelm all others. Affected competitors may not be able to mount an adequate counter-attack individually; but a coalition of them, in an NOA, would be in a much better position to respond. This would be similar to a rapid deployment force necessary for dealing with trouble spots, which most armies lack but would like to have (Armistead and Mapes, 1993; Chan and Heide, 1993; Fitzgerald and Daly, 1993; Golich, 1992; Gunter, 1993; Magee, 192).

Flexible response
A wide-reaching survey of manufacturing firms has identified two highly de-sired characteristics of responses to competitive challenges: flexibility and multiple capability. Flexibility, by many accounts is, 'a bright corporate vision, but attaining it is filled with many obstacles' (Cook, 1990). Firms are networks of people and activities, confined to their own corporate culture and con-strained by resources and other limitations. They are hence not very flexible in the short term (Gadde, 1993). In contrast, a network of firms is the sum total of its members' flexibilities. The network is capable of relieving a member's limitation through the added diversity and increased scale and scope due to the pooling of resources. In the era of mass demand for tailor-made goods and services at mass production prices (because of 'globally localized markets'[11]), the availability of nearly unlimited choice combined with fast changing tech-nologies and instantly available information, flexibility is absolutely necessary.

Once in an NOA, a member can be mandated or empowered by partners to organize or perform a specific task(s), including shielding of the NOA partner(s) against adverse conditions before the NOA can collectively match and mount a counter-attack, especially in a turbulent environment. Little has documented the NOA's ability to offer much of the requisite flexibility and extra capabilities (Little, 1987). This is similar to intrafirm backup and support for a unit or division under stress. To the extent that a portion of a division's goods and services are intrafirm traded, the division is shielded from external turbulence (for example, fast exchange fluctuations, political risk, rapid policy change or intense competition). Although the firm as a whole bears the cost and pays the price for such protection, a division under stress can be shielded for a while to recover. It is argued that Japanese firms have used their network-like relationships, well established through *keiretsu* arrangements, to shield their exports from the US government's protectionist measures (Harbrecht, 1994, p. 45; Little, 1987, p. 58).

Other NOA-specific flexibilities range from adding to the breadth and depth of product lines and complementing them with some extra reach and presence (in markets in which only one partner previously possessed some strength), and strengthening their offering by complementary services, especially where one partner is particularly weak and the other unusually strong (Chapman, 1992; Gilbert, 1991; Saxenian, 1991). Gladkowski documents the case of Alliance Productive Technologies (APT), a Vendor Network Association formed by its investing members to provide a wide range of previously unavailable products and services which APT would make available to each of the members. Membership fees and sales proceeds finance new R&D which is expected to lead to new products (or services) for most members. These new joint capabilities were to be utilized in response to competitive pressures or for increased profits (Gladkowski, 1993).

Rapid, inexpensive and pre-emptive expansion

Many successful firms have used NOAs coupled with a combination of mergers, acquisitions, joint ventures and licensing agreements to expand rapidly without drawing upon much resources (Peterson, 1993; Schnerken, 1991). With such arrangements Asea Brown Boveri (ABB) is reported to have expanded rapidly in the Eastern European and ex-Soviet bloc countries without much expenditure, acquiring 58 plants in 17 countries with 20,000 employees. It has sales in the $30 billion range and profits in excess of one-half billion ($860 million in 1993 after a $560 million one-off write-off). ABB has indeed accomplished several strategic objectives: pre-emptive expansion into Eastern Europe, building a global product/production network, and building a powerful platform for further rapid expansion in other markets with newly acquired local expertise, resources and flexibilities unlikely to become available to its competitors (Hofheinz, 1994). Without such an expanded network supported by foreign direct investment (FDI) the Eastern European presence would have been slow and expensive (UN report, 1993).

Glaxo's expansion strategy has reportedly been based on a combination of NOAs coupled with joint ventures. This strategy has made Glaxo the second largest pharmaceutical company world-wide and has been equally beneficial to small firms joining its network. The alliance of IAF Biochem International Inc. (Canada) and Glaxo is a case in point. For the successful, small R&D firm, short of expansion funds and without much access to international pharmaceutical markets, an alliance with Glaxo was an expansion strategy made in heaven (Willis, 1991, pp. 28–30). Roches became the fourth largest world pharmaceutical company (just after Merck Frost & Co., Glaxo Holdings and Bristol Myers-Squibb[12]) through the acquisition of a large distribution network in the US, formerly controlled by Syntex (Corporate Growth Reports, 9 May 1994). For Roches, the establishment of such large networks would have required tremendous effort and funds in the US's competitive pharmaceutical environment.

For small to medium sized enterprises (SMEs), NOAs are equally valuable. Aside from large-scale production in Japan and South Korea by *keiretsus* and *chabeols*,[13] Japanese and Korean trading companies export considerable volumes of products manufactured by SMEs in these countries (Sasseen, 1993). Through NOAs, with or without cross-directorship or equity holdings by the large firms in both countries, SMEs produce many parts, components and subassemblies for flagship firms. They then push them through production or assembly channels for final manufacturing or assembly at flagship companies such as Mitsubishi, Toshiba, Toyota, Mitsui, Sumitomo, Dae-Woo Hyundai, Lucky-Goldstar, Samsung and so on (Friedland and Smith, 1994; Stone, 1992; Gadde, 1993).[14] A similar network structure is observed in countries with traditional Chinese family business practices, which also rely on intertwined alliances and networks of family-led or family-run firms with and without equity involvements.

The literature has attributed the tremendous success of Japan, South Korea and the South East Asian NICs to traditional structures of production[15] without much recognition of NOAs as viable production structures, regardless of their cultural context. It is only recently that the contributions of small and medium sized firms and their harmoniously coordinated network actions and allied practices have come to light. Faced with the pressures of such staunch competitors, large firms and SMEs alike in North America have begun to explore mutual synergies. The example of many SMEs as network partners of Nike Incorporated is well documented. Nike's success is reported to be solely based on its management of a 'legion of SMEs' as its suppliers and distributors. Manufacturing all over the world through an NOA (Harrison, 1994), Nike has achieved global distribution through a similar network of independent distributors. Nike is characterized as a hollow headquarters (no manufacturing of its own), busy coordinating many production and distribution SME networks (ibid. p. 40).

The Erie Bolt Corporation (EBC), a manufacturer of metal parts and components (based in Erie, Pennsylvania), is also a good example of small firms using NOA for expansion and growth. Through a simple network of similarly minded firms in the region, EBC has proven that the combined synergic effects of a number of similarly sized companies, sharing resources and coordinating their activities, can accomplish much more than that which a company with comparable aggregate size can achieve. Its network achieved 50 per cent growth and 300 per cent customer-based expansion a year after the network began to function (Richman, 1988).

Internationalization of services
For worldwide expansion of services, especially when a firm is incapable of producing them on demand in many sites (for example, SMEs), the NOA is the *only* feasible instrument of presence and expansion. Even before the popularity of NOAs, a loose network of affiliates, working and coordinating technical and professional standards in consulting, engineering and technical services (such as logistics), produced the desired quality services on and across locations (Andren, 1994). Licensing and franchising of certain knowledge and know-how or other assets provided a formalized structure in some cases. The current practice is not much different. For a service SME, a network with some skeletal support appears to be the only feasible, quick and inexpensive vehicle for worldwide presence and expansion (Bress, 1994; Robins, 1994; Sentinery, 1994). The FTD's worldwide flower delivery service is an example of independent flower shops supported by a simple order communication and fund-clearing system.

International distribution, viewed as a service, shares similar characteristics.[16] Most members of distribution and sales networks are independents who have developed a finely tuned cooperative system for providing vital marketing services (for example, before- and after-sales support). Standard services in distribution – unpacking, sorting, repackaging, delivery, billing, accounting, collection, inventory control, promotion, advertising and after-sales maintenance and services – are produced locally as parts of a broader network of production and distribution. Although not traditionally considered as production networks, such services (for example, distribution) are produced on site and on demand. Service networks have proven to be instrumental in moving goods and producing services internationally. They act as international accelerators if they behave cooperatively, but are insurmountable bottlenecks (or even entry barriers) and very expensive to avoid or replicate if they act uncooperatively. They have assumed a vital role in international trade and investment; and have also made important contributions to local economies, sometimes with FDI stimulation (Borrmann and Jungnickel, 1992; Gadde, 1993; Solonitskii, 1993; Van Oldenborgh, 1993).

Many aspects of newly emerging systems of supply–manufacturing–distribution, especially by a large number of Asian Pacific SMEs, are worthy of examination. They collectively point to a very strong trend towards further formalization and structuring of their respective NOAs, combined with some equity or technology infusions to strengthen the linkages in what are formally known as supply and manufacturing networks (Dubois, Toyne and Oliff, 1993; Fawcett, 1992). In line with the equally strong trends of worldwide out-sourcing and distribution, similar structures and trends are observable in distribution, sales and after-sales service (Hitomi, 1991, 1993; Schroath, 1993; Witt and Rao, 1992). As to their specific objectives, they generally fall into the categories covered above.

Strategic Concerns

Strategic concerns also span a very wide range. As stated earlier, the rapidity with which policy environments and technology have been changing is making proactive strategic initiatives increasingly more complex and yet more vital to economic survival. At the same time, due to interacting strategic initiatives, the effective life of all initiatives is reduced and the cost of each cycle increased. In such environments, prudence, insight and genuine strengths are essential to support a strategy's effectiveness. For a strategy to succeed, the sequence of events and activities must receive adequate support from actors and resources to stay on track and reach its final destination (Gadde, 1993).

Rivals are usually determined to do everything in their power to disrupt the sequence. They may even attempt to destroy it. Then, either a new course has to be taken rapidly or intermediate changes must be made. Any slow-down or stop will lead to lost time, require extra resources and reduce efficiency. In the face of hostility, the alternative of finding new strategic routing through uncharted terrains can entail additional time and expenditures, if not a fatal risk.

The terrain analogy is appropriate because of the high stakes in a hostile, rapidly changing, highly competitive global technological environment. Traditionally large and powerful firms with heavy vested interests, due to their developed constellations of subsidiaries, affiliates and sales offices, are laden with large negative momentum. They are increasingly overtaken by a network and loose alliance of (flexible) fast-moving smaller firms, with new products, new technologies or greater efficiencies.

The rapidity of change has introduced, comparatively speaking, a degree of perishability into most goods and services. High technology products are rendered obsolete with time. Therefore the quicker they are delivered to markets, the higher the realized value (a combination of time value of money and high-tech perishability) and the lower cost of delivery. The smaller, faster-moving and more flexible firms are indeed analogues to flexible alliances and networks. They are bound to dominate the strategic sphere of globalized supply–manufacturing–distribution of the future as they can better optimize their portfolio of activities, actors and resources (Gadde, 1993).

Practically all surveys of large and small firms acknowledge the increasing importance of strategic linkages. All indications show that these have positive effects (Hagedoorn and Schakenraad, 1993). A survey of 500 firms documented that the majority were using networks and alliances. Because of their potency and importance, decisions dealing with them are increasingly centralized (Burns, 1994).[17] It also indicated that achieving excellence and gaining a competitive edge required diverse multiple capabilities combined with a strategic flexibility to respond in time; NOAs were increasingly used.

Total quality and just-in-time performance philosophies, which require excellent performance at every step, are expected to embrace all aspects of business conduct, including office work (Dangerfield, 1992). Chapman indicates that there is an increasing worldwide emphasis on just-in-time responsiveness, with real quality complemented with customer service, both before and after sales (Chapman, 1992). Chapman further observes that NOAs are playing a critical role in achieving just-in-time quality, while modern information technology is used in managing the NOA. Modern information systems, as a result of a fast-changing environment, have become vital for the management of groups based on a service concept that he calls 'flexible deployment' (Chapman, 1992, p. 61).

Teece has shown that NOAs have been used strategically by various firms for accessing resources and capabilities unavailable to them due to their size. He further adds that with the advent of NOAs, the old concept of a firm's size as a proxy for power and capabilities has become very fuzzy and almost meaningless. Constellations of bilateral and multilateral agreements enlarge a coalition's capabilities and resources to an extent unreachable by any given firm independently (Teece, 1992).

Malincoe (1992) argues that the fast-changing environment (policy, technological, trade and so on) is exposing firms to new, costly options. These are strategic options not previously considered feasible. A good example is the alliance between IBM and Apple, with each firm previously set to harm the other beyond repair. The coalition in a highly competitive environment forced other competitors such as Unisys and Hewlett-Packard (HP), to search for a strategic redirection, to make at least as strong a coalition, and to amass enough strategic power to counter other potential coalitions. Malincoe reviews both the IBM–Apple coalition and that of Unisys, HP, Motorola, Informix, Cray Research and Sun Micro Systems (Malincoe, 1992). Motorola has become a chip manufacturer involved in several potentially rival NOAs, causing fears of strategic instability in such coalitions as firms' strategies evolve differently. Malincoe has already foreseen such life-shortening instabilities (*ibid.*).

An implicit game-theoretic framework is active in the background. It appears that the flexible instruments of coalition formation have forced an action–reaction–feedback into the open as the emerging paradigm to provide strategic direction for further movements. Although the literature has yet to view them in this light, NOA examples of such behaviours abound. Consider, for example, the context of American Telephone and Telegraph (AT&T)'s breakup, leading to the formation of the current telecommunications industry in the United States.

The protracted litigations leading to the break up of AT&T, then the world's largest telecommunications company, were interpreted as a sign of the US government's resolve to enforce its anti-trust policy to avoid, or slow down, concentration (that is, coalitions, alliances, and combines and cartels of the old parlance). In other countries, such as France, Japan and Korea, concentration was allowed or even encouraged. Furthermore, government–industry dialogues produced policies which were effective and fostered growth and expansion towards dominance in some cases. In the face of generally supportive governmental policies elsewhere, the massive government regulatory machinery in the US has proven to be too slow and not proactively responsive. In a game-theoretic framework, German and French support for their industries compromised the interests of US firms in the worldwide industry.

The evolving regulatory environment in the US telecommunications industry within which the so-called Baby Bells are now increasing their power and concentration, is taken as a new signal pointing towards a gradual reorientation of past policy.[18] Practically all Baby Bells are pursuing their strategic objectives through a constellation of NOAs. More importantly, however, similar behaviour is observable in both the allied industries and also other countries. The rapid convergence of members of the telecommunications, entertainment, information and computer industries (to name a few) into several giant coalitions reflects a strategic offensive–defensive sequence.[19] In a parallel fashion, the newly emerging NOAs are creating strategic flexibilities which are enhancing their strengths in the industry's formation process (Golich, 1992; Magee, 1992; Olesen, 1993; Sasseen, 1993; Saxenian, 1991; Teece, 1992; Wolf, 1994).[20]

Aside from the most recent developments in the pharmaceuticals,[21] telecommunications and computer industries, the automobile industry (especially in the early 1990s) in Europe experienced similar coalition formation, mainly through mergers and acquisitions (and, to a lesser extent, through NOAs) just before the Single European Act came into force. The prospect of change in the policy environment provided sufficient impetus for what was called the European merger–acquisition mania. No major European auto firm remains unaffiliated today. Even the largest European auto manufacturer, Daimler Benz, has a Japanese alliance partner.

In the expected battle of American and Japanese 'auto titans' for world dominance, no strategically minded European auto firm can afford to remain unprotected. It is important to note that any single auto flagship firm already has large NOAs of suppliers and distributors. A coalition between two or more flagship firms creates a complex hierarchical web of NOAs with their own multiple tasks or multipurpose links, capable of increasing scale and scope economies as well as new flexibilities, all necessary in strategic battles.

PART III: TOWARDS A TAXONOMICAL STRUCTURE

The structure of production has not been immune to change. Forces of change, as outlined earlier, have gradually created an environment which is making the old structure weak and vulnerable. Most aspects of what previously confined total production to one or a handful of sites have changed dramatically.

Most of the modern tools of production and manufacturing did not exist a mere quarter century ago. Computer assisted processes which are now integral parts of manufacturing (for example, multiple generations of CAD, CAM, CAE and production resource management and planning programmes) and a host of other computer-driven and -controlled devices, played very little to no role in production. The gradual penetration of modern tools, all assisted by computers, into most aspects of supply–production–distribution, followed by the advent of flexible manufacturing and industrial robots (driven and controlled by computers) have changed production and production planning. These devices have increased the accuracy of production and the fitting of interfaces to a degree that production engineers could only dream about a quarter century ago.

Detailed technical production specifications, which used to fill reams of paper and technical drawings, can now be easily transmitted to a numerically controlled manufacturing island with a flick of a computer key, regardless of distance. The infrastructure and superstructure of design, procurement and production have changed from mainly human-driven, geographically bound and locally controlled processes to computer-designed and -controlled processes, centrally, locally or remotely located. The early attributes of such evolving systems are divisibility, transportability, accuracy and increased capability for scale and scope economies. In spite of their tremendously expensive price tags, they are becoming indispensable, as demand for higher quality and value escalates continuously.

A parallel technological development in worldwide transportation and logistic management has also accelerated the evolutionary speed all around. Super-efficient logistic management for the movement of parts, assemblies and general cargo, combined with a continuous drop in real costs of air, land

and marine transport, have paved the road for a wholesale change in various aspects of production.

It seems as if the stage was well planned for a quiet and continuous change from all-inclusive, massive and on-site production facilities, mostly owned and controlled by one company, to dispersed manufacturing integrated by information and logistic systems, but not necessarily on one site or controlled by one owner. Highly flexible manufacturing (with high scope economies) can now be serially coordinated (like long assembly lines) for scale economies. Computer technology was the vehicle of change and the glue for integration, offering prospects for increased efficiency, quality, value, manageability, flexibility and so on.

Computer penetration and the consequent production transformation have led to a gradual financial transformation. The introduction of computers and computer-assisted processes, at high fixed and lumpy costs, caused dramatic reductions in variable components such as labour, material, energy and even transportation. Modern manufacturing has become a high fixed cost proposition. Its direct impact on worldwide management is either to avoid, share or otherwise amortize unavoidable fixed costs at the fastest possible rates.

These emerging conditions have led to a production environment which could not be engineered or managed without NOAs.

Escalating fixed costs and declining competitiveness in the West, while North America and European gates were steadily closing, caused Japanese and Asian producers to seek each other's cooperation and coordination through NOAs. When North American and European producers were eventually forced (for their own survival) to concede a small portion of production and distribute some of their goods and services to Japanese and Asian NICs, entry barriers to the rich North American and European markets had begun to fall. North American and European producers, in turn, had to ally with their Japanese and Asian counterparts to help reduce increasing production costs and gain competitiveness (that is, quality) and establish access to the burgeoning Asian markets. Production NOAs now span the globe and cover all industries, and are complemented by supply and distribution NOAs. NOAs include small and large firms of all colours that can contribute to the aggregated sums of value generated by the constituent NOAs in supply, production and delivery of the highest possible quality products and services throughout the value-chain.

If one can abstract from reasons for use of NOAs in order to construct a taxonomy, four prominent characteristics – the nature of power relations and the locus of control, the form of structure, the nature of the mission and the ultimate degree of formality – can be used to delineate several archetypes (see Figure 6.1).

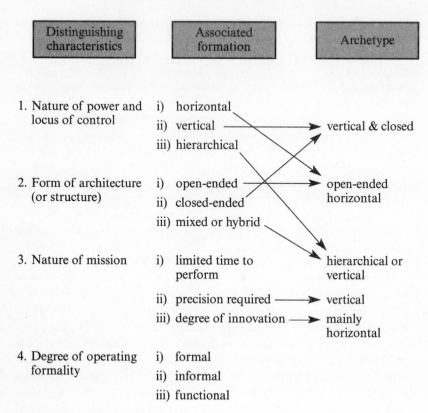

Figure 6.1   NOA archetypes

The Nature of Power Relations and the Locus of Control

Power relations and shifts in the locus of control can best be characterized by horizontal, vertical and hierarchical configurations.

Horizontal

This is a type of NOA configuration formed by *similar* firms' desire to expand their reach beyond current limits without any power trade-off. Member firms are attracted to each other through a horizontal arrangement when subjugation is remote or adequate safeguards are in place to avoid a shift in the locus of control from one member to another. In general, member firms have similar power structures, resources and capabilities, but are focused differently. They contemplate joining or forming an NOA to take advantage of benefits from synergies, expanded scales and better coordination at very low to no marginal cost. The relationships within NOAs are not based on power distance (vertical) or one-way dependence, but on lateral movements and mutual interdependence. It is not necessary for the partners to be linked and hence no power struggle is foreseen. Cross-licensing, co-production and cross-agreements for distribution in regions or fields which a particular firm had not contemplated before are typical. All partners benefit from such alliances or networks without much cost. Most justifications for such formations are smaller to those for horizontal integration, and the quest for power and dominance is not among these reasons.

Vertical
A sense of dependency is at the root of vertical configurations and some control is exercised by a member over others. A relationship between a part supplier and an assembler (or manufacturer) is viewed as a more vertical than horizontal relationship, because of the dependence. Although mutual dependence for survival is at the root of all NOA configurations, some shifts in the locus of power and control occur due to the dependencies involved. In the coalition of supplier(s)–manufacturer–distributor(s), there is an implied locus and direction of power. The manufacturer has traditionally exercised stronger power – everything being the same – than others in the coalition. But the traditional direction of power seems to be shifting away from the manufacturer, as suppliers and distributors are allying themselves differently.

Hierarchical configurations
These are complex constellations of NOAs which have developed to accomplish different objectives, and hence include horizontal and vertical NOAs within them. Most older and functional groupings are of this kind. Due to the reasons discussed in Parts I and II, the locus of power is actually moving towards the periphery from the centre (Bloom, 1992). Most coalitions in the past have been based on a very loose relationship, resembling voluntary organizations. This relationship seems to be evolving towards shared or common visions, more formal agreements and understandings, higher controls for better coordinations, and shared or common information systems, to offer the entire coalition a higher sense of purpose (and better chance of success) against similarly minded groupings.

The Form of Structure

The form of structure impacts the architecture of an NOA almost independently of its power relationships. For example, all of the above configurations could be open-ended, closed or mixed. The open-ended configuration is the most flexible and, regardless of its original nucleus, is bound to evolve into a hierarchical one with some vertical (or functional) concentrations. An open-ended structure does not bar members from joining others; while close-ended structures impose certain restrictions. In closed structures, for example, all members are theoretically required to consent to possible changes of configuration, policy, mission and so on, while the open structure does not have many such limitations. An open-ended and hierarchical structure could flexibly expand its functionally oriented NOAs to include many resources and activities.

Nature of the Mission

The length of time in which partners have been involved in an NOA and the character of their objectives suggest another dimension: the nature of their mission. Consider project-based alliances of partners for construction ventures. The main characteristic of such alliances or consortia is commitment to a set of objectives within certain constraints and in a given time. As a result the project influences everything else: when an open structure serves the purpose that is adopted; when there is a strong need for coordination and control, a project management company is designated to exercise the necessary controls for the duration, and hence it may adopt a vertical profile. Practically all large firms (for example, in construction, consulting and engineering, especially those based in Japan and Korea) find it necessary to form quickly a structure to suit the project. This requires a large degree of flexibility before and during the project which only NOAs can accommodate. The so-called flagship companies with their constellations of NOAs call on participating members to adopt a configuration adapted to the task, based on past experience. Large hydroelectric projects and petrochemical complexes around the world are managed successfully by South Koreans using a hierarchical and open structure. Japanese have used their traditional *keiretsu* structure to produce automobile assemblies, iron and steel mills and petrochemical complexes, usually led by a *keiretsu* flagship member.

Technologically oriented alliances may adopt a loose, flat and professional structure (that is, horizontal) early on in order to create certain innovations, and then shift to another more structured one for implementation, production and distribution. The alliance for resolving technical problems associated with the new generation of RISC chips by IBM, Motorola, Apple and others initially adopted such open and task-oriented structures, but their future arrangements remain to be seen.

The Degree of Formality

Another distinction commonly used for classifying production NOAs is their degree of formality. It appears that the degree of formality is influenced by power relationships (that is, the first dimension) and is formalized by the structure (that is, the second dimension). The various degrees of formality may also result from other dimensions, determined in response to some prior considerations. The horizontal network structure is more likely to be loose and informal, while the vertical ones are bound to adopt more formality, within more rigid structures.

Structurally, production NOAs, within the broader field of NOAs, can be classified in a taxonomy characterized by the first three dimensions specified above.[22] These dimensions, each with two polar extremes, give rise to eight (that is, $2 \times 2 \times 2$) distinct theoretical categories, which can also be combined to various extents to create many more hybrid ones. But not all these types are observable or can be empirically distinguished.

PART IV: TOWARDS A THEORETICAL EXPLANATION OF NOAS

A theoretical attempt to portray NOAs as a distinctively different class of organizational arrangements and as instruments of conducting business cross-functionally or internationally, must look into the changes in the broader environment. The explosive frequency of their appearances in recent years across industry and country boundaries is the consequence of new forces. These have impacted the policy environment, accelerated the technological race and transformed the economies of supply–manufacturing–distribution. As outlined schematically in Figure 6.2, several processes have systematically caused a dynamic cascade of subsidiary change.

Time pressure seems to be a prominent force. Falling market barriers have necessitated prompt action to protect one's own as well as other future potential markets. Market opportunities cannot be left unattended for long, as other competitors would eventually exploit them to gain immediate scale, first-mover and other locally derived advantages, and raise higher entry barriers. To minimize insurmountable future troubles, and to cope with constrained resources, NOAs for sharing, delegation and extension have served as appropriate options.

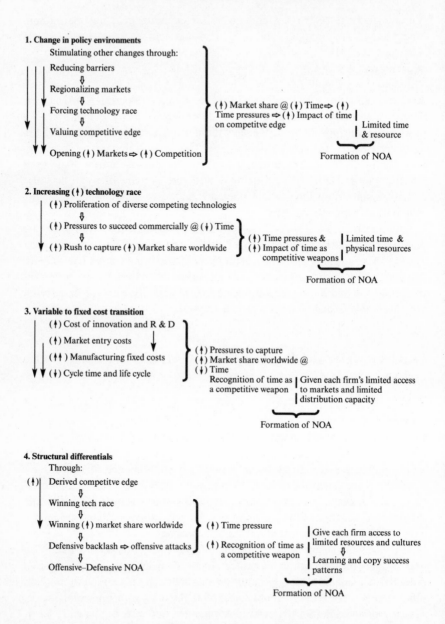

Figure 6.2   Brief schematic of change dynamics leading to increased formation of NOAs

Time appears to be the dominant factor in the escalating technological race. Participants are forced to pool resources and share expertise and proprietary assets, including some of their own technologies, to ensure higher chances of success. In the fixed cost transformation, time applies tremendous pressure to switch to highly efficient modes of operation and amortize costs rapidly to protect against technological obsolescence. This has been a major force pushing manufacturers to all corners of the world for additional market shares, using NOAs.

The second prominent underlying mechanism of change appears to be a quest for competitive advantage, for assured survival. In the face of high risk and uncertainty, this intense struggle for survival with constrained resources serves as a major driving force in the formation of NOAs. For those who have developed some competitive advantage already, keeping or increasing it in the face of constrained resources, shrinking time, and escalating risk and uncertainties is always a fight to stay ahead. For others facing disadvantages and similarly handicapped by operating constraints, the rising competitiveness of others causes an intense struggle for survival. Sharing, coordinating, borrowing, learning and, more importantly, relying on others' comparative advantage, in the face of adversity, is sound logic.

Structural differentials can thus be viewed as a set of inherent advantages that East Asian societies had accumulated. Gaining access to such advantages, however limited, appears to be worth its associated price – a trade-off between one giving up a part of one's own advantage in order to learn about, emulate and operate likewise; and hence the high incidence of NOAs between North American, European and East Asian firms. These alliances can be expected to form along the value-chain anywhere from supply, procurement and co-production to co-marketing and co-distribution. For the chain to deliver maximum load with maximum strength, and deflect competitive damage from others, all parts have to be strong in the face of all operating adversities and constraints.

For those disadvantaged on one dimension, NOAs offer other advantages. Outsourcing and subcontracting to minimize costs (for those in the West) and co-marketing and co-distribution (for those in the East) are logical choices. This explains why a world-class manufacturer in the US or Europe is outsourcing and co-distributing through NOA(s) in Asia and at the same time co-marketing and co-distributing Asian products in Europe and North America.

In the final analysis, the forces of change have gradually deprived market participants of some of their previous advantages (for example, time, technological edge, size and so on) which allowed them to decide their course of growth and evolution independently. Reliance on others for their contribution to mutual survival has become the dictate of time; hence the high prevalence of NOAs everywhere along the value-chain, especially around production (where most value is created). These are shown schematically in Figure 6.2. Finally, all indications point to a further expansion of intertwined NOAs everywhere, especially around production. In the case of services, NOAs may turn out to be the dominating organizations of the future.

NOTES

1. It should not therefore be difficult to see why the West had felt righteous in defining and then advocating a general and loose system of international law, order and institutions without specifying and developing a rigid framework for the particulars of *fair* conduct in international transactions. It is precisely this latter lack of a micro framework which has allowed the rise and support of certain national practices (for example, structural differentials).

2. Little (1987) reports that 40 per cent of Japanese imports to the US are intrafirm purchases and hence somewhat shielded from the Japan–US hostile trade environment. Harbrecht's (1994) figure for Japanese imports, 'bought by the US affiliates of Japanese MNCs', is about 80 per cent. US sanctions and policies have proven ineffective against large Japanese complexes.

3. While the West as a whole had prevailed in defining the general rules of the game (the macro framework), some of the Asian nations have found corporate cultures and coordinated industrial structures better attuned for winning the game of international trade and investment (at the micro level).

4. Except for those instances where a clear distinction is necessary, this chapter treats network and alliances similarly.

5. The critical point concerning discontinuities is that a cross-sectional observation of any given arrangement may not fully portray the whole picture; it may have been based on a previous arrangement, or yet lead to another complementary or evolving arrangement – each bridging certain discontinuities or gaps at the time. A longer-range perspective is at times more illuminating or necessary.

6. The environment of telecommunications has traditionally been regulated and wide regulatory gaps exist in different regions and countries. This topic will therefore be revisited when examples of telecommunications industry are discussed.

7. In the emerging competitive–cooperative environment, in order to join or service large cooperative alliances or networks, a firm must achieve a certain size of its own for obvious economic advantages and competitive bargaining power. Weiss (1993) reports on one such telecommunications firm's (Ameritech) effort to set up a large network of its own alliance to command multiple technologies, have access to many suppliers and control a large network. Ameritech is cooperatively competing in the hope that it can expand its geographical reach and range of services in the full audio-video range of radio-telephone-satellite-based information technology of the future.

8. Gandy reports a wide range of services, not previously available. He observes that they will have to be provided by numerous alliances, mergers, acquisitions and networks of European and non-European firms. The European Commission is expected to come down with pan-European policies similar to the HDTV one before the industry assumes its shape and character (Gandy, 1993).

9. The current telecommunications industry is likely to evolve into the emerging 'information highway' industry. For more details on the information industry formation process, see Part III (especially sections on the offensive–defensive actions of telecommunications firms).

10. As indicated earlier, only the particular detailed condition of each case can give the full picture and bring out ancillary details.
11. 'Globally localized' is a term, coined by the Chairman of the Sony Corporation, which refers to localized fragmentation in otherwise global markets. This allows world-class producers with scope economies to produce tailor-made products (for fragmented markets) at scale economies.
12. Bristol Myers-Squibb and Elf Sanofi, after some protracted courtship, have recently decided to engage in joint development, clinical testing, co-production and co-marketing of a family of pharmaceuticals (see Back and Jackson (1993) for more details).
13. *Keiretsus* and *chabeols* have their own constellation of small and medium sized suppliers and parts manufacturers. They should therefore be viewed as networks and alliances of a large number of SMEs and large firms with cross-directors and equity holdings.
14. The inner workings of Japanese *keiretsu* (or Korean *chabeols*) and *sogoshosha* are of immense interest to alliances and networks. But their cultural specificity, coupled with their complexities, puts them beyond the scope of this chapter. These organizations establish a wider global network with other multinationals. Samsung and Lucky-Goldstar still sell over 50 per cent of their production under the brand names of large customers (Bloom, 1992).
15. This is an integral part and a tangible manifestation of structural differentials presented in Part I of this chapter.
16. Driza-Bone, a Queensland (Australia)-based wet clothing company changed its approach to manufacturing and distribution in the early 1990s. Reportedly, Driza-Bone began to treat manufactured goods and their distribution worldwide as a service industry in need of a strong distribution pipeline. Driza-Bone consequently adopted a just-in-time philosophy and began to deliver orders nationwide in Australia overnight, fortnightly to the US and weekly to other markets in Europe and Asia.
17. This distinction could be used to distinguish between strategic NOAs and others. When an NOA is not playing a strategic role, the necessity of centralized decisions are reduced; and hence NOAs can be formed by decentralized units as they see fit.
18. Should this be a false reading of the intended signals, a regulatory redirection would be prohibitively costly and disruptive for US concerns; while Asian and some Europeans (Germany to some extent) have been encouraged. Their companies are less likely to change just because of US desires. The above is especially the case in the emerging 'information highway' industry.
19. The Canadian giant, Roger's telecommunications takeover of McLean Hunter, a publishing and TV and cable company, is presented to CRTC as 'necessary' for survival in the emerging industry.
20. The real salvation seems to come from the rapidity and the speed with which certain events have taken place. There is the hope that the US regulatory bureaucracy and its counterparts elsewhere are caught off guard; and by the time the bureaucracy truly catches up to the reality, the level of change will be too massive and complex to be redirected.
21. Ayerst's purchase of Sterling Drugs from Kodak also supports the offensive–defensive strategic framework at work. Although Sterling manufactures and distributes popular over-the-counter pharmaceuticals such as Bayer Aspirin, it was too small to compete effectively in spite of its large distribution network. Ayerst and Sterling combined have formed an alliance which even major world-scale pharmaceuticals companies must contend with.
22. Upon closer examination, well beyond the scope of this chapter, it turns out that the first three dimensions can account for most variations in the degree of formality. This suggests that the degree of formality is not an independent dimension. Conversely, one may be able to combine any of the *three* dimensions to capture the variance of the fourth dimension (omitted). For this reason, this chapter will concentrate on the first *three* dimensions.

BIBLIOGRAPHY

'Air Frame Makers Weigh Benefits of Expanded Coproduction', *Aviation Week and Space Technology*, **128** (11), 14 March 1988, 183–9.

Andren, Emily (1994), 'Standards Empower Distribution Network', *Transportation and Distribution*, **35** (3), March, 76.

Armistead, Collin and John Mapes (1993), 'The Impact of Supply Chain Integration on Operating Performance', *Logistics Information Management*, **6** (4), 9–14.

'ATR May Locate Assembly Line in China', *Aviation Week and Space Technology*, **140** (8), 21 February 1994, 83.

Back, Rolf and Debbie Jackson (1993), 'Elf Sanofi and Bristol-Myers Squibb Form Drug Pact', *Chemical Week*, **152** (22), 9 January, 19.

Bloom, Martin (1992), 'Technological Change in Korean Electronics', *OECD Observer*, No. 175, April/May, 32–4.

Bond, David (1990), 'Korea Picks F/A-18 for Coproduction, Cites Capabilities, Industry Benefits', *Aviation Week and Space Technology*, **132** (1), 1 January, 34–5.

Borrmann, Axel and Rolf Jungnickel (1992), 'Foreign Investment as a Factor in Asian Pacific Integration', *Inter Economic*, **27** (6), November/December, 282–8.

Bress, Marcia (1994), 'Mack Malaise', *Forbes*, **153** (8), 11 April, 73.

Burns, Christine (1994), 'Corporations Align Enterprise Networks with Competitive Edge', *Network World*, **11** (6), 7 February.

Chan, Peng Si and Dorothy Heide (1993), 'Strategic Alliances in Technology: Key Competitive Weapon', *SAM Advanced Management Journal*, **58** (4), Autumn, 9–17.

Chapman, Paul T. (1992), 'Flexible Deployment: Making Decisions that Optimize Service and Costs', *Journal of Business Strategy*, **13** (4), July/August, 59–64.

Cook, Brian M. (1990), 'Flexible Manufacturing: Something that People Do', *Industry Week*, **239** (21), November, 36–43.

Cottril, Ken (1993), 'Transnational Building Global Production Lines', *Cash Management News*, No. 93, October, 10–12.

Cunningham, Malcolm and David Ford (1993), 'Technology Networks and Purchasing Strategy', *Advanced International Marketing*, **5**, 205–19.

Dangerfield, Nick (1992), 'Just in Time for the Office', *Accountant's Journal*, **71** (61), July, 43–4.

Del Nibletto, Paolo (1992), 'Competition Makes Strange Bedfellows', *Info. Canada*, **17** (11), November, 9, 36.

Dornheim, Michael A. (1994), 'Industry Grapples with Low Deliveries', *Aviation Week and Space Technology*, **140** (5), January, 40–41.

Dubois, Frank L., Brian Toyne and Michael D. Oliff (1993), 'International Manufacturing Strategies of US Multinationals: A Conceptual Framework Based on a Four Industry Study', *Journal of International Business Studies*, **24** (2), 2nd Quarter, 307–33.

Eckerson, Wayne and Bob Wallace (1991), 'Open System Executives Dispel Industry Myth', *Network World*, **8** (33), 19 August, 4, 64.

Farr, C. Michael and William A. Fischer (1992), 'Managing International High Technology Cooperative Projects', *R&D Management*, **22** (1), January, 55–67.

Fawcett, Stanley (1992), 'Transportation Characteristics and Performance Maquilodora Operations', *Transportation Journal*, **31** (4), Summer, 5–16.

'Fine Tuning's the Difference in Making TQM Work', *Managing Office Technology*, **38** (10), October 1993, 35–6.

Fitzgerald, Michael and James Daly (1993), 'PC Factions Re-Arming', *Computer World,* **27** (16), 19 April, C.16.

Friedland, Jonathan and Charles Smith (1994), 'Japan: Producing Value for the Money', *Far Eastern Economic Review,* **157** (1), 30 December – 6 January, 50–51.

Gadde, Lars-Erik (1993), 'Evolution Process in Distribution Networks', *Advances in International Marketing,* **5**, 43–66.

Gandy, Tony (1993), 'Product File', *The Banker Journal,* **143** (809), July.

Gilbert, Nathaniel (1991), 'Strategic Alliance Spur Small Business R&D', *Financier,* **15** (6), June, 18–21.

Gladkowski, Chester (1993), 'APT – Another Profit Taker', *Rough Notes,* **136** (11), November, 42–5.

Glasmeier, Amy (1991), 'Technological Discontinuities and Flexible Production Networks: The Case of Switzerland and The World Watch Industry', *Research Policy,* **20** (5), October, 469–85.

Golich, Vicki L. (1992), 'From Competitive to Cooperation: The Challenge of Commercial Class Aircraft Manufacturing', *International Organization,* **46** (4), Autumn, 899–934.

Gunter, Toddi (1993), 'Dinosaur', *Super Food Services Inc.,* **151** (4), 15 February, 156–8.

Hackney, Holt (1994), 'Strategic Alliances', *Financial World,* **160** (22), 29 October, 20–22.

Hagedoorn, John and Jos Schakenraad (1993), 'R&D Partnership in the European Information Technology Industry', *Journal of Common Market Studies,* **31** (31), September, 373–90.

Hamill, Jim (1992), 'Employment Effects of Changing Multinational Strategies in Europe', *European Management Journal,* **10** (3), September, 334–40.

Harbrecht, Douglas (1994), 'The Secret Weapon that Won't Start a Trade War', *Business Week,* No. 3361, 7 March, 45.

Harrison, Bennett (1994), 'The Dark Side of Flexible Production', *Technology Review,* **97**, May/June, 38–45.

'High-Value Parts Draw Interest in Bank', *Transportation & Distribution Journal,* **35** (1), January 1994, 62.

Hitomi, Katsundo (1993), 'Manufacturing Technology in Japan', *Journal of Manufacturing System,* **12** (3), 209–15.

Hitomi, Katsundo (1991), 'Strategic Integrated Manufacturing System: The Concept of Structure', *International Journal of Production Economics,* **25** (1–3), December, 5–12.

Hofheinz, Paul (1994), 'You Can Win in Eastern Europe', *Fortune,* **129** (10), 16 May, 110–12.

Keefe, Patricia (1991), 'Users Gain Possible in IBM/Lotus Deal', *Computer World,* **25** (27), 8 July, 37, 43.

Kuratko, Donald F. and Frank Sabatine (1989), 'From Incubator to Incubation', *Economic Development Review,* **7** (4), Fall, 42–5.

Larson, Paul (1994), 'Venture Capital, Montana Style', *Montana Business Quarterly,* **31** (4), Winter, 18–22.

Levine, Jonathan B. (1992), 'HDTV: Europe May Already be an Also-Ran', *Business Week,* No. 3247, 13 January, 46.

Little, Jane Sneddon (1987), 'Intra-Firm Trade: An Update', *New England Economic Review,* May/June, 56–61.

Magee, John F. (1992), 'Strategic Alliances: Overcoming Barriers to Success', *Chief Executive*, No. 81, November/December, 56–61.

Malincoe, Alan H. (1992), 'These Alliances Aren't Forever', *Computer World*, **26** (9), 2 March, 33.

Mason, Charles F. (1992), 'Cellular Carriers Join Hand for Wireless Data Standard', *Telephony*, **222** (17), 27 April.

Mayere, Anne and François Vinot (1993), 'Firm Structures and Production Networks in Intellectual Services', *Service Industries Journal*, **13** (2), April, 76–90.

Morrocco, John D. (1989), 'Korean Air Negotiates Agreement to Coproduce Sikorsky Att-60', *Aviation Week and Space Technology*, **130** (24), 12 January, 225–7.

Musich, Paula (1988), 'GM Canada to Build MAP 3.0 Net on Fiber', *Network World*, **4** (51), 4 January, 3.

O'Leary, Mick (1993), 'TINS Boots Texas High Tech. Transitions', *Information Today*, **10** (3), March, 11–12.

Olesen, Douglas E. (1993), 'The Future of Industrial Technology', *Industry Week*, **242** (24), 20 December, 50–52.

Ophisanwo, A.O. and P.P. Dasiewicz (1987), 'MAPPS: A VLSI Multiprocessor for the Execution of Production System Programs', *Microprocessing and Microprogramming*, **21** (1–5), August, 251–8.

Pastin, Mark and Jeffrey Harrison (1987), 'Social Responsibility', *Society Review*, (63), Fall, 54–8.

Pesmen, Sandra (1993), 'Time Warner Seeks Driver for Electronic Super Highway', *Business Marketing*, **78** (3), March, 13.

Peterson, Robin T. (1993), 'Speed is Important in New Product Introduction', *Marketing News*, **27** (5), 7 March, 4.

Pinnington, Ashly (1992), 'Managing Technology Partnership', *Journal of General Management*, **17** (3), Spring, 46–55.

Richman, Tom (1988), 'Make Love not War', *INC*, **10** (8), August.

Robins, Gary (1994), 'Less Work, More Speed', *Stores*, **76** (3), March 24–6.

'Roche to Create Fourth Largest Drug Co', *Corporate Growth Reports*, No. 793, 9 May 1994, 7231–42.

Rosenthal, Thomas M. (1989), 'McDonnell Douglas in China', *Journal of Global Trade*, **109** (2), February, 22–4.

Ross, Madelyn (1987), 'Foreign Trade Offensive', *China Business Review*, **14** (4), July/August, 30–35.

Rugman, Alan M. and Alain Verbeke (1992), 'The Transnational Solution and the Transaction Cost Theory of Multinational Strategic Management', *Journal of International Business Studies*, **23** (4), 4th Quarter, 761–71.

Sasseen, Jane (1993), 'Seoul Traders', *Journal of International Management*, **48** (7), September, 42–3.

Saxenian, Ann Lee (1991), 'The Origin and Dynamics of Production Networks in Silicon Valley', *Research Policy*, **20** (5), October, 423–37.

Schnerken, Ivy (1991), 'O'Connor Lifts the Cover', *Wall Street Computer Review*, **9** (1), October, 34–6.

Schroath, Frederick W., Michael Y. Wu and Haiyan Chen (1993), 'Country of Origin Effects of Foreign Investment in the People's Republic of China', *Journal of International Business Studies*, **24** (2), 2nd Quarter, 277–90.

Sentinery, Robert (1994), 'Build a Network of Small Distributors', *Folio*, **23** (7), 15 April, 86.

Smith, Bruce (1994), 'Trunkliner Production Signals New Phase for Douglas China', *Aviation Week and Space Technology*, **140** (8), 21 February, 62–7.

Solonitskii, A.S. (1993), 'Possible Aspects of Comparing USSR and Its Successor States with Third World Countries', *Problems of Economic Transition*, **36** (1), May, 6–18.

Spangler, Todd (1993), 'Alliance Dominate Marketing Race on the Information Highway', *Business Marketing*, **78** (7), July, 8.

Stone, Eric (1992), 'Tricks of Japan Trade', *Asian Business*, **28** (2), February, 20–25.

St-Pierre, Antoine (1993), 'Forging Links in the Information Age: An Interview with Jocelyne Cote-O'Hare', *Canadian Business*, **20** (4), Winter, 6–13.

Sylla, Cheickna and Bay Arinze (1991), 'A Method for Quality Precoordination in Quality Assurance Information System', *IEEE Transactions on Engineering Management*, **38** (3), August, 245–59.

Teece, David (1992), 'Competition, Cooperation and Innovation: Organizational Arrangements for Revive of Rapid Technological Progress', **18** (1), June, 1–25.

'UN Report: MNCs are Key to Growth of World Economy', *Crossborder Monitor*, **1** (19), 18 August 1993, 1.

Van Oldenborgh, Marita (1993), 'Argentina's Draw', *International Business*, **6** (5), May, 65–8.

Weiss, William (1993), 'LEC Courts Consumers with Bold Moves', *Telephone Engineer and Management*, **97** (8), 5 April, 41–2.

Willis, Rod (1991), 'An R&D Success Story', *Financier*, **15** (6), June, 28–30.

Witt, Jerome and C.P. Rao (1992), 'The Impact of Global Sourcing on Consumers: Country of Origin Effects on Perceived Risk', *Journal of Global Marketing*, **6**, 105–28.

Wolf, Michael (1994), 'Building Trust in Alliances', *Research-Technology Management*, **37** (3), May/June, 12–15.

7. Competitive and cooperative macromanagement

Gavin Boyd and Peter J. Buckley

Macromanagement refers not just to macroeconomic policies but to the implementation of an entire policy mix in the governance of a national political economy. It conveys a sense of the range and complexity of technocratic functions which have become necessary in conditions of high structural interdependence. These functions involve advisory, regulatory, supportive and infrastructure activities through which governments assist the commerce of national and foreign firms, to promote growth and employment with financial stability. Such commerce is assuming very large dimensions, with flows of goods, services and capital, and – as the foreign operations of firms become more regional and global – the scale of national technocratic functions has to expand. Much of this expansion remains at the national level, but some regional forms of economic cooperation are developing. The most advanced of these is the European Union, a system of *regional macromanagement*. Ranking next, at a lower level of regional economic integration, is the North America Free Trade Area (NAFTA).

Macromanagement is generally considered to be primarily competitive: governments become identified with the efforts of their firms to gain larger shares of world markets, and rivalry over such market shares is developing between the European Union and NAFTA. All the competition, however, is facilitated by various forms of cooperation, primarily to ensure manageable degrees of market openness and to assist transactions. Diverse combinations of competitive and cooperative activity are evident, and they raise questions about efficiency, equity, and systemic development, at the national, regional and global level. Competition gives impetus to performance but can be wasteful and destructive unless restrained by goodwill and trust. Cooperation can amount to collusion but, if highly motivated, can result in complementary growth at levels that would not otherwise be possible; cooperative macromanagement can be very actively entrepreneurial, giving impetus to achievement by the managements of firms, through information-sharing, guidance and solidarity-building.

The interaction of macromanagement endeavours that are in varying degrees competitive and cooperative affects the evolution of national economic structures, regional systems and the world economy. States influence each other's policy mixes, sometimes through demonstration and first-mover effects, as well as through bargaining, while also influencing the activities of firms which are shaping national economies and their structural interdependencies. In this vast multifunctional process labour markets remain mostly national, but markets for goods and services become mainly regional, while capital markets become global. The most active agents of change and development are multinational enterprises, which are acquiring wider scope for independent decision-making as they secure assets, produce, set prices, make alliances, set up entry barriers, develop new technologies and drive weaker firms into declines.

There is much complementarity and conflict between the strategies of multinationals and the policies of governments. Managements striving for larger market shares comes into conflict with, but can also benefit from, anti-monopoly, price control and environmental measures, as well as minimum wage legislation and expansions or contractions of state sectors. For governments, multinationals can increase growth, raise employment, earn foreign exchange, contribute to technological advances and provide additional revenue. All this tends to be increasingly significant as governments cooperate and compete in regional contexts and endeavour to cope with trends in global capital markets.

Figure 7.1 depicts the interrelated levels of government and multinational activity in the world economy. The patterns of regional economic integration are assuming more and more significance as their forms of intrazonal market separation diminish, allowing freer movement of goods and factors of production. As a system of regional collective management develops in Europe it, moreover, becomes a challenge for the development of increased economic cooperation in NAFTA, and for the promotion of trade and investment liberalization in the Asia Pacific area. The integration of capital markets on a global scale, however, which has gone very far, has reduced governmental capacities to implement regional expansionary or contractionary policies through changes in interest rates: individuals and firms can move funds across the exchanges. Nevertheless, states with very responsive domestic financial sectors are able to retain considerable economic sovereignty, with resultant advantages in contests for regional markets.

The economic sovereignty of most states is constantly affected by volatility in world capital markets, which persists because of failures to cooperate for the introduction of comprehensive international regulatory measures. Meanwhile, even routine capital mobility, affecting regionalized product markets and their transregional linking, makes macromanagement difficult. Fiscal,

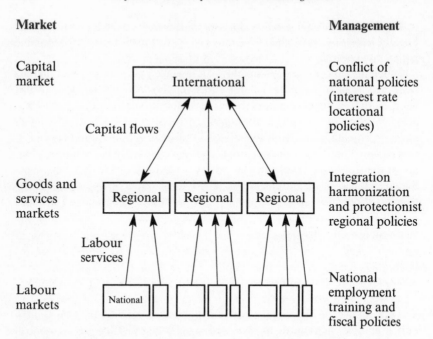

Market   **Management**

Capital market — International — Conflict of national policies (interest rate locational policies)

Capital flows

Goods and services markets — Regional / Regional / Regional — Integration harmonization and protectionist regional policies

Labour services

Labour markets — National — National employment training and fiscal policies

Figure 7.1   Internationalization of firms – conflict of markets

social and employment policies cannot be managed independently: effective macromanagement requires cooperation by other governments and by multinationals. Problems which hinder the evolution of both types of cooperation are causing a 'crisis of management'. The activities of multinationals are especially significant in this context because of the increasing degrees to which they are affecting the spread of gains from trade between the national economies whose structures they are shaping. For governments, accordingly, the implementation of 'national' industrial policies thus tends to become predicated on the cooperation of multinationals, which is not always received. Yet through political action multinationals contribute to the removal of barriers to trade and investment, thus in effect enhancing their scope for independent implementation of their strategies.

While governments have to operate in contexts which limit their economic independence, they endeavour to regulate labour markets and implement preferred fiscal and monetary policies. To the extent that competition results at the policy level the gainers tend to be multinational firms: they benefit from investment-bidding rivalry between governments which results in cheap loans, subsidies and tax concessions. They can also benefit from competition in social policies as governments use these to ensure lower production costs that will attract foreign direct investment. Britain's decision not to join in the Social Chapter of the Maastricht Treaty has been seen as an example of social policy competition.

Cooperation between governments would make policy harmonization possible and reduce opportunities for firms to play off one country against another. In a common market labour costs, social overhead costs and taxes affect location advantages, and accordingly the common interests of member states in sharing gains from liberalized intrazonal trade require harmonization of social policies. This need not discourage externally based multinationals, as the size of a common market would have considerable drawing power. Social policies in the European Union are, however, contributing to escalations of production costs relative to those in North America, and are thus posing a difficult problem of collective management, with intrazonal and transregional dimensions.

MACROMANAGEMENT IN A GLOBALIZING ECONOMY

The macromanagement endeavours of governments are becoming more difficult over time, as failures to cooperative sufficiently at the policy level in effect leave the way open for the development of strong international production and distribution structures by multinational enterprises that limit regulatory exposure and acquire substantial bargaining resources. The large-scale manufacturing, commercial and financial operations of these firms have strategic significance because they tend to dominate higher technology sectors and assume dimensions that reduce the contestability of national markets for domestic firms. With the reductions in national macromanagement *capacities* there are virtual shifts of macromanagement *functions*.[1] The capabilities of individual multinational enterprises, meanwhile, are being augmented by strategic alliances for market- and technology-sharing.[2] Some national clusters of these enterprises, moreover, in effect collectively enhance their firm-specific advantages through relational ties in industry groups, with benefits in terms of risk-sharing and sustained entrepreneurial cooperation.[3]

National macromanagement can assume strong external salience if clusters of relationally linked firms have close bonds with their national administrations.[4] Economic policy instruments have weaker external effects if a government deals at arm's length with its national enterprises. They also have weaker effects if there are conflicts between those instruments, and if on the whole they give those national enterprises incentives to move industrial capacity abroad, source products from foreign locations, and reduce home country tax exposure.

COMPETITIVENESS

Figure 7.2 shows a model of international competitiveness which includes three key elements: performance, potential and (management) process.[5]

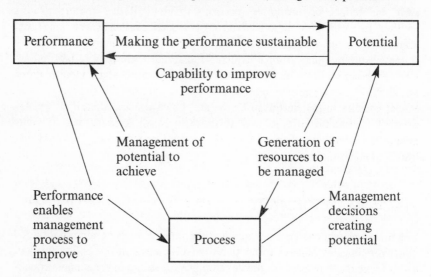

Figure 7.2   Aspects of competitiveness

It depicts competitiveness not as a state but as a *process*, resulting from the interaction in the model. As an analytical scheme it is applicable at the firm level as well as the national level. There are possibilities for 'virtuous circles' in which good performance leads to the investment of resources in future potential (training, R&D and so on) and efficient management leads to improved performance. There can also be 'vicious circles' in which declining performance, badly managed, leads to inadequate investment in future potential.

Several important issues emerge. Competitiveness is a wider concept than efficiency. Efficiency is the optimum allocation of resources to achieve desired objectives. Competitiveness results from the choice of the most important objectives, and includes both efficiency (reaching goals with optimum use of resources) and effectiveness (having the right goals). Competitiveness is, however, relative, as it can refer to sequences over time, differing economic contexts, or some counterfactual situation which would have existed if some action had not been taken.

The utility of the scheme for study of the competitiveness of an enterprise is straightforward, as the typical firm is a substantially unified actor, although it may be affected by organizational manipulation. An international firm will, however, be competitive, in different degrees, within the areas of its regional and global operations, in which it may encounter varying challenges and may resort to discriminatory pricing. It may increase its competitiveness across those areas at some cost to the competitiveness of its home economy, for example through relocations of industrial capacity that disrupt sectors in that economy.

For the study of national competitiveness the scheme has to be used with some understanding of the dynamics of policy-making, which can be affected by problems of governance as well as by the consequences of losses of economic sovereignty to multinational enterprises. Government performance can be hindered by unresolved conflicts within and between policy communities, and the intended results of economic policies can be prevented by the declines of domestic firms under pressure from transnational enterprises with superior competitiveness.

The competitiveness of the entire organization of an international firm, reflected in Figure 7.3, while varying within the markets which it links, can become an increasing problem for its home government because intensifying challenges in those markets tend to force single-minded concentration on

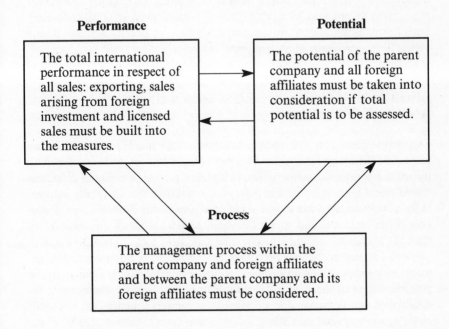

Figure 7.3   Measuring competitiveness in a global market-place

struggles to maximize global performance. This concentration weakens managerial home country attachments, and successes in global markets, it must be reiterated, provide resources for deployment in widening ranges of strategic options. Meanwhile, the identity of an international firm can change, through cross-holdings and the development of enduring links through corporate alliances,[6] or through acquisition by a foreign enterprise. Industrial policy choices can thus become complicated for each national administration as the home government of international firms with uncertain future affiliations. Where international enterprises have stable identities and home country ties, however (as in Japan), industrial policy choices involve fewer hazards.

In states whose international firms retain home country social and political bonds, the national character of labour markets can pose relatively manageable policy problems, unless there are rigidities that lower X efficiency and occasion high overhead costs which discourage entrepreneurial innovation. Where firms lose home country ties as they move into international operations, however, the immobility of the national labour-force is a source of policy problems. Adjustment to the highly independent restructuring strategies of the international firms is difficult, and awareness that it will remain difficult tends to motivate concessions to those firms (on taxation and financing issues) in order to have a favourable influence on their restructuring. Such restructuring, it must be stressed, tends to be constantly associated with quests for larger shares of regional markets for goods.

REGIONAL ISSUES: THE EUROPEAN UNION, NAFTA AND THE PACIFIC

Corporate production and trading activities, with much restructuring, are increasing the integration of the European Single Market, as it expands with the inclusion of new members. The established pattern of regional collective management is ensuring further policy harmonization that facilitates increasingly comprehensive intrazonal trade and investment liberalization. European firms are intended to be the main beneficiaries of this venture in regional economic integration, but many of them lack competitiveness in rivalries for market shares with American and Japanese enterprises. Engagement with this regional macromanagement problem will evidently not be possible unless stronger institutions for European collective management are established. At the national level, macromanagement practices are not sufficiently concerted, and thus allow multinational firms to take advantage of the diverging preferences of member governments. The differences in policy preferences have sources which are expressed, with linkages, in several areas, including monetary and financial management, and thus relate to the structuring of a regional monetary authority. Such an authority would have to play an important role in the regulation of global capital markets.

The European Union encounters competition from NAFTA, which may extend into Central and South America. NAFTA is at an elementary level of regional integration, but the USA, its core member, is the economic equivalent of an integrated regional bloc, and is advantaged by strong bargaining power as well as a very large role in the world economy. Atlantic economic rivalry can be managed more effectively from the American side, because of collective decision-making problems in the European Union and the generally weaker competitiveness of its firms. Macromanagement issues are more difficult to resolve in the Union, because of major differences between the policy preferences of member states. In NAFTA there is no regional macromanagement, but the USA's dominant role ensures the resolution of issues in separate dealings with Canada and Mexico.

The formation of NAFTA has strengthened the USA's influence in the large Asia Pacific Economic Cooperation forum (APEC) which includes Japan, China and the industrializing market economy East Asian states, together with Australia and New Zealand. In this extensive region trade and investment liberalization is being promoted, mainly by the USA, and a modest regional consultative system is being established. The industrializing market economy East Asian states are, however, being linked by trade and investment more with Japan than with the USA, because of very active expansion by Japanese firms, and because Europe remains the principal focus of US corporate strategies. In the East Asian area of the region, *intrazonal* capital flows are potent sources of growth.[7] A Greater China economic system is being formed by rapidly growing commercial links between mainland China, Taiwan and Hong Kong. Because of the size and dynamism of this system it overshadows the Association of South East Asian Nations, a loose grouping which is slowly liberalizing trade between its members.

Asia Pacific regional macromanagement is not in prospect, for the present, because of the ethnic, cultural, economic and political diversity of the APEC members, and the vast distances across which interactions have to be managed. At the regional level, therefore, the main economic rivalry is that between NAFTA and the European Union, but the principal contests are between US and European firms for shares of the Single European Market. Japanese firms are entering into these contests, with the advantages of large resources gained through the penetration of the US market. The most demanding macromanagement challenges, then, are those confronting the European Union, and these concern especially the technological dimensions of competitiveness.[8]

GOVERNMENTS AND FIRMS

Commitments to intrazonal collective management are being maintained in Europe mainly in response to losses of competitiveness in the Union and in world markets.[9] Such commitments are not emerging in NAFTA because of its more hierarchical configuration, which allows the USA wide scope for initiative,[10] and in this setting there is emphasis on giving market forces very extensive freedom to shape economic structures. The resulting pattern of production and trade contrasts with a more patterned linking of East Asian economic structures which is dominated by a regional extension of the Japanese system of guided entrepreneurship.[11]

Uneven rivalry between the Japanese political economy and the liberal American system is evident across the Pacific and has occasioned much theoretical and policy literature dealing with problems of competitiveness and cooperation. Most of this literature is American and it deals with losses of competitiveness by US firms. American exporters are seen to be disadvantaged by close linkages between firms in Japanese industry groups, in violation of what are considered to be basic principles of competition policy. One strand of the literature argues that the US administration must resort to trade policy activism, especially by using pressure to open Japan's domestic market. Political problems hindering reduction of the US fiscal deficit[12] are factors in the rationale for the market-opening leverage.

Some of the literature advocates increased cooperation between US firms, for enhanced competitiveness in the rivalry with Japan.[13] Such cooperation could balance the advantages derived by Japanese firms from membership in their industry groups and would ease the tasks of competitive liberal macromanagement for the US administration. Emphasis on the need to strengthen US corporate competitiveness is very prominent in the literature, and tends to be persuasive partly because of warnings, in other areas of the literature, that sound domestic policies are basic requirements for effective involvement in the world economy and cannot be substituted for by ventures in international economic cooperation.[14] Trade liberalization is identified in much of the literature as the most important objective of international collaboration, but tends to be seen as more feasible for the USA in the regional context of North America and Central and South America, than in the Pacific.[15]

The evolution of competitive pressures and concentrations of economic power in Europe has not been significantly affected by US policy shifts induced by economic advice and internal pressures.[16] The main US policy initiatives have been attempts at market-opening leverage, directed principally against Japan, and these appear to have had only minor effects on the strategies of Japanese, US and European firms. The USA's choices of leverage have been limited by vulnerabilities associated with asymmetries in its structural interdependencies, worsened in some respects by its macro-management problems. Like other states, the USA has had to reckon with the retaliatory capacities of major trading partners. The interests of American states in attracting foreign direct investment, moreover (especially by Japanese firms), have necessitated restraint in economic diplomacy.[17]

In the literature on competitiveness in the Triad context, dealing mainly with the problems of US and European firms, considerable attention has been given to questions of government–business cooperation. Special interest has been shown in the efficiency effects of such cooperation in the rather highly integrated Japanese political economy. In Japan the policy environment for national firms is very supportive, as it is responsive to aggregated corporate interests, and contributes to the maintenance of a business culture which causes a blending of cooperative and competitive activities by firms. This is uniquely functional because of the impetus given to entrepreneurship by intense rivalries but also by solidarity that ensures risk-sharing.[18] The American policy environment is a sharp contrast, because of weaker responsiveness between a less functional policy mix and a less cohesive pattern of intercorporate relations.[19]

European policy environments are more conducive to government–business cooperation than those in the USA, but with efficiency effects weaker than those in Japan. There are complex national variations which are reflected in an uneven distribution of gains from liberalized commerce within the Union. The German policy environment, which has the broadest significance in the region, is very responsive to business interests, which are effectively aggregated to provide functional inputs into policy.[20] The French policy environment has evolved with less responsiveness between the administration and corporate managements, and these are less united by associational ties than those in Germany.[21]

Pressures for policy changes have been evident mainly in the USA, as has been noted, because of losses of international competitiveness, but advocacy of increased cooperation between US firms and between such firms and the US government has conflicted with the aggressive individualism of the national business culture. The record of attempts at government–business collaboration in the USA has evidenced much rent-seeking, as well as extensive incentive conflicts influencing the activities of government economic agencies and interested legislators.[22]

Imperatives to achieve greater corporate competitiveness without major policy changes are felt intensely in Europe, but the options for policy-makers and managements are very complex. The formation of the Single Market has given impetus to national efforts to achieve greater structural competitiveness, thus complicating and hindering the development of the Union system of collective management.[23] National interests tend to be given higher priority than Union interests, in a context in which Germany is consolidating a dominant regional market position. For firms based in other Union member countries there are incentives to develop bonds with US and other non-European enterprises, for more competitive intra-Union operations and for more active expansion outside the Union.[24]

LIBERAL MACROMANAGEMENT

Concepts of limited government, aloof from industry and commerce, are expressed in liberal policies intended to allow wide scope for market forces. In principle, liberal foreign economic policies are not competitive, and there is openness to cooperation with other liberally oriented governments. Leverage against neomercantilist administrations is, of course, considered necessary to protect vital interests and encourage shifts towards liberal policies.

Liberal macromanagement in the Triad pattern encounters several challenges. Other governments advantaged by close links with their business communities assist their firms with subsidies and discriminatory trade measures, while enterprises in states under liberal macromanagement generally have to operate without such assistance and must make investment decisions with much caution. Liberal macromanagement can be manipulated by corporate political action to secure shelter for domestic market positions and assistance for export promotion, but improved competitiveness often does not result because limited government tends to be an ineffective source of performance requirements. Decision-makers typically operate with little sense of responsibility for the functioning of the economy, because of expectations about the efficiency of free market forces.[25] Yet weak allocative control, in the face of broad representations of interests, tends to allow fiscal expansion to approach, if not exceed, sustainable limits, with negative effects on competitiveness more serious than those attributable to corporate extraction of administrative favours.

Liberal macromanagement became a well-established tradition in the USA after World War II because of confidence in the superior international competitiveness of American firms. Initial export successes were, however, reduced after the 1950s by German trade expansion, which was aided by membership of the European Community. Subsequently Japan began to make larger and more rapid gains in world markets. The German and Japanese export achievements were facilitated by very active collaboration between the exporting firms, and between those firms and their administrations. The tradition of limited government, however, remained strong in the USA, despite growing awareness of increasing German and Japanese competitiveness which could not be countered by liberal policies.[26]

The danger of fiscal laxity under liberal macromanagement became very evident during the 1980s as large budget deficits contributed increasingly to large trade deficits, through the effects on internal demand and through the effects of necessary monetary contraction on exchange rates. The organizational weaknesses of US political parties and business associations prevented the emergence of a sufficiently strong consensus for fiscal discipline. By the middle of the decade, however, administrative policy learning was forced by warnings from economists that international confidence in the appreciated dollar could drop sharply.[27] A depreciation was thus encouraged, with German and Japanese cooperation, and was facilitated by monetary loosening, but the fiscal deficits remained high.

Liberal macromanagement has become a highly interdependent process for the USA since the 1980s, because of considerable dependence on external financing of the fiscal deficits, the exposure of the dollar to speculative attacks in world financial markets,[28] the foreign trade effects of the fiscal deficits,[29] and growth problems, which were motivating quests for German and Japanese macroeconomic and commercial cooperation. The maintenance of stability in the US economy became more necessary to sustain international investor confidence as the risk of a financial crisis was evident, due to the accumulation of government debt and relatively high levels of speculation which had been weakening the financial sector.[30] In the unfavourable pattern of interdependence which was evolving, however, German and Japanese policy-makers were not inclined to adopt measures that would ease difficulties of adjustment for the USA while its basic problem of inadequate fiscal discipline remained serious.

The adverse effects of the fiscal problem have made it more difficult for US firms to compete against Japanese and German enterprises that benefit from strong ties with their industry groups and with their administrations. There have been significant losses of competitiveness across several sectors.[31] These have reflected pressures on managements to achieve short-term profits, while avoiding long-term investments in advanced technology.[32] The losses of competitiveness have been assessed on the basis of trade flows, but there has been high volume production by US firms at foreign locations (especially in Europe because of the opportunities of its Single Market[33]), and this has evidenced the significance of international manufacturing for corporate competitiveness.[34] Improvements in competitiveness have been more difficult for firms producing in the USA for export, as they have been more disadvantaged by the intercorporate ties of Japanese and German enterprises and by the diverse effects of fiscal laxity in the home economy.

American higher technology firms producing mainly in the USA have been exposed to severe Japanese competition in their home market. This has happened principally in the automobile and electronics industries. US firms in more mature technology sectors with substantial market strengths at home and in Europe have been less seriously challenged, as have US resource-based enterprises.[35] In the services sector, American financial enterprises, communications firms and air transport companies have relatively secure global market positions, with domestic and European concentrations, but the financial enterprises are vulnerable to potentially destabilizing dangers in their home country sector.[36]

Macromanagement in the United Kingdom has a liberal orientation similar to that in the USA, but has had to contend with more significant losses of competitiveness by national firms, while adjusting to the challenges of the Single European Market and to the strains of collective management in the European Union. In part the losses of competitiveness have been attributable to currency appreciation resulting from a restrictive monetary policy that benefited financial rather than manufacturing interests. London's importance as a major international financial centre was enhanced by financial deregulation in the mid 1980s, but a high exchange rate policy became difficult to maintain during subsequent membership of the Exchange Rate Mechanism of the European Monetary System. The adverse trade effects of losses of competitiveness exposed sterling to speculative attacks which caused abrupt withdrawal from the Exchange Rate Mechanism on 17 September 1992. Monetary loosening followed, as high interest rates had caused much unemployment, social disruption and export losses. The sequence reflected slow policy learning in the liberal macromanagement process, and this was in part a consequence of insufficiently forceful representations of manufacturing interests by business associations.

Conservative administrations have endeavoured to reduce taxes and public spending, to assist private sector growth, but fiscal discipline has been relaxed in recent years. British firms, meanwhile, have encountered increasing competition in the Single Market and have sought to reduce costs by shedding labour, thus adding to the administration's welfare expenditures. The ideological stance of the government has been based on expectations that free market forces will oblige corporations to operate with greater efficiency. As in the USA, however, the absence of strong relational ties between firms has tended to hinder competition against German, Japanese and other foreign enterprises operating in industry groups and aided by close links with their national administrations. Cost advantages have been gained by the Conservative government's decision against participation in the Social Chapter of the Maastricht Treaty, but the structural effects of losses of competitiveness caused by the period of high interest rates and high exchange rate policy remain serious.[37]

NEOMERCANTILIST MACROMANAGEMENT

The most significant external challenges encountered by states under liberal macromanagement are posed by states less affected by domestic pluralism that have attained greater structural competitiveness and that are thus able to implement neomercantilist policies. Japan, the most dynamic of these rival states, has superior structural competitiveness which has made possible deep penetration of higher technology markets in the USA. Germany ranks next as a state under neomercantilist macromanagement and as a contender for shares of US higher technology markets. Japanese and German neomercantilism challenges liberal policies and the strategies of firms based in liberal states, but the responses at the governmental level have not been sufficiently constructive to achieve more balanced interdependence. The overall scope for neomercantilism has indeed increased, through cumulative processes in which Japan and Germany have continued to gain competitiveness and have acquired additional bargaining strengths. The building of policy consensus in the USA and Britain has been hindered by fragmented interest representation and adversarial relations between major political parties.

Neomercantilist macromanagement strives for efficiency effects through coordinated corporate strategies, with informal protection of domestic markets. Strong ties between firms enjoying and helping to maintain that protection facilitate collaborative investment and production activities for competitive ventures into world markets. The Japanese political economy is well structured for aggressive neomercantilism, and its distinctive culture resists penetration by potentially disruptive foreign influences. The German political economy is somewhat less internally cohesive, but is highly competitive relative to partners in the European Union. Both states have used monetary and financial measures to exert downward pressure on their currencies, as these have tended to appreciate on the basis of export successes. These successes, meanwhile, have evoked broad corporate and public support for governments in office.

Neomercantilist macromanagement in Japan has a history of administrative guidance, in which technocrats have given and received much advice in close and very extensive consultations with the managements of outward-oriented manufacturing firms. This guidance has been accepted, for the most part, because of managerial respect for the expertise and dedication of the technocrats, and because a high degree of continuity in policy has facilitated the development of trustful long-term cooperation. Export achievements, aided to an extraordinary degree by US fiscal expansion and currency appreciation during the 1980s, strengthened commitments to information-sharing and consultations between technocrats and managements, although managements became capable of operating more independently as their export gains increased. In the penetration of the US and other foreign markets many Japanese enterprises derived competitive advantages from affiliations with their industry groups. Collaboration between firms in these groups was a major feature of the large-scale Japanese manufacturing and services investment in the USA that followed the depreciation of the US dollar in the mid 1980s. This structural penetration resulted in increased Japanese control over much of the commerce between the two countries.

Corporate vitality, as a potent factor in Japanese neomercantilism,[38] has been significant because of its contributions to, and benefits from, collaborative entrepreneurship. Moreover, this has made possible rapid pre-emptive advances in applied technology. Associated with these have been large investments in R&D, with shared benefits, which have limited dependence on government funding of work at the frontiers of industrially related science. Technological imperatives have, however, necessitated some modification of neomercantilist practices to ensure access to advanced American and European R&D, and to allow entries into strategic alliances with US and European firms. Such alliances can be managed with considerable discretion, because of the new technology generated within Japanese industry groups, and the increasing strength of these groups in foreign markets.[39]

Neomercantilist macromanagement in Germany has been aided by the strengths which national firms have gained in their domestic market and in the European Union market, where most rival firms have been weaker and Japanese penetration has been less extensive than in the USA. Technological advances ahead of most of those in other Union member countries have assisted consolidation of the positions secured in the domestic and other Union markets, although these technological achievements have lagged behind those in Japan. Extensive financial sector involvement in the ownership and advising of manufacturing enterprises has facilitated much long-term planning, with considerable risk reduction because of continuing identities of interest. However, technocratic guidance of the manufacturing sector has been much less significant in German macromanagement than it has in Japan's.

The basic orientation of German economic policy is stable, because of broad elite consensus, but adaptation to the European Union's advances towards a higher level of regional integration is obligating choices that can restrict the scope for neomercantilism. Competitive pressures in world markets, together with US and Japanese penetration of the European market, are posing questions about the possible benefits of a common industrial policy, which would substantially expand current European technological cooperation projects. German firms could derive large benefits from the prominent roles which they could expect to have in the implementation of such a policy, but would have to participate in much technology-sharing. Informal bonds between these firms could be weakened, and the largest share of the funding for the new policy would have to be assumed by Germany, because of the size of its economy. In the collective decision-making on industrial policy issues, moreover, Germany could confront a coalition of less industrialized Union states. All the issues relating to Union industrial policy options have become more complicated than they would otherwise have been because of the heavy costs of financing economic recovery in the former East German states. In the absence of a common industrial policy for the Union, Germany's present competitive advantages remain secure.[40]

TOWARDS COOPERATIVE MACROMANAGEMENT

The European Union's advances from an elementary to a more comprehensive form of regional economic cooperation have provided a setting for policy convergence in which there will be less scope for German neomercantilism but in which other Union states will encounter stronger competitive pressures to enhance the efficiencies of their firms. More cooperative macromanagement will be in prospect if there is sufficient consensus, across borders, for structuring a stronger system of intergovernmental decision-making and building an integrated regional economy. A regional political culture is beginning to develop with the Europeanization of several areas of what have been domestic politics, and the economies of member countries are becoming highly interdependent. The continuing enlargement of the Union increases the complexities of collective decision-making, but extends consensus on the importance of maintaining the Single Market.[41]

The main source of strain in the recent history of the region has been slackening growth and rising unemployment, attributable principally to German monetary tightening related to the costs of absorbing the former East German states. Economic decline throughout the region discouraged optimism about achieving growth in the Single Market and roused concerns about German influence in a future Union monetary authority. The stresses in the European Monetary System during 1992 were consequences of shifts in fundamentals, related to the trade performance of several member states, which reflected the adverse effects of German monetary policy and the capacities of German firms to maintain their competitiveness. Imbalances in the spread of gains from freer commerce in the Union market became sources of friction that influenced attitudes towards the structuring of a more advanced system of collective management.[42]

The European Monetary System has been a difficult venture in cooperation, intended to provide a zone of monetary stability and prepare the way for a regional monetary union that would be appropriate for the Single Market. A

German concern has been to use the system for moderation of upward pressures on the mark, resulting from trade surpluses, but weaker trade performance by other states has caused downward pressures on their currencies. Where these have been countered by monetary tightening, as in France, the negative effects on growth have hindered better trade performance. Changes in balances of payments have then exposed the weaker currencies to speculative attack. After the system had been strained by British and Italian withdrawals in 1992 speculation against the franc led to a widening of fluctuation margins to +/−15 per cent. As the Union was experiencing the effects of slack growth in Germany, and ratifications of the Maastricht Treaty had been slow, advances towards the full monetary union envisaged in the Treaty did not seem probable.

Progress towards full monetary union will require much policy convergence, which will be difficult for inflation-prone countries hampered by weak trade performance. The development of a common political will to achieve the necessary policy convergence will be doubtful in these countries, especially because of concerns about the negative growth effects of shifts to monetary discipline. Differing interests and preferences are dividing countries that have linked their currencies tightly to the Deutschmark from those (Britain, Italy and Spain) whose currencies have been floating. Strains in the Franco–German monetary relationship (which developed when the franc came under speculative attack in 1992) have, moreover, persisted, because of the costs of sustained monetary tightening which has pushed the French inflation rate very low but raised unemployment.[43]

For effective operation of the Single Market full monetary union is recognized to be necessary, and in its absence European firms tend to be more disadvantaged than larger American and Japanese enterprises with more substantial resources and more extensive regional organizations that facilitate the spreading of currency risks and costs. The establishment of the Single Market has been a regional macromanagement achievement, facilitated by general elite recognition of the exposure of European firms to increasingly severe US and Japanese competition in their own area and in world markets. More and more substantial gains from free intrazonal commerce have been expected to result from the elimination of obstacles to the movement of goods, services, capital and labour between member states, and from the adoption of common technical specifications, value-added taxes and other sales taxes. This comprehensive liberalization has opened up wide scope for economies of scale, which are being exploited by multinational firms, including European corporations which have expanded through mergers and acquisitions. Uneven national gains from the freer commerce are, however, influencing the attitudes of member governments to issues of regional monetary cooperation, and to the prospect of pressures for fiscal convergence under a European monetary authority.

The deepening integration and expansion of the European Union has not inspired increased cooperation within NAFTA, in which questions of regional macromanagement have been excluded by the dynamics of interactions in its more hierarchical configuration. For Canada and Mexico NAFTA has been primarily a safe haven arrangement, to avoid vulnerability to US protectionism on terms necessarily acceptable because of weak bargaining power. Perceptions of interest guiding US policy have been influenced by awareness of a capacity to relate to Canada and Mexico from a position of strength, and thus to benefit from advantageous asymmetries in regional trade liberalization without losing scope for independent decision-making in a system of collective management.[44]

In the Pacific, the USA has opportunities to promote regional trade liberalization, because of the dependence of Japan and the industrializing East Asian states on access to its large internal market, and because of the concerns of these states about imbalances in their economic relations with Japan. The political costs of neomercantilism have limited Japan's scope for regional trade liberalization initiatives, and the industrializing East Asian states do not constitute an effective coalition for regional cooperation. High growth rates in East Asia encourage US efforts to negotiate freer trade arrangements, but American estimates of the prospective benefits are influenced by awareness of tight links between national administrations and firms in Japan and the rest of that area. As Japan's economic ties with the industrializing East Asian states are growing faster than their commercial bonds with the USA, moreover, they have incentives to avoid causing Japanese displeasure by accepting US trade liberalization proposals. As their degrees of dependence on trade with, and investment from, Japan increase they are obliged to exercise caution regarding options for collaboration with the USA. Japanese policy is guided by tacit preferences for bilateral dealings with the industrializing East Asian states, rather than for the evolution of a system of regional economic cooperation.

The degree of regional macromanagement in Europe thus remains unique, despite the strains hindering the development of a more integrated system of collective management. European markets for goods and services have become more fully regionalized than those in North America because of very active regional cooperation, setting up high levels of interdependence which, by general agreement, require continued regional collaboration. The regionalization of markets for goods and services in North America is developing mainly under two unequal bilateral relationships, rather than through a process of regional cooperation, and on present indications will not lead to the structuring of a system of regional macromanagement. In the Pacific the regionalization of goods and services markets is evolving with marked asymmetries between the East Asian pattern of government–business links and the basically liberal North American pattern. American efforts to secure East Asian shifts to liberal policies are the most active causes of interactions on trade issues, but are not successful and are not encouraging support for the building of a system of regional macromanagement.

The contrasting regional patterns of interaction and market-linking provide an uneven basis for the support of economic cooperation ventures at the global level, where problems of stability in world financial markets have assumed large dimensions. The level of institutionalized functional and representative cooperation in Europe *can* support constructive involvement at the global level. However, NAFTA is not yet and may never become a system for political cooperation, and on global issues the USA acts alone. Japan also acts alone on such issues, without involvement by the East Asian industrializing states that are being linked closely with its economy. The European Union has exceptional significance because of its progress, despite stresses, in the evolution of its system of regional macromanagement, and because the dynamics of its collective decision processes generate pressures for monetary stability. This is extremely important, for Europe and for world financial markets, because of the potentially destabilizing effects of large fiscal deficits in the USA.

NOTES

1. See John H. Dunning, 'Governments, Economic Organisation and International Competitiveness', in Lars-Gunnar Mattsson and Bengt Stymne (eds), *Corporate and Industry Strategies for Europe*, Amsterdam: Elsevier, 1991, 41–74.
2. On strategic alliances, see Peter H. Cowhey and Jonathan D. Aronson, *Managing the World Economy*, New York: Council on Foreign Positions, 1993; and Peter J. Buckley, 'Alliances, Technology and Markets: A Cautionary Tale', in Peter J. Buckley, *Studies in International Business*, London: Macmillan, 1992.
3. On industry groups, see W. Carl Kester, 'Industrial Groups as Systems of Contractual Governance', *Oxford Review of Economic Policy*, **8** (3), Autumn 1992, 2–44. On management cultures and capabilities for global operations, see Allen J. Morrison and Kendall Roth, 'The Regional Solution: An Alternative to Globalisation', *Transnational Corporations*, **1** (2), August, 1992, 37–56.
4. See Dennis J. Encarnation, *Rivals Beyond Trade*, Ithaca: Cornell University Press, 1992, particularly Chapters 3 and 4.
5. Peter J. Buckley, C.L. Pass and Kate Prescott, *Servicing International Markets: Competitive Strategies of Firms*, Oxford: Blackwell, 1992.
6. Robert B. Reich, 'Who Is Us?', *Harvard Business Review*, **68** (1), January–February 1990, 53–65. Robert B. Reich, 'Who Is Them?', *Harvard Business Review*, **69** (2), March–April, 1991, 77–88.
7. Peter J. Buckley and Hafiz Mirza, 'The Strategy of Pacific Asian Multinationals', *The Pacific Review*, **1** (1), 1988, 50–62.
8. See *Technology and the Economy: The Key Relationships*, Paris: OECD, 1992.
9. On the competitiveness of European firms, see Kirsty S. Hughes, 'Trade Performance of the Main EC Economies Relative to the USA and Japan in 1992 – Sensitive Sectors',

Journal of Common Market Studies, **XXX** (4), December 1992, 437–54, and Kirsty S. Hughes (ed.), *European Competitiveness*, Cambridge: Cambridge University Press, 1993.

10. See Carlo Perroni and John Whalley, *The New Regionalism: Trade Liberalization or Insurance*, Cambridge, Mass.: National Bureau of Economic Research Working Paper No. 4626, 1993.

11. References to the integrated Japanese regional production systems in Asia are contained in *World Investment Report 1991: The Triad in Foreign Direct Investment*, New York: UNCTC, 1991, 44–52.

12. See Alan J. Auerbach, *The US Fiscal Problem: Where We Are, How We Got There, and Where We're Going*, Cambridge, Mass.: National Bureau of Economic Research, Working Paper No. 4709, 1994.

13. Kester *op. cit.* and Thomas M. Jorde and David J. Teece, 'Competition and Cooperation: Striking the Right Balance', *California Management Review*, **31** (3), Spring 1989, 25–37.

14. Martin Feldstein (ed.), *International Economic Cooperation*, Chicago: Chicago University Press, 1988, particularly pp. 1–10.

15. Gavin Boyd, 'Potentials for Collective Action in the Pacific', International Studies Association Annual Meeting, Acapulco, 21–29 March, 1993.

16. Alexis Jacquemin and David Wright, 'Corporate Strategies and European Challenges Post 1992', *Journal of Common Market Studies*, **31** (4), December 1993, 525–38.

17. Domestic opposition to protectionism has also been a factor. See Stanley D. Nollen and Dennis P. Quinn, 'Free Trade, Fair Trade, Strategic Trade, and Protectionism in the US Congress, 1987–88', *International Organization*, **48** (3), Summer 1994, 491–525.

18. Kester, *op. cit.*

19. Kester, *op. cit.*; and see Laurence J. White, 'Competition Policy in the United States: An Overview', *Oxford Review of Economic Policy*, **9** (2), Summer 1993, 133–50.

20. Christel Lane, 'European Business Systems: Britain and Germany compared', in Richard Whitley (ed.), *European Business Systems: Firms and Markets in their National Contexts*, London: SAGE, 1992, 64–97.

21. Jeffrey A. Hart, *Rival Capitalists: International Competitiveness in the United States, Japan and Western Europe*, Ithaca: Cornell University Press, 1992, 87–138; and William D. Coleman, 'State Traditions and Comprehensive Business Associations: A Comparative Structural Analysis', *Political Studies*, **XXXVIII** (2), June 1990, 231–52.

22. Roger G. Noll, 'Structural Policies in the United States', in Samuel Kernell (ed.), *Parallel Politics: Economic Policymaking in Japan and the United States*, Washington D.C.: Brookings Institution, 1991; and Terry M. Moe, 'Political Institutions: The Neglected Side of the Story', *Journal of Law, Economics and Organization*, **6**, Special Issue, 1990, 213–54.

23. Stephen Young and Neil Hood, 'International Investment Policy in the European Community in the 1990s', *Transnational Corporations*, **2** (2), August 1993, 35–62.

24. Young and Hood *op. cit.*; Jacquemin and Wright, *op. cit.*

25. Andre de Jong and Gerrit Zalm, 'Scanning the Future: A Long Term Scenario Study of the World Economy, 1990–2015', in *Long Term Prospects for the World Economy*, Paris: OECD 1992, 27–74.

26. Douglas Nelson, 'Domestic Political Preconditions of US Trade Policy: Liberal Structure and Protectionist Dynamics', *Journal of Public Policy*, **9** (1), January–March 1989, 83–109; and I.M. Destler, *American Trade Politics*, second edition, Washington D.C.: Institute for International Economics, 1992.

27. I.M. Destler and C. Randall Henning, *Dollar Politics: Exchange Rate Policymaking in the United States*, Washington D.C.: Institute for International Economics, 1989.

28. Destler and Henning, *op. cit.*

29. Greatly increased sourcing from foreign production bases by US firms contributed to these deficits. See Masaaki Kotabe and K. Scott Swann, 'Offshore Sourcing: Reaction, Maturation and Consolidation of US Multinationals', *Journal of International Business Studies*, **25** (1), 1994, 115–40.

30. Martin Feldstein (ed.), *The Risk of Economic Crisis*, Chicago: Chicago University Press,

1991; and Allen B. Frankel and John D. Montgomery, 'Financial Structure: An International Perspective', *Brookings Papers on Economic Activity*, **1**, 1991, 257–310.

31. On the sectoral losses of competitiveness see Maria Papadakis, 'Did (Does) the United States have a Competitiveness Crisis?', *Journal of Policy Analysis and Management*, **13** (1), Winter 1994, 1–20.

32. See *Technology and the Economy: The Key Relationships*, Chapters 10 and 11, Paris: OECD, 1992.

33. See Raymond J. Mataloni, Jr, 'Us Multinational Companies: Operations in 1992', *Survey of Current Business*, **74** (6), June 1994, 42–62.

34. For the figures on US direct investment in Europe see Sylvia E. Bargas and Jeffrey H. Lowe, 'Direct Investment Positions on a Historical Cost Basis, 1993: Country and Industry Detail', *Survey of Current Business*, **74** (6), June 1994, 72–7.

35. See Papadakis *op. cit.*

36. See Feldstein (ed.) *op. cit.*; and Frankel and Montgomery *op. cit.* For comparative figures on foreign market servicing strategy of firms by nationality, see Peter J. Buckley and Gordon E. Smith, 'An International Comparison of the Structure of Foreign Market Servicing Strategies', *International Business Review*, **3** (1), 1994, 71–94.

37. See *Oxford Review of Economic Policy*, **9** (3), Autumn 1993 – Symposium on UK Economic Policy.

38. For a critical account of Japanese management see Peter J. Buckley and Hafiz Mirza, 'The Wit and Wisdom of Japanese Management: An Iconoclastic Analysis', *Management International Review*, **25** (3), 1985, 16–32.

39. For a critical view of Japanese strategic alliances see Robert B. Reich and E.D. Mankin, 'Joint Ventures with Japan Give Away our Future', *Harvard Business Review*, **64** (2), March–April 1986, 78–86.

40. See Kirsten S. Wever and Christopher S. Allen, 'The Financial System and Corporate Governance in Germany: Institutions and the Diffusion of Innovations', *Journal of Public Policy*, **13** (2), April 1993, 183–202.

41. See Andrew Moravcsik, 'Preferences and Power in the European Community: A Liberal Intergovernmentalist Approach', *Journal of Common Market Studies*, **31** (4), December 1993, 473–524.

42. See Niels Thygesen, 'Towards Monetary Union in Europe – Reforms of the EMS in the Perspective of Monetary Union', *Journal of Common Market Studies*, **31** (4), December 1993, 447–72.

43. *Ibid.*

44. Perroni and Whalley, *op. cit.*

8. Political change, macromanagement and economic cooperation

Gavin Boyd

As the linking of markets through transnational production and trade continues there are increasing efficiencies, resulting from economies of scale and scope, but there are also problems of internationalized market failure. These are associated with disparities in the spread of gains from transnational production and trade. They are increasing, moreover, with those disparities, because of inadequate cooperation between governments, and because governments are losing elements of economic sovereignty to the transnational enterprises that are securing larger shares of world markets. The disparities in economic gains and the problems of internationalized market failure cause stresses for the less advantaged states: they experience slack growth, structural dislocations and high unemployment. Hence in their political processes there are pressures for change. The more advantaged states, enjoying higher growth and achieving competitive structural adjustment to the challenges of intensifying global competition, exhibit considerable political continuity: their macromanagement achievements reinforce the strengths of their political economies.

The contrasts reflect differences between national political economies *as advanced systems*. The less advantaged industrialized democracies in the Euro-Pacific pattern experience problems of structural competitiveness because they are less integrated. Destructive political competition tends to increase problems of governance while the stresses resulting from intensifying competition in world markets obligate improved macromanagement. Concerted entrepreneurship in response to these stresses is not sponsored, the home country loyalties of national firms are lost and heavy fiscal expansion, driven by political competition, becomes the most serious problem of governance. The more advantaged industrialized democracies operate as more advanced systems, with higher degrees of integration because of domestic political cooperation and corporate cooperation. Resulting efficiencies, possible because of restraints on competition, facilitate further systemic development, with collaborative entrepreneurship for effective involvement in the unevenly integrating world economy.

The disparities in gains from international production and trade activate leverage by disadvantaged states. Individually or in groups they may have sufficient bargaining strength to press for changes in the terms on which trade and direct investment policies influence commerce and transnational production. Forms of managed trade and managed direct investment may result. Problems of governance, however, may not be overcome, and there may be no gains in structural competitiveness. Corporations operating out of disadvantaged states will tend to continue international strategies focused on maximizing the exploitation of foreign location advantages. Meanwhile, high costs of government associated with fiscal expansion in these states will continue to burden firms manufacturing for export in the disadvantaged states.

The overall effects of activities by firms are not reducing the disparities in the integrating world economy. Global oligopoly power is being gained, principally by American and Japanese enterprises, and especially at the expense of weaker European companies. Continual relocations of industrial capacity associated with the growth of global oligopoly power have adverse consequences for many sectors and communities: production operations are shifted from higher wage and more industrialized to lower wage and less industrialized states, often with exploitation of investment bidding by host governments. Trade flows, related more and more to the changing pattern of international production, benefit mainly the industrialized democracies with superior structural competitiveness and with capacities to maintain this competitiveness through intensive investment in advanced technology.

The less advantaged states are challenged to achieve more efficient macromanagement. Policy shifts in line with the demonstration effects of the growth strategies implemented by the more integrated political economies are, however, difficult. They are especially difficult in the USA, because of its very aggressively competitive political tradition, which hinders consensus and the development of policy learning in the public interest. Pressures to externalize the costs of failures to improve macromanagement tend to be strong in the USA. They increase if growth and welfare issues assume larger dimensions because of worsening imbalances in structural interdependence.

Imperatives for comprehensive integrative international economic cooperation can be seen in the problems of structural interdependence that cause strains between leading industrialized democracies in the Euro-Pacific context. Current policy orientations are generally unfavourable and reflect hardening of adversarial attitudes, especially in the US–Japan relationship, but the range of common interests that would be served by integrative collaboration is very wide. All transnational linking of sectors and communities is an elementary form of system-building which sets requirements for further development, responsive to concerns that presently cannot be expressed effectively across borders.

CHANGE AND CONTINUITY

The policy orientations and macromanagement capacities of governments evolve through phases of political business cycles, involving industrial development and decay, gains and losses in international trade and production, and shifts in patterns of interest representation. There is often policy learning, but it is usually not cumulative unless there is considerable integration in the political economy that ensures continuity in consensus. In the leading industrialized democracies of the Euro-Pacific pattern, processes of political continuity and change are strongly influenced by the positive and negative effects of foreign commerce and production on growth and employment. These effects, however, are seen with a strong domestic focus, in the context of interactions within and between contending groups seeking approval from sectoral and community interests. National patterns of political rivalries are mostly inward-looking, relating to particularistic attachments and loyalties, and often the issues are grossly simplified and distorted in the media. If the rivalries are very divisive, problems of consensus formation and interest aggregation can be perpetuated. This danger is evident in the USA:[1] although its political processes are less inward-looking than those in Japan, they are nevertheless very divisive, while Japan's are mainly consensual. In the European Union national political processes are traditionally quite inward-looking, but are being gradually Europeanized as deepening regional economic integration continues. Where political cultures are oriented towards consensus, as in Germany, divisive effects can be prevented, but this is not always feasible in member states with individualistic political traditions.

States with very divisive political processes, due to individualistic political cultures and/or sharp ideological cleavages, experience strong pressures for changes of power and policy. These can be intensified when problems of growth and employment are made very serious by macromanagement failings and losses of structural competitiveness. There can be vicious cycles in which migrations of industrial capacity to better managed states contribute to further losses of structural competitiveness, and thus to welfare losses which add to the burdens of government but also to conflicted and disjointed policy-making.

In more integrated industrialized democracies solidarity-building macromanagement contributes to political continuity, moderating and narrowing ideological cleavages. Firms tend to achieve greater efficiencies through concerted entrepreneurship in more supportive policy environments, and retain ties with cohesive national intercorporate systems. Consensual policy-making responsive to functionally aggregated corporate interests and community interests assists advances in structural competitiveness and facilitates collective adaptation to strains in foreign economic relations.

The less integrated industrialized democracies experience serious problems of advanced political development which adversely affect, and are adversely affected by, stresses associated with losses of external markets, import surges, deindustrialization, declines in investor confidence and speculation against their currencies. The collaborative adjustment to these problems which becomes increasingly necessary is more and more difficult to achieve. Decisive engagement with the issues is hindered by individualistic and group endeavours to manipulate the institutions of economic policy. Manipulation by distributional coalitions, meanwhile, tends to push fiscal expansion beyond sustainable limits, with increasingly negative effects on structural competitiveness.[2]

States functioning as more integrated systems, at more advanced levels of political development, with cohesion based on relational political contracting and relational business contracting, operate with consensual rationality. Macromanagement achievements tend to reinforce consensus as growth and employment levels are raised with gains in external markets, restraints on potentially disruptive imports, restructuring into higher technology manufacturing, increases in investor confidence, and continued currency stability. Adjustment to major external problems is aided by extensive intercorporate cooperation, as was illustrated by the adaptation of the Japanese economy to the large rises in oil prices during the 1970s.[3]

Considerable political continuity has been achieved in Germany, at an advanced level of political development, with very broadly consensual rationality in decision-making. Internal cohesion in support of a functional policy consensus has made possible a long record of sustained outward-oriented growth, with recovery from the heavy costs of rehabilitating the former East Germany. The objective of the policy consensus has been orderly growth, achieved through harmonizing managerial, labour and community interests, with allocative discipline, and through efficiencies resulting from extensive intercorporate cooperation.[4] Much political continuity has also been maintained in Japan, on the basis of a broad and very functional but insular policy consensus, and of very competitive achievements by a more dynamic and tightly organized business community. Elite factionalism and corruption, however, have disrupted the continuity in recent years. These failings have indicated the perverse effects of traditional patron–client relationships on institutional development,[5] and have suggested that the Japanese political system would benefit from the establishment of a strong independent advisory council, to which the administration would be informally accountable.

Pressures for political change have been strong in the United States during recent years because of growth and welfare problems.[6] The commonly recognized domestic source of these problems has been prolonged unsustainable fiscal expansion, burdening the nation with heavy debt, raising the costs of government, diverting investment from productive use, and posing uncertainties about the stability of the economy. Strains resulting from unemployment, trade deficits, losses of industrial capacity, import surges and currency depreciation, however, have tended to activate more aggressive individual, corporate and community endeavours to further economic objectives through political action. Policy processes have thus become more conflicted, making improved macromanagement difficult to achieve. Altogether, the dysfunctional effects of hyper-pluralism have made the nation's problems of advanced political development more serious.

STATES UNDER PRESSURE

Change without political development, and sometimes with political decay, is a threatening trend in the United States and in other less integrated industrialized democracies. The trend is a multilevel process, affecting all dimensions of each political economy. Individual pursuits of interests manipulate organizations that are necessary for collective action, and hinder their development. This happens in enterprises, interest groups, political parties, legislatures and administrative structures. Business transacting is mainly an arm's length process, with major risks of opportunism, moral hazard and adverse selection. Political transacting is also mostly done at arm's length, with similar but greater risks. Hence there are social limits to institutional evolution and performance.

Transacting costs, related to risks, are appreciably lowered if exchanges are internalized within a firm, but in an instrumental business culture this tends to remain an arm's length rather than a relational process. To lower *political* transacting costs through organization-building in an interest group or political party is very difficult in an instrumental culture, as arm's length *political* exchanges inevitably amount to very incomplete contracts, with more serious dangers of opportunism and adverse selection, as well as moral hazards. Interest groups, political parties, legislatures and administrative structures can be extremely vulnerable to organizational manipulation.[7]

Individualistic utility-maximizing in an instrumental business culture is expressed in ruthless labour management practices, and in predatory intercorporate relations with hostile takeovers. Distrust thus becomes pervasive, limiting possibilities for productive long-term business cooperation, as well as for the development of stable identities by firms.[8] The typical enterprise becomes a temporary nexus of expedient and unequal arm's length contracts. Possibilities for collective political action are also affected, as the representation of corporate interests, although aggressive, is fragmented, and is thus largely responsible for very conflicted policy processes.

In the United States, multiple incentive conflicts deriving from individualistic pursuits of instrumental values hinder decision-making in its system of divided government, while perpetuating aggregating weaknesses in its corporate associations and political parties. The decisional problems, it must be reiterated, necessitate numerous expedient compromises, resulting in pluralistic issue evasion and, more seriously, in fiscal laxity that tends to become unsustainable.[9] In the United Kingdom, policy-making is less difficult, because of a tradition of obligation to the public interest that moderates individualism in the national culture. The policy style is, however, rather conflicted and reactive, and the representation of business interests is fragmented because of organizational weaknesses in the corporate associations.[10]

The dysfunctional effects of intense pluralism, straining the capacities of weak institutions, tend to persist in the USA because of vicious cycles in which problems of governance have cumulative effects, contributing to, and being adversely affected by, stresses in external economic relations. Political figures are socialized in an atmosphere of pervasive adversarial advocacy. Administrative agencies and regulatory authorities tend to be structured with intra-organizational and inter-organizational conflicts, mainly because of the perverse behaviour of legislators with opposing constituency interests.[11] Assertiveness on behalf of such interests by individual legislators interacts with administrative quests for political support, causing the problem of fiscal laxity to become politically intractable.

Corporate planning does not anticipate improved government performance or increased intercorporate cooperation. Traditional business distrust of government tends to become stronger as its major deficiencies persist and as these contribute to losses of structural competitiveness. Distrust also persists because of proliferating litigation problems that managements see themselves risking because of actual or possible dealings with government agencies by their own firms or by rivals. Litigation risks, meanwhile, tend to reinforce aversion for intercorporate cooperation that expresses the aggressive individualism of the business culture.[12] The political economy is thus seriously affected by the evolution of corporate strategies along very independent lines, with emphasis on avoidance of interactions with the administration, and on minimizing regulatory and tax exposure. There is selective use of opportunities to advance business interests through political action, but this does not contribute to the development of functional aggregations of business interests, and is managed at arm's length.[13]

Resourceful leadership is a basic development need in the American political system, but elite socialization and selection processes do not produce politicians with substantial executive capabilities. Success in contests for administrative power depends very much on the popular projection of personal qualities in presidential campaigns, rather than on experience of higher organizational work and policy formulation in an institutionally well-developed political party. Organizationally the major political parties are weak, and because their capacities for generating knowledge-intensive policy consensus are weak, there tend to be wide idiosyncratic variations in the political psychology of contenders for high office. Performance potentials are thus very uncertain, as the cognitive and motivational attributes of the contenders have not benefited from collegial assessments associated with organizational experience. The successful contender, moreover, typically does not emerge as the leader of a team with an organizational base that can act as a collective executive. The president structures his administration with arm's length political contracting, endeavouring to retain much personal power. Under information overload and demand overload, a cybernetic policy style tends to evolve – experimental, disjointed and incremental, with alternating biases.[14]

Potentials for continuity in policy are often limited by shifting requirements to seek Congressional and public support. Each incoming president usually shows compulsions to demonstrate that potentially decisive new approaches are being taken to outstanding problems. Successive quests for general approval restrict the attention given to substantive issues. Possibilities for policy learning based on the experience of the permanent bureaucracy are, moreover, less significant than they are in several other industrialized democracies because of the common US practice of filling large numbers of higher posts with often inexperienced political appointees. These individuals have to build their own consultative links with each other and with career officials, and most of them have to plan for futures outside government after their short terms in office.

The United States may be entering into vicious cycles in which growth and welfare problems increase, intensifying and being intensified by problems of governance and by trade- and investment-related stresses. The difficulty of achieving allocative discipline, which is the nation's most serious problem of governance, may well become more serious because of legislative and executive efforts to maximize support through favours to communities and sectors. Demands for such favours may become more numerous and more insistent while debt-related costs of government slow the economy, national firms increase foreign rather than domestic production, trade deficits remain large, and the competitiveness of high technology exporting firms is eroded. Because the fiscal deficits are unsustainable, moreover, and because the usually large volume of speculative activity in the home economy tends to rise in conditions of strain and uncertainty, the risk of a financial crisis may indeed become very great.[15]

Britain's growth and employment problems are sources of pressures for change similar to those in the USA, but executive authority in its parliamentary system is stronger, and a less aggressively individualistic political culture poses fewer difficulties for interest aggregation. A tradition of obligation to the public interest is pervasive, but considerable social polarization along class lines is perpetuated by general strains in management–labour relations and is reflected in a relatively wide divergence between the policy orientations of the two major political parties. The pressures for political change deriving from stresses in the economy pose large uncertainties because of the contrasts between these major parties and because their relationships tend to be entirely adversarial. The Conservative Party's emphasis on limited government is opposed by the Labour Party's interventionist policy of direct administrative engagement with problems of industrial development and welfare.

The nation's economic difficulties are more serious than those of the USA, because of considerable deindustrialization, resulting from losses of structural competitiveness and outflows of direct and portfolio investment.[16] Shifts in voter attitudes related to the state of the economy and the popular status of the two main political parties tend to intensify their competition for support, thus driving fiscal expansion. As in the USA this has pushed government debt to high levels, while slowing growth by raising the costs of administration and diverting investment from productive use into the support of deficit-financing. The possibility of shifts of power between the two main political parties, however, poses economic uncertainties greater than those to be reckoned with by firms in the USA. The danger of further economic decline is, moreover, assuming larger dimensions because of Britain's exposure to intensifying competition in the European Single Market.

Sufficiently adaptive political change to cope with growth and employment problems is difficult to promote because of the lack of integration in the national political economy. The system of intercorporate relations is not sufficiently cohesive to make possible concerted entrepreneurial responses: corporate strategies are directed with much individualistic management, and the fragmentation of corporate interests in business associations prevents aggregations of sectoral concerns that could become constructive inputs into policy. Large manufacturing firms are attracted by opportunities to produce at foreign low cost locations, in or near major markets. Dynamic foreign centres of innovation, moreover, exert attractions for research-intensive industrial activity.

Legislative inputs into policy are relatively weak and do not compensate for the fragmentation of corporate interest representation. Bureaucratic inputs into policy, moreover, tend to be impartial contributions by generalists giving expression to Cabinet preferences. Leadership functions thus assume much potential significance, but elite personality factors tend to perpetuate Cabinet pluralism, which obscures basic macromanagement tasks. The most urgent task at present is to achieve fiscal restraint, for a longer-term reduction of the costs of government and of diversions of investment into deficit spending.[17] This task demands strong resolve because its neglect would entail more unequal sharing in the gains from trade within the Single Market, and more exposure to pressures for policy convergence in Europe which are resulting from German fiscal discipline.

France experiences pressure for political change because of growth and welfare problems almost as large as those in Britain. These are failing to evoke sufficiently constructive administrative responses, while the constitutionally powerful executive tends to keep the weak and fragmented intercorporate system in a subservient role, limiting entrepreneurial vitality. The individualistic business culture tends to perpetuate the existence of numerous relatively inefficient small and medium sized firms unwilling to form affiliations with each other. The general absence of relational ties prevents the development of a functional balance between competition and cooperation, thus necessitating cautious entrepreneurial planning. Politically the representation of business interests reflects the lack of intercorporate cohesion, which in effect allows the administration to deal very authoritatively with national firms, especially large ones dependent on state subsidies.[18]

The growth and welfare problems causing economic discontent in recent years have been attributable primarily to the European recession, during which a deflationary policy has been implemented in order to strengthen the competitiveness of French firms. These enterprises, while disadvantaged by failures to engage in productive collaboration, have been adversely affected by the general economic costs of what has been a large inefficient state sector. Slow privatization over the past decade has opened the way for renewed growth, but with the formation of the Single Market French firms have been encountering stronger competition from German, American and Japanese enterprises rationalizing their European operations.

Potentials for change through electoral shifts have been reduced in some respects over the past half decade by a narrowing of policy differences between the major conservative political parties and the Socialist Party. The latter's policy has been moving towards the centre, especially since a severe defeat at the polls in 1993. Because of the great importance of executive power, contests for the presidency assume much importance, and the outcomes depend very much on the projection of images by leading contenders, rather than on the approval and support of political organizations.[19] Such organizations dominate contests for control of the legislature, but their institutional weaknesses and the restricted powers of the legislature limit opportunities for the effective representation of sectoral and community interests.

Current policy under a conservative Cabinet with a majority in the legislature emphasizes the significance of market forces as agents of growth.[20] Restraint is intended to be imposed on interventionist measures that tend to induce corporate dependence on official support. As this conflicts with what has been accepted bureaucratic practice, however, the intended increases in autonomous managerial performance may well be less than expected. Interventions to restrict foreign penetration of higher technology sectors through acquisitions and new investments, moreover, may well have secondary effects that cause managements to continue seeking ministerial approval and assistance.

HIGHER PERFORMING STATES

Adaptive continuity, in response to moderate pressures for change, is a trend in the more integrated industrialized democracies. This results from stable, broad and functional policy consensus; responsiveness between policymakers, technocrats and cohesive intercorporate systems; and aggregations of interests on an extensive scale by representative organizations. Efficient macromanagement, sustained by these factors, tends to ensure the maintenance of each political economy as a dynamic system, deriving above average gains from international trade and production while achieving high domestically based growth. Costs of government are held down by allocative discipline, and adjustment to stresses in external economic relations is facilitated by wide-ranging administrative–corporate collaboration.

Among the more integrated industrialized democracies, Germany has attained the most advanced level of political development, through broadly consensual macromanagement based on an inclusive social partnership for orderly growth. The partnership has been under strain because of the recession caused by monetary tightening to overcome inflationary pressures associated with the costs of reunification, but general elite agreement on the orientation of economic policy has been maintained. Multilevel and multifunctional cooperation involving the two major political parties has become well established, in line with the functional requirements of the German federal system. The integrated pattern of intercorporate relations sustains representation of well-aggregated interests, in harmony with those of organized labour, which accord with the established principles of economic management. Allocative discipline is one of the most fundamental of these principles, and it has been possible because of rather high growth levels.[21] These have evidenced entrepreneurial dynamism generated within the relational ties of the intercorporate system, under guidance from banks deeply involved in the ownership of German manufacturing firms.

Political continuity has been possible because the overall performance of the social market economy has tended to reinforce the consensus in support of collaboration between government, business and labour. Adaptation to internal and external strains is facilitated by this collaboration, especially because it operates with much informal accountability. The extent of this informal accountability, involving advisory councils, state governments, the national legislature, peak business associations and labour unions, is much greater than that of any other major industrialized democracy.[22] Executive performance, however, is not significantly hindered, because of the breadth of policy consensus. Strains in the consensus resulting from the costs of rehabilitating the former East German economy have been less than might have been expected because the Socialist Party, out of office during the reunification process, has not been well placed to profit from dissatisfactions with the burdens of the process.

Political continuity in Germany has assumed much significance for the development of collective management in Europe, as Germany is the dominant economic power in the Union and its main source of monetary stability. Before the post-unification recession Germany had gained general acceptance as the core member of the then European Community, because of strong growth, fiscal and monetary discipline, and effective leadership of the European Monetary System. The disruption of that system during 1992/3, linked with difficulties experienced by most European states because of the spread of the German recession, had alienating effects. European Union governments became more cautious about implementing commitments to work towards a regional monetary union in which Germany would be the strongest member.[23]

Japan's political economy is on the whole more tightly integrated than Germany's, and tends to remain so because its political processes are quite inward-looking, as its insular culture has not been significantly penetrated by external influences. Policy-making is not complicated by issues of cooperation in a context of regional integration, as has been happening to some degree in Germany. Forceful American leverage on trade issues tends on balance to increase general consensus in support of maintaining strong internal cohesion in the political economy. The level of advanced political development attained on a broadly consensual basis, however, has been endangered by high level factionalism and corruption. Political loyalties and behaviour in Japan are intensely personal, evolving in patron–client relationships, and accordingly structures for interest representation tend to be very much affected by the divisive consequences of such ties. Leadership to build organizational strength is generally difficult because of the pervasive factionalism, but also because a culturally based emphasis on consensus discourages assertiveness among the top figures of a typical organization.

In the political system effective administration has been mainly the responsibility of the traditionally powerful bureaucracy, which has been distinguished because of its high levels of task orientation and competence. General elite acceptance of a dominant policy role for the senior officials in the administration, and especially in the leading economic ministries, has allowed much bureaucratic autonomy while in effect restricting legislative involvement in policy-making. Hierarchical discipline and the strong task orientations have limited the potentially disruptive effects of factionalism in the bureaucracy. Much political continuity has resulted, despite the destabilizing effects of factionalism that weakened the largest political organization, the Liberal Democratic Party, which lost power in 1993. This continuity has sustained major macromanagement achievements, which have been possible because of the dynamism of the nation's intercorporate system.[24]

In Japanese firms factionalism has not seriously affected organization-building, on a basis of strong normative integration. Managerial practices stressing working-level autonomy have fostered widely shared and very strong task orientations. Moreover, the formation of large industry groups, comprising numerous firms, has not been hindered by factional ties. The benefits of relational bonds in these groups, facilitating concerted entrepreneurial planning, with risk-sharing, have strengthened intercorporate links transcending factional connections. Within major firms, moreover, standard managerial cultures have evolved without factional cleavages that could result in major problems of organizational manipulation.

Prolonged entrepreneurial achievements, resulting in high growth and low unemployment, have tended to sustain broad elite consensus in support of the pattern of government–business relations. In this pattern the major economic ministries relate principally to peak corporate associations. The weakening of the Liberal Democratic Party's role in recent years has, however, widened opportunities for political groups to influence infrastructure ministries awarding public works contracts. Campaign contributions from favoured firms are in demand for the support of vote-mobilizing networks.[25] Political groups tend to have less interest in influencing the Ministry of International Trade and Industry, as its interactions with firms and business associations are primarily consultative.

A serious deficiency in macromanagement that developed in the late 1980s was a failure to control a speculative property boom, which caused a recession when it collapsed in the early 1990s. The financial sector was subjected to considerable stress, from which it gradually recovered under the guidance of the Ministry of Finance. The recession was made more serious by some losses of export revenue caused by appreciation of the yen against the dollar, especially after the Clinton Administration assumed office. Substantial gains in world markets continued, however, and the welfare problems posed by the recession remained small compared with those experienced in the other leading industrialized states.

MACROMANAGEMENT ISSUES

The industrialized democracies under pressure have basically similar problems of governance that hinder the achievement of allocative discipline. The costs of this failing weaken structural competitiveness by increasing government debt burdens, thus making national firms disadvantaged in rivalries with foreign suppliers. Asymmetries in the sharing of gains from international trade and production tend to increase because the losses of structural competitiveness are cumulative, and the negative effects of rising government debt are also cumulative. While the deficit spending remains large, efforts can be made to restrict imports and incoming as well as outgoing direct investment, and to strengthen corporate competitiveness through industrial policies. Import restraints, however, allow the inflationary pressures of deficit spending to operate with greater effect. Restrictions on incoming direct investment can protect the domestic market positions of national firms, but in conjunction with import restraints can allow inflationary pressures to become stronger. Restrictions on outward direct investment are difficult to apply when the foreign direct investment position is already large and corporate interest in outward investment is very active. Industrial policies can strengthen firm-specific advantages, but are likely to be flawed because of the problems of governance responsible for failures in allocative discipline.

Strong leverage against trading partners is feasible only for the USA, because of the size of its internal market. Substantial import restraints, while deficit spending remained large, would contribute to serious inflation. Hence leverage for wider access to the markets of states with trade surpluses can be exerted. In Atlantic commerce, however, leverage has to be attempted against the European Union as a whole, and it has potent bargaining strength because of its continuing enlargement and the deepening of its integration process. Japan is a more vulnerable target, but is strengthening its position in the global economy while competing against the USA in third country markets, especially in the high growth industrializing East Asian states. Unequal financial interdependence with Japan is, moreover, limiting the USA's options, and this will continue while Japanese investor confidence becomes more critical for the stability of the US economy.[26]

Restraints on incoming direct investment could be politically feasible for the US administration if directed against Japan, but of course would cause losses of Japanese investor confidence and would be difficult to implement. Sectoral dislocations and employment losses would activate protests, and there would be opposition from US firms linked with Japanese enterprises through strategic alliances. Restraints on outward direct investment from the USA would be largely ineffective, because of the diversity of channels for international funding through financial markets and intrafirm transfers. Foreign production by US firms for the home market could be reduced through tax methods, thus somewhat lowering trade imbalances, but the political costs of this option could be large because of corporate opposition.

Industrial policy innovations, in so far as they require allocations from the federal budget, tend to become dysfunctional in the American system because of the influence of vote-maximizing concerns on legislative decisions about aids to industry.[27] Corporate cooperation is invited on a short-term basis, and can be discouraged by shifts of priorities and political affiliations as each new administration assumes office. Managements of non-participating enterprises typically oppose the awarding of subsidies, and have interests in political action to terminate them. Export gains resulting from US industrial policy innovations are difficult to measure, partly because these innovations can also contribute, directly or indirectly, to increased service of foreign markets through overseas production. The possible rises in exports will always tend to be followed by greater foreign production and, more importantly, cannot be expected to offset the import drawing effects of heavy deficit spending.

Britain's options are more restricted than those of the USA, because of membership of the European Union and weaker structural competitiveness. Restraints on imports and direct investment from Union members cannot be considered, and efforts to limit US and Japanese market penetration are possible only within the framework of Union policies. Openness to American and Japanese direct investment is greater than in most other Union member countries, and as this investment continues the costs of any possible restraints on it tend to become larger. Endeavours to reduce outward direct investment, so as to prevent further deindustrialization, would encounter difficulties similar to those that would have to be expected in the USA. Industrial policy options deserve earnest consideration because of the degree of deindustrialization that has been experienced, but the record of administrative efforts in this area of policy indicates persistent problems of planning and implementation.[28]

France's options are not as restricted as Britain's, because membership of the European Union is based on a political partnership with Germany that ensures considerable influence on Union decision-making, and because the domestic intercorporate pattern, although fragmented like Britain's, is responsive to administrative preferences. Capacities for technocratic direction of trade, investment and industrial policies moreover tend to be stronger in the French system because of the more limited scope for legislative intrusions, and the influence of economic nationalism on bureaucratic task orientations. Corporate responsiveness to administrative preferences can restrain imports and inflows of direct investment, while limiting outward direct investment. The industrial policy record includes some significant achievements, indicating potentials for more active administrative–corporate collaboration if bureaucratic methods can become more respectful of managerial autonomy.[29]

Germany and Japan, as higher performing industrialized states, are well constituted to continue strengthening their structural competitiveness, but have to reckon with the external political costs of successful neomercantilism. The vigorous penetration of global markets by their firms tends to provoke retaliation against their export-led growth policies. Prudential options would be to work towards more balanced structural interdependence with the less integrated industrialized states, but strong domestic forces tend to drive policies and corporate strategies aiming at greater shares of world markets.

Pressures to moderate neomercantilism are experienced by Germany within the European Union, and can be managed from a position of considerable strength, especially because of France's favourable alignment and the lack of unity between other Union members. While the cohesive intercorporate system restrains imports and inflows of foreign direct investment, it also restrains outflows, and the dynamism generated in the system ensures efficiencies that limit requirements for an industrial policy. Increasing shares of the Union market, however, are won by German firms pushing weaker enterprises into declines. Other Union governments are thus challenged to strengthen and protect their corporations, and are given incentives to work for the introduction of Union policies that would offer relief. The attitudes of other Union administrations towards the structuring of a more integrated system of regional governance are also affected, as it is clear that a sufficiently representative federal arrangement could introduce a common industrial policy, to which Germany would have to make the largest contributions. More moderate market-seeking by German firms in Europe could make consolidation of their present strengths more acceptable. A policy for this purpose could be combined with the promotion of German manufacturing in less developed Union countries for export to the rest of the world. This could be a very effective way of increasing the social acceptability of the German corporate presence.

Japan's options are not constrained by regional ties, but have to be considered under severe pressure from the USA for a more balanced trading relationship. The Japanese surpluses in bilateral trade are being gradually reduced by incremental concessions to American demands for market access and by manufacturing in the USA for its market and for export. The market entry concessions can be made in the light of phases in the American political business cycle; for example, with many delays when dealing with an unpopular president committed to trade policy activism, but with greater willingness when responding to the concerns of a less aggressive US administration enjoying wider domestic support.

American pressure obligates intense efforts further to diversify Japan's foreign economic relations. Commercial links with the industrializing East Asian states, which are larger than those with the European Union and are growing faster, clearly have high priority. Each of these East Asian links can, moreover, be managed bilaterally, and with much bargaining strength, because the regional American corporate presence is much weaker than in Europe: Japan has the stronger regional corporate presence in East Asia and, while this is an integrated extension of the home business community, its activities are assisted by a large official aid programme.[30]

Japanese macromanagement planning can anticipate further expansion of the nation's corporate presence in the industrializing East Asian states, with a relative decline in US commercial involvement. Host governments and business communities are influenced by the resources and dynamism of Japanese firms, and by the strength of their intercorporate bonds, the stability of their long-term interests, and their willingness to enter joint ventures. The USA's economic status in the region has been affected by its trade deficits, the depreciation of its currency and its debt levels; moreover, some diversion of US direct investment from East Asia to Mexico is expected because of the formation of the North America Free Trade Area.

Competition against the USA is difficult in the European Union, as the American direct investment position is very large and socially more acceptable, while enjoying considerate treatment because of extensive European direct investment in the United States. Britain's openness to Japanese direct investment is an exceptional advantage and, in conjunction with the similar degree of openness in Germany, encourages deepening penetration of the European market. The capacities of Japanese firms for strategic pricing, which have been evident in East Asia and North America, may well ensure increasing competitive advantages in operations within the European Union.[31]

MARKET EFFICIENCY PROBLEMS

The challenges of the higher performing industrializing democracies and the responses of those under pressure are evolving as their markets are becoming more international, with asymmetries related to contrasts in structural competitiveness, and while segments of these markets are being internalized by firms and groups of firms, across borders. Increasing concentrations of market power, especially in higher technology sectors, are resulting as weaker enterprises are overcome by competitive pressures. The intercorporate systems of the higher performing industrialized democracies and their national administrations have significant degrees of influence and control over the market changes. The substantial degrees of integration in the higher performing states are sources of superior efficiencies, and are responsible for collective entry barriers that protect the expanding market shares which are being gained. The shifting balances of economic power in the Euro-Pacific context are, however, very complex, and a very critical area of competition is the European Union, where the weak structural competitiveness of several member countries provides opportunities for intensifying US–Japan rivalry.

Foreign trade and transnational production make markets less domestic: supply and demand conditions are less country-specific and are altered with changes in foreign production and import requirements. Moreover, the proportion of arm's length trade in each country's commerce decreases as transfers within international firms expand. When these firms lose their home country identities another dimension of market internationalization is added. The processes of internationalization and internalization are restrained in varying degrees by the trade and investment barriers maintained by national administrations and by corporate entry barriers, resulting in many asymmetries. Some markets are more internationalized than others, often with vulnerabilities to external concentrations of market power.

The intensifying competition which drives the internationalization and internalization of markets results in market efficiencies but also in market failures. The efficiencies are consequences of economies of scale and scope, while the most pervasive type of market failure is the growth of oligopoly power, acquired mainly by firms with superior competitiveness because of those efficiencies. The principal rivalries are between American and Japanese enterprises achieving regional and global market gains at the expense of mostly European and Third World firms. The markets which are being internationalized are significantly contestable, in varying degrees, but are becoming less so, notably in several higher technology sectors, including electronic products, automobiles and aerospace products. Outlays for research and development, and for advanced equipment, are becoming feasible only for very large corporations in all higher technology sectors.[32] The evolution of these very large enterprises involves extensive internalizations of market processes, and further internalizations occur as international corporate alliances are formed.

The Japanese market is the least internationalized in the Euro-Pacific pattern, as it is relatively closed. In this market oligopoly power is almost entirely a national phenomenon, accepted largely because of the scale of cooperative corporate behaviour. Many of the domestically dominant firms are acquiring external oligopoly power in the industrializing East Asian states, the USA and, to a degree, in Europe. This, it must be stressed, is an intercorporate process, using industrial group links on a scale which cannot be matched by US or European firms. While the extensive market internationalization continues, there is ongoing market internalization as Japanese firms expand their structures. There is also market internalization at another level as many of these firms collaborate to set up what are virtually internal markets within industry groups.[33] These have more permanent and wider-ranging effects than the strategic alliances which Japanese firms contract at arm's length with American and European enterprises.

The American market is highly internationalized, because of foreign penetration through exports and direct investment, external sourcing by US firms, and linkages between the domestic and the very large-scale overseas operations of US firms, as well as because of losses of home country identities by some of these firms, especially through foreign cross-holdings. Associated with this extensive internationalization is considerable market internalization, which results as firms extend their organizations vertically, horizontally and through diversification. In the absence of industry groups there is secondary internalization only through strategic alliances. Oligopoly power in the home economy is mainly national but, as challenged by the Japanese corporate presence, is maintained with support derived from the foreign operations of the dominant firms, many of which are acquiring oligopoly power in Europe. Increases in domestic oligopoly power have been facilitated over the past decade and a half by relaxed anti-trust enforcement, which has in effect widened the scope for tacit collusion.[34]

European Union markets, while being regionalized within the Single Market, are being internationalized primarily through the operations of American and Japanese firms, and secondarily through the activities of German and other Union enterprises. There are large asymmetries, because of the lagging competitiveness of many European corporations. Market internalization processes resulting from mergers, acquisitions and rationalizations, tend to be consequences of American and Japanese corporate expansion, although there is considerable intra-Union restructuring.[35] US and Japanese oligopoly power is assuming large dimensions, while forms of Union oligopoly power are mainly German.

The concentrations of market power in the European context are both national and collective macromanagement problems. Union governments tend to protect national firms dominating their domestic economies as these enterprises contend for shares of the Single Market, and questions of efficiency and equity in that market tend to be obscured by concerns about national benefits from its operation. The common competition policy of the Union is recognized to be liberal, but dependent in specific cases on exercises of divided authority in the European Commission that can reflect rivalries between its directorates.[36] The increasing severity of competition within the Single Market, which is resulting in greater acquisitions of oligopoly power, tends to make governments more anxious to strengthen the home and Union market positions of their national firms.

The unevenly internationalized advanced country markets are affected in different ways by the efficiencies and deficiencies in the pattern of internationalization. The most extensive consequences, which entail high risks for the global economy, are those resulting from the very high volume speculation in world financial markets, which far exceeds that associated with the real transactions of trade and international production, and which has some negative effects on the efficiencies with which trade and production are funded. The pattern has asymmetries because of major contrasts between the more responsibly managed financial sectors of the more integrated industrialized democracies and those of the pluralistic states under pressure. Associated with these asymmetries are the differences in trade and transnational production fundamentals between the two types of states which provide opportunities for speculators to promote and exploit volatility in currency markets. The extraordinary volume of anarchic rent-seeking in these markets is an acute market failure problem because of the resultant uncertainties affecting the transaction and reserve functions necessary for productive investment and for exchanges of goods and services.[37] The risks posed by these uncertainties have inhibiting effects on entrepreneurship, but more for small than for large firms with extensive international operations. While overall growth potentials are thus affected, the evolution of forms of global oligopoly power is also indirectly aided.

The volatility generates pressures for short-term returns in stock markets as well as currency markets, adding especially to the pressures for such returns in the stock markets of the less integrated industrialized democracies. Longer-term productive investment decisions become more risky for the firms in the fragmented intercorporate systems of these states than for enterprises in the industry groups of the more integrated states. The governments in these states have incentives to strengthen cohesion within, and controls over, their financial sectors. They also have incentives to continue neo-mercantilist policies that sustain domestic and foreign investor confidence and that encourage speculators to focus on the weaker currencies of the less integrated and less effectively managed states.

Externalities in the real economy include internationalized market failure problems variously influenced by the speculation in financial markets. The most prominent externalities associated with activities in the real economy are the dislocations experienced by communities and sectors caused by major relocations or deactivations of industrial capacity as international firms rationalize their operations for increased competitiveness. Adjustments are managed rather effectively in Japan through corporate innovations and cooperation (with administrative support), but are difficult in the USA where failures in this regard become very serious during recessions, especially because of entrepreneurial orientations towards the use of foreign rather than domestic production bases for service of the home market. In the European Union large adjustment problems are being encountered as Union and foreign firms restructure for enhanced competitiveness and absorb or eliminate weaker rivals, thus contributing to the region's high unemployment.[38] The externalities causing adjustment problems in the USA and Europe are becoming more and more interconnected with the expansion of global operations by very large firms striving to maximize their exploitation of location advantages. Their strategies are facilitated by the extraction of concessions from host governments engaged in investment bidding.

Oligopoly power gained by very large transnational enterprises is an international market failure problem of increasing dimensions. The global organizations and large resources of these firms enable them to push weaker corporations into declines, while serving markets which they are linking with greater efficiencies but also making them less contestable and extracting higher profits from them.[39] The contests for market shares have become very intense in the European Union, and strengths gained here by large American enterprises can assist their competition against Japanese firms for domination of the markets in industrializing East Asian states.

The greater efficiencies associated with gains in oligopoly power can diminish as competition becomes less challenging and strategy shifts to maximizing profits from positions of secure market power. It must be stressed, moreover, that the greater efficiencies can often be gained through restructuring and predatory activities that disrupt sectors in several countries, making it necessary to weigh the externalities against these market efficiencies. Questions of equity have to be confronted, because of the commonly recognized use of oligopoly power for exploitation, and these questions indicate requirements for widely coordinated competition policies, especially because governments can operate in collusion with transnational corporations acquiring international oligopoly power. Administrations in the more integrated political economies tend to become involved in such collusion, as an extension of their alignment with the competitive strategies of their transnational enterprises.

Public goods concepts have to become more comprehensive in recognition of the effects of general, although uneven, market internationalization. An orderly international social market economy is not emerging. While the international financial markets are dominated by very high volume rent-seeking activity which threatens to have destabilizing consequences, and forms of global oligopoly power assume larger proportions, the public goods issues for governments have to be identified with full understanding of their transnational dimensions, which result in extended accountability. Imperatives for cooperation are evident, and it is clear that the cooperation should be integrative rather than instrumental. This will require national and international discipline to reduce and eventually eliminate forms of administrative collaboration with financial enterprises deeply involved in the exploitation of volatility in currency markets, and with firms gaining oligopoly power in markets for goods and non-financial services.

For orderly growth with equity in conditions of high but uneven structural interdependence there is an increasing need for broadly coordinated entrepreneurship, to make full use of productive potentials without destructive and inhibiting forms of competition. The opportunity for governments is to foster integrative international corporate cooperation through collaborative sponsorship of information-sharing and concerted corporate planning, for example through continuing international direct investment conferences. Problems of industrial fragmentation and excess capacity, and the dislocations caused by large-scale restructuring, originate in uncoordinated and competing investment decisions, and remain serious because of failures in integrative adjustment. The potential for high levels of harmonious growth through concerted and substantially integrative entrepreneurship has been evident in Japan.[40] This can provide orientation for endeavours by governments to sponsor wide-ranging cooperation between transnational enterprises, in line with harmonized policies for infrastructure development. Of course the sponsorship of collaborative international corporate planning could be manipulated by firms and governments, but the attainable international public good would be significantly more balanced and less stressful structural independence. With this there could be higher levels of understanding, trust and goodwill between firms and governments.

Restraints on the growth of global oligopoly power could develop through ventures in government-sponsored collaborative international corporate planning. The evolution of a transnational intercorporate system with some self-regulating capabilities could be possible, while the degrees of fragmentation in the intercorporate systems of the less integrated states could be reduced. Cooperation between national administrations for the coordination of competition policies, meanwhile, could develop with the general increases in levels of international trust and goodwill.

Informational market failure problems become evident in an international public goods perspective. The planning and management of operations in widely linked markets has become highly knowledge-intensive, and smaller firms tend to be disadvantaged by their difficulties in matching the information-processing capacities of larger enterprises. An increasingly important function for cooperating governments would be to combine their efforts to provide commercial intelligence for their firms, and their endeavours to project sectoral trends and potentials for corporate planners. The efficiency effects of pervasive information-sharing in the Japanese intercorporate system can assist understanding of the potential benefits of a common commercial information policy which could be implemented by a group of governments. The international market failure problem which could thus become more manageable is currently assuming larger dimensions because of the increasing concentrations of market power which result in virtual monopolies of much commercial intelligence. Market solutions are not emerging, as consulting firms tend to service the more powerful enterprises with superior resources for the funding of research-intensive planning.[41]

Unemployment, finally, must command recognition as a market failure problem, in an international public goods perspective. Many discussions of market efficiencies fail to identify unemployment as a failure of market forces, but the presently large numbers of workless people, especially in Europe but also in the USA, indicate serious deficiencies in the advanced market economies. These deficiencies have international dimensions, many of which are related to the externalities associated with restructuring by firms acquiring global oligopoly power.[42]

The advanced market economies are affected because unemployment reduces internal demand as a spur to growth, while raising welfare burdens for governments and thus giving firms incentives to produce abroad rather than at home. Considerable unemployment is caused by the migrations of industrial capacity to developing countries, and there is also unemployment resulting from vast economies of scale by large enterprises that have absorbed or eliminated smaller rivals. Further, there is unemployment attributable to restraints on growth caused by the inhibiting effects of destructive competition on entrepreneurship.

Socially responsible intercorporate systems with capacities for harmonious adjustment to structural strains are becoming more necessary in industrialized democracies as unemployment and other market failure problems with international dimensions become more serious. The basic remedy for unemployment is highly innovative concerted entrepreneurship within integrated intercorporate systems, as has been demonstrated by the Japanese experience. Fiscal expansion in states with extremely competitive and minimally cooperative intercorporate systems is not a remedy, and tends to become less effective for the promotion of growth because of the rising government debt levels that result. Such expansion, moreover, as must be reiterated, tends to give impetus to the movement of industrial capacity to lower wage areas.

MACROMANAGEMENT AND ECONOMIC COOPERATION

Government failures with international effects add to the complexities of many of the problems of international market failure, while significant macromanagement achievements by governments contribute to both efficiencies and failures in the variously linked markets. The most significant government failures in the pattern of relations between the leading industrialized democracies are the losses of allocative discipline in the less integrated states, especially the USA. The effects on trade and investment fundamentals provide opportunities for the exploitation of volatility in world financial markets. Incentives for US firms to produce abroad are increased, while strong internal demand draws large imports. Meanwhile the potentially destabilizing stresses of unsustainable fiscal expansion and of balance-of-payments difficulties are made more serious by continuing regulatory failures in the financial sector.

The macromanagement achievements of Japan and Germany, assisting major gains in world market shares by their firms, are indirectly responsible for efficiencies in the markets which these firms penetrate, but also for resulting increases in oligopoly power. Sectoral dislocations in the penetrated economies are indirectly attributable mainly to Japanese policies, but are also consequences of restructuring by American firms that is influenced by deficiencies in US economic policies.

The Triad pattern of market efficiencies and failures, and government achievements and failures, can divert attention from imperatives for integrative economic cooperation posed by asymmetries in the rising levels of structural interdependence. These imperatives can be obscured because of the proliferation of competitive strategies and policies and the established orientations of decision processes activating those strategies and policies. With increasing structural interdependence, however, the policies of governments, interacting with the activities of firms, have extensive transnational externalities. Shifts of economic power to firms as they operate with greater independence meanwhile limit the macromanagement capacities of governments in ways that can be overcome only through collaboration between national administrations.

Basic questions about state functions have to be considered in the context of structural and policy interdependencies and of the related patterns of market and government operations. Governments have to recognize responsibilities for the common good of the diverse communities that are being linked across borders by trade and international production, and that are affected directly and indirectly by policies influencing the activities of firms. Issues of international social justice are assuming more and more moral significance, while the functioning of what are still largely national economic structures is becoming increasingly dependent on gains from external commerce. Political processes remain basically national, and government responsiveness to 'domestic' interests tends to increase with achievements and difficulties in foreign economic relations, but the transnational externalities of policy mixes continue to assume larger dimensions. Political competition for the support of 'domestic' interests tends to motivate concentration on the service of those interests in foreign economic policy, but in the resulting economic rivalries the less integrated states are disadvantaged. Trade conflicts, then, adversely affect general growth prospects. Resolution of these conflicts, however, depends very much on the USA, the largest of the disadvantaged states, as it has a potential for global leadership.

The USA has been the only major advocate of international economic cooperation, which has been sought for trade liberalization on favourable terms and for the adoption of expansionary fiscal policies by trade surplus states, principally Japan and Germany.[43] The persistence of trade deficits, with perceived disruptions of domestic industries, has been responsible for domestic pressures on US administrations to achieve more balanced external commerce through market-opening leverage against protectionist foreign governments. Applications of this leverage have been expected to be more effective than the use of dispute settlement arrangements under the General Agreement on Tariffs and Trade and its successor, the World Trade Organization. Reliance on this leverage, however, has tended to cause protectionist shifts in European Union policies, while increasing Japanese government and corporate concerns to limit foreign penetration of their economy. Triad support for general trade liberalization, in line with formal commitments made at the end of the Uruguay Round of multilateral trade negotiations, has thus been heavily qualified. The structuring of dispute settlement arrangements provided for in the results of those negotiations will depend principally on bargains struck in Triad interactions, mainly between the USA and the European Union.[44]

A US quest for regional trade liberalization has resulted in the North America Free Trade Area agreement, on significantly advantageous terms that have reflected the use of superior bargaining strength in dealings with Canada and Mexico. Weak political links between these two states enable the USA to deal separately with them. The agreement has been entered into without interest in moving towards a more advanced level of regional economic integration: collaborative management of the structural interdependencies evolving in the free trade area has not been envisaged.[45]

The establishment of the North America Free Trade Area has enhanced the USA's status in the Asia Pacific Economic Cooperation forum (APEC), in which the main interactions are with Japan, the industrializing market economy East Asian states and China. APEC is a loose association which allows scope for bilateral dealings, and US preferences for these have been evidenced in opposition to Malaysian proposals for the formation of an East Asian Economic Caucus, in which Japan would be associated with members of the Association of South East Asian Nations. In the APEC setting, however, the USA's regional influence is tending to become relatively weaker, as Japan's trade and investment links with industrializing East Asian states are larger and are growing faster. The USA's European bonds thus remain dominant concerns in its foreign economic relations, but interactions with the European Union have to be managed with recognition of its rough equality in bargaining strength.

The fiscal cooperation sought from Japan and Germany, which encounters resistance, has lower priority than the promotion of trade liberalization, in part because it promises less visible economic and political benefits for the US administration. It is clear, however, that reduced deflationary emphasis in Germany, which would have effects throughout the European Union, would have greater significance for the US economy than fiscal expansion in Japan, where the increased consumer demand would have positive effects almost exclusively for Japanese firms.

Emphasis on strengthening political and economic ties with the European Union would accord with the configuration of the USA's structural interdependencies: these are larger and have more favourable asymmetries than those in the Pacific, especially because of the volume of American direct investment in the Union. The evolution of a more integrative orientation in US quests for international economic cooperation could well begin in the Atlantic context. For the present the evolution of a favourable common European external policy is hindered by multiple engrossing differences between member states over the structuring of institutions for collective management in the Union. Resolution of these differences could be aided by constructive US contributions to Union deliberations that would affirm support for deepening integration, on the ground that common European interests would be served. Such contributions to European policy-making are lacking, however, even though a more united Europe linked more closely with the USA could help to induce accommodative shifts in Japan's policies.

There is a large potential for US policy learning and conversion to principles of integrative cooperation in the Atlantic setting. On the European side the deliberative, consensual and diffusely accountable German policy style can become active for leadership in constructive dialogue with the USA. This would be feasible provided the German partnership with France remained harmonious, and would be aided if Britain's political cooperation with Germany and France became more active, while complementing US contributions to the dialogue. On the US side an important source of motivation for dialogue could be the fundamental but inadequately recognized interest in establishing a firm basis for cooperation with the projected monetary union in Europe. This is becoming increasingly necessary for the international role of the US dollar, which is threatened by persistently adverse balances of payments and by the high debt levels caused by heavy deficit spending.[46]

Pending the formation of a European monetary union intensive macroeconomic consultations with Germany are becoming more and more essential for stability and growth in the US economy over the medium term. German policies have potent effects on growth in the European Union and will have very strong influence on the structuring of the Union's projected monetary system. German interest in Atlantic monetary stability can be expected to become more active as trade and investment links with North America expand. The prospects for such stability will be increasingly significant for US firms constituting the large American corporate presence in Europe, and for the US administration's efforts to cope with the pressures tending to force further depreciation of the dollar.

Through the learning experiences and socialization effects of intensive interactions with German policy-makers, the US policy style could become more consensually rational. This could open the way for more integrative and less instrumental cooperation, with knowledge-intensive rapport on basic issues of collective management. This would be possible if there were very frequent high level exchanges and industrial conferences that could link US and German business associations.

The intensive interactions with Germany could cause difficulties in US relations with France and Britain. Such difficulties, however, would be less serious if the interactions were managed by Germany with careful regard for French and British interests, and if similar regard were evident on the American side. Much would depend on the ways in which the interactions began, and it can be suggested that they could begin on a semi-official basis, with increasing exchanges between the German Council of Economic Experts and the US Council of Economic Advisers. As the German Council of Economic Experts is autonomous and operates with greater status and continuity, it could be the main source of initiatives. The US Council of Economic Advisers would have to enter into dialogue under executive direction, which could be restrictive and very much subject to change, but executive understanding of the need for intensive exchanges could be deepened by in-house advising related to the high vulnerabilities in the USA's structural interdependencies.

The proposed Atlantic consultative link could be viewed with much concern in Japan, but it could be accompanied by German initiatives to develop very active exchanges with Japanese semi-official advisory groups. These have had low profiles, and the German endeavours could encourage the formation of an autonomous high status economic council with members drawn from these advisory groups. US policy, meanwhile, could become more constructive and less demanding in exchanges with Japan, while indicating readiness to draw Japan into the Atlantic consultations. A German advisory role, it would be clear, could have beneficial effects on the US–Japan relationship.

NOTES

1. See John E. Chubb and Paul E. Peterson, 'Political Institutions and the American Economy', in Samuel Kernell (ed.), *Parallel Politics: Economic Policymaking in Japan and the United States*, Washington D.C.: Brookings Institution, 1991, 17–49; and Philip G. Cerney, 'Political Entropy and American Decline', *Millennium*, **18** (1), Spring 1989, 47–64.
2. See tables on government debt levels in *Government Securities and Debt Management in the 1990s*, Paris: OECD, 1993.
3. On the efficiency effects of integration in the Japanese political economy, see Michael L. Gerlach, *Alliance Capitalism: The Social Organization of Japanese Business*, Berkeley: University of California Press, 1992.
4. See Kirsten S. Wever and Christopher S. Allen, 'The Financial System and Corporate Governance in Germany: Institutions and the Diffusion of Innovations', *Journal of Public Policy*, **13** (2), April 1993, 183–202; and *Germany*, Paris: OECD Economic Survey, 1994.
5. See Gregory W. Noble, 'Japan in 1993', *Asian Survey*, **XXXIV** (1), January 1994, 19–29; and comments on factionalism in Raymond V. Christensen, 'Electoral Reform in Japan: How it was Enacted and Changes it may Bring', *Asian Survey*, **XXXIV** (7), July 1994, 589–605. See also Michio Muramatsu, 'Patterned Pluralism under Challenge: The Policies of the 1980s', in Gary D. Allinson and Yasunori Sone (eds), *Political Dynamics in Contemporary Japan*, Ithaca: Cornell University Press, 1993, 50–71.
6. On trade-related job losses in the USA see Jeffrey D. Sachs and Howard J. Shatz, 'Trade and Jobs in US Manufacturing', *Brookings Papers on Economic Activity*, **1**, 1994, 1–84. On the distributional aspects of improvements in manufacturing productivity during 1985–92, see Barry Bosworth and George L. Perry, 'Productivity and Real Wages: Is there a Puzzle?', *ibid.*, 317–35.
7. On problems of organizational manipulation see Paul Milgrom and John Roberts, 'Bargaining Costs, Influence Costs, and the Organization of Economic Activity', in James E. Alt and Kenneth A. Shepsle (eds), *Perspectives on Positive Political Economy*, New York: Cambridge University Press, 1990, 57–89.
8. See Mark Casson, *Enterprise and Competition: A Systems View of International Business*, Oxford: Oxford University Press, 1990.
9. See Chubb and Peterson, *op. cit.*, and Mathew D. McCubbins, 'Party Politics, Divided Government, and Budget Deficits', in Kernell, *op. cit.*, 83–118. On the fragmentation of business interests see William D. Coleman, 'State Traditions and Comprehensive Business Associations: A Comparative Structural Analysis', *Political Studies*, **XXXVIII** (2), June 1990, 231–52.
10. See Coleman, *op. cit.*
11. See Terry M. Moe, 'Political Institutions: The Neglected Side of the Story', *Journal of Law, Economics and Organization*, **6**, Special Issue, 1990, 213–54.
12. On the risks of exposure to anti-trust enforcement, see Lawrence J. White, 'Competition Policy in the United States: An Overview', *Oxford Review of Economic Policy*, **9** (2), Summer 1993, 133–53.
13. See Mark S. Mizruchi, *The Structure of Corporate Political Action: Interfirm Relations and Their Consequences*, Cambridge, Mass.: Harvard University Press, 1992.
14. See Gavin Boyd, *Corporate Planning and Policy Planning in the Pacific*, London: Pinter and St Martin's Press, 1993, 163–94.
15. See Martin Feldstein (ed.), *The Risk of Economic Crisis*, Chicago: Chicago University Press, 1991.
16. See *Oxford Review of Economic Policy*, **9** (3), Autumn 1993 – Symposium on UK Economic Policy.
17. See comments by Buiter and Currie, *ibid.*, 62–8.
18. See Coleman, *op. cit.*, and Jeffrey A. Hart, *Rival Capitalists: International Competitiveness in the United States, Japan, and Western Europe*, Ithaca: Cornell University Press, 1992, 87–138.

19. See Alastair Cole, 'The Presidential Party and the Fifth Republic', *West European Politics*, **16** (2), April 1993, 49–66.
20. See *France*, Paris: OECD Economic Surveys, 1994; and Olivier Jean Blanchard and Pierre Alain Muet, 'Competitiveness through Disinflation: An Assessment of the French Macroeconomic Strategy', *Economic Policy*, **16**, April 1993, 11–56.
21. Until the post-unification recession, from which recovery has begun. See *Germany*, Paris: OECD Economic Surveys, 1994.
22. See Norbert Kloten, 'West Germany', in Joseph A. Pechman (ed.), *The Role of the Economist in Government*, New York: New York University Press, 1989, 47–72.
23. See C. Randall Henning, Eduard Hochreiter and Gary Clyde Hufbauer (eds), *Reviving the European Union*, Washington D.C.: Institute for International Economics, 1994.
24. See Gerlach, *op. cit.*
25. Electoral reforms enacted in January 1994 restricted the scope for political fund-raising. See Raymond V. Christensen, 'Electoral Reform in Japan', *Asian Survey*, **XXXIV** (7), July 1994, 589–605.
26. See Eric Helleiner, 'Money and Influence: Japanese Power in the International Monetary and Financial System', *Millennium*, **18** (3), Winter 1989, 343–58; and 'States and the Future of Global Finance', *Review of International Studies*, **18** (1), January 1992, 31–49. On the influence of the Ministry of Finance see Stephen K. Vogel, 'The Bureaucratic Approach to the Financial Revolution: Japan's Ministry of Finance and Financial System Reform', *Governance*, **7** (3), July 1994, 219–43.
27. See Paul M. Romer, 'Implementing a National Technology Strategy with Self-Organizing Investment Boards', *Brookings Papers on Economic Activity*, **2**, 1993, 345–89.
28. See Keith Cowling and Roger Sugden, 'Industrial Strategy: A Missing Link in British Economic Policy', *Oxford Review of Economic Policy*, **9** (3), Autumn 1993, 83–100.
29. See Hart, *op. cit.*, 87–138.
30. On the Japanese regional corporate presence see *World Investment Report, 1991: The Triad in Foreign Direct Investment*, New York: United Nations Centre on Transnational Corporations, 1991, 44–52.
31. See Gary R. Saxonhouse, 'Do Japanese Firms Price Discriminate in North America?', *The World Economy*, **17** (1), January 1994, 87–100.
32. On the growth of global oligopoly power see John Stopford and Susan Strange with John S. Henley, *Rival States, Rival Firms: Competition for World Market Shares*, Cambridge: Cambridge University Press, 1991; and *Technology and Productivity: The Challenge for Economic Policy*, Paris: OECD, 1991, Part IIIB.
33. See Dennis J. Encarnation, *Rivals Beyond Trade: America versus Japan in Global Competition*, Ithaca: Cornell University Press, 1992, 97–146.
34. See comments by Ray Rees, 'Tacit Collusion', *Oxford Review of Economic Policy*, **9** (2), Summer 1993, 37, 38. See also Lawrence J. White, *op. cit.*
35. See Matthew Bishop and John Kay (eds), *European Mergers and Merger Policy*, Oxford: Oxford University Press, 1993.
36. See Andre Sapir, Pierre Buiges and Alexis Jacquemin, 'European Competition Policy in Manufacturing and Services: A Two-Speed Approach?', *Oxford Review of Economic Policy*, **9** (2), Summer 1993, 113–32. See also Matthew Bishop and John Kay, *op. cit.*, 313.
37. See Helleiner, *op. cit.*, and *Bank for International Settlements 64th Annual Report*, Basle, 1994, 160–71.
38. Large-scale restructuring has been anticipated. See Stephen Young and Neil Hood, 'Inward Investment Policy in the European Community in the 1990s', *Transnational Corporations*, **2** (2), August 1993, 35–62.
39. See John Stopford *et. al.*, *Rival States, Rival Firms, op. cit.*
40. See Gerlach, *op. cit.*
41. See Dorothy I. Riddle, 'Business Services in the Pacific', in Gunnar K. Sletmo and Gavin Boyd (eds), *Pacific Service Enterprises and Pacific Cooperation*, Boulder: Westview Press, 1993, 217–44.

42. Unemployment problems are reviewed in *Bank for International Settlements 64th Annual Report*, *op. cit.*, 16–28.
43. See I.M. Destler, *American Trade Politics*, Washington D.C.; Institute for International Economics, 1992.
44. Vague language in the Uruguay agreements leaves the way open for coalition-building to influence the structuring of the World Trade Organization. See *The Results of the Uruguay Round of Multilateral Trade Negotiations: The Legal Texts*, Geneva: GATT Secretariat, 1994.
45. See Carlo Perroni and John Whalley, *The New Regionalism: Trade Liberalization or Insurance?* Cambridge: National Bureau of Economic Research, Working Paper 4626, 1994; and Alan M. Rugman (ed.), Foreign Investment and NAFTA, Columbia: University of South Carolina Press, 1994.
46. On the need for monetary and fiscal cooperation in the Triad see Val Koromzay, 'Monetary and Fiscal Policies', in John Llewellyn and Stephen J. Potter (eds), *Economic Policies for the 1990s*, Oxford: Blackwell, 1991, 163–82.

9. Long-range planning: policies and corporate strategies

Gavin Boyd

Cooperation between the leading industrialized democracies is generally instrumental and strategic, within rules given qualified assent for governance of the international trading and monetary systems. The rules are understandings of variable significance about the benefits of substantial openness in commercial relations and of working for stability in world financial markets. As competing firms shape national economic systems and structural interdependencies, the objectives of governments are affected, and accordingly new issues are posed for growth, trade, investment and welfare policies. Meanwhile bargaining strengths in relations with international firms are altered. Under the pressures of domestic political competition and of rivalries for shares in the gains from external commerce, the policy imperative normally given high priority is the attainment of increasing structural competitiveness. Consciousness of collective identity based on large and rising structural interdependencies does not develop.

Under-representation of the interests of communities and sectors affected by the cross-border consequences of national policies and corporate activities is a 'democratic deficit' of increasing international dimensions: a problem of international political development. This necessitates recognition of the obligations of governments to accept extended accountability. They have to recognize responsibilities for externalities associated with their policies, and for failures in the markets which their policies are affecting.

To reduce the international 'democratic deficit' and promote comprehensive integrative cooperation, transnational networks of concerned elites will have to become very active, to function on a long-term basis, for systemic development in the international political economy. Such elites will have to contribute to the formation of an international political culture, capable of sustaining institutions for collective management, without weakening authentic values in national political cultures. The need for such elites has become evident in the European Union, where understandings of the principle of subsidiarity have to reconcile requirements for local and state autonomy with those for macromanagement at the evolving federal level. Equitable transnational interest aggregation for collective decision-making at that level has become necessary for advanced political development in the Union.[1]

Concerned elites active in Europe will have to collaborate with others in the USA and Japan, to promote long-term Triad planning on the basis of a doctrine of collective management. Such a doctrine will be necessary in the evolution of the international political culture, to set principles for the integrative coordination of policy mixes. For this purpose the doctrine could inspire convergence between the policy orientations of major political parties contending for office in the leading Triad states. A spirit of relational collaboration could meanwhile be encouraged to develop in Triad industrial development conferences that could be sponsored by the European Union, the USA and Japan. An immediate objective for concerned Triad elites will have to be the mobilization of broad high level support for the establishment of greater stability in world financial markets. This must be promoted with earnest concern about the danger of an economic crisis in the USA, as this remains serious because of fiscal deficits and declining international confidence in the dollar, as well as because of heavy corporate debt and stresses in the financial sector. A crisis in the US economy would have severe effects throughout the world economy, and indications that it may occur can increase inclinations towards cautious decisions about long-term foreign trade and foreign direct investment options. The need for caution, it must be stressed, is greater for small and medium sized firms operating without affiliations than for larger enterprises and for those of all sizes working within integrated intercorporate systems, as in Japan and Germany.

POLICY PLANNING CAPACITIES

The tasks that can be envisaged for an emerging transnational policy community of Triad elites can be indicated by a review of policy planning capacities in the Euro-Pacific context. These capacities differ greatly, because of contrasts in national political dynamics that are reflected in conflicted reactive vote-maximizing or more consensual and holistically rational decision-making. The latter policy style engaged with basic long-term issues, responding to the aggregated interests of cohesive intercorporate systems, but typically with a neomercantilist orientation. The former policy style has a short-term focus on responsiveness to issues of shifting salience in fragmented patterns of interest representation. Of the leading Triad states Germany has the most significant policy planning capabilities, but their current European focus will have to be expanded to facilitate the development of a larger role in the Euro–Pacific setting.

Japanese policy planning capabilities are substantial, and are active in large policy communities that include very functionally oriented peak business associations as well as dedicated technocrats. There is little openness, however, to inputs from transnational elites. Linguistic and attitudinal factors associated with the national culture limit interactions with foreigners, although exhaustive efforts are made to obtain information about other states and markets. Policy planning is an intensive in-house activity, principally within the policy communities dominated by the Ministry of Finance and the Ministry of International Trade and Industry. Extensive cross-functional information-sharing generates much innovative potential, which develops with emphasis on working-level autonomy, but with apparent technocratic reluctance to use inputs from independent policy research institutes.[2]

The focus of policy planning is evidently somewhat narrowed by concepts of departmental mission, in the Finance and International Trade and Industry Ministries, as these structures have neomercantilist orientations. Their roles have evolved primarily in response to the foreign trade and transnational production interests of the intercorporate system.[3] The Foreign Ministry's participation in decision-making on the larger issues of external economic relations appears to be relatively weak, because of the very large aggregations of interests identified with the Ministries of Finance and International Trade and Industry. Problems regarding foreign political acceptability of deep Japanese market penetration, especially in the USA, tend to receive inadequate recognition in the macromanagement process.[4]

Established strategy in trade dealings with the USA is to grant incremental market-opening concessions which tend to be more than balanced by continuing gains in the American market. There is a danger of miscalculation, which a stronger Foreign Ministry could help to avoid, because perceptions of the political risks by the Ministry of International Trade and Industry may be too optimistic. The strengthening of Japan's large-scale involvement in the world economy ensures increases in bargaining strength that can cause less consideration for the goodwill of trading partners and undue optimism about accommodating shifts in their policies. This is possible because of the long social distances across which Japanese decision-makers relate to other governments and because, as relatively closed systems, the major Japanese policy communities generate solidarity partly with emphasis on successes gained in contests for world market shares.[5]

American policy planning capabilities are less inward-looking and more open to advocacy by transnational elite networks, but are affected by divided government and by the pluralism responsible for a conflicted and reactive policy style, oriented towards short-term options. Planning is directed from the higher levels of the administration by political appointees with extraneous career interests, and this limits autonomous working-level engagement with fundamental policy issues.[6] Working-level planners, moreover, experience incentive conflicts because they are attracted to operational responsibilities that will advance their interests. As members of the permanent bureaucracy they cannot move into the political levels with higher management functions unless they are assisted by patronage, and in these levels they risk displacement by the next administration.

Substantively, the planning tends to be concerned mainly with strategies for policies favoured by the executive, which can be based on subjective preferences formed in restricted high level exchanges, with very active vote-maximizing concerns. The common executive style is to avoid the informal accountability of intensive collective decision-making while controlling separately the various branches of the administration, in line with displays of resourceful engagement with all politically prominent issues.[7] Media treatment of current events influences choices of these issues, in conjunction with proliferating demands in the fragmented national system of interest representation. Streams of advisory papers from numerous policy research institutes contribute to thinking at the working levels, but generally have little influence on the emergence of politically salient topics that attract executive attention. Working-level attitudes to policy issues, while guided by higher level directives authorizing planning endeavours, have to reckon with possible idiosyncratic shifts in the objectives of those endeavours. Executive preferences tend to change, especially in response to opportunities and problems posed by the strong pluralism of the American system.

The most urgent fundamental issue of unsustainable fiscal expansion has been a challenge for budget planners over the past decade and a half, but they have been obliged to work within executive allocative preferences. The focus of these has related primarily to quests for legislative support, and thus to large assortments of constituency interests.[8] In the absence of executive commitments to coordinate fiscal policy with other leading industrialized democracies, the planning evidently involves little interaction with their decision-makers. The scope for inputs into this policy area by transnational elite networks is small, but could become more significant if they were able to contribute to the shaping of monetary policy, in which channels of influence based on expertise are significantly open.

Trade policy planning, influenced very much by pressures for protection and for strong market-opening leverage, especially against Japan, has a very short-term emphasis, and evidently excludes consideration of issues posed by the foreign production of US firms for the home and other markets. The planning clearly has to reckon with the trade effects of fiscal deficits, further likely depreciations of the dollar, and relatively slow results from the current technology enhancement programme.[9] The strong domestic pressures allow little openness to foreign advice, and this problem, together with the intense domestic forces shaping fiscal policy, makes the potential for openness to external influence in monetary decision-making especially significant.

US monetary policy planning, much less subject to domestic pressures, has to be responsive to imperatives for expedient cooperation with other leading industrialized states, particularly Japan and Germany, because of requirements to control exchange rate fluctuations. Efforts to plan, however, have to proceed without substantially functional aggregations of financial interests and preferences, but must work within narrow limits set by needs for inflation control and for overall growth, while meeting financial sector hopes for high interest rates and manufacturing sector hopes for low interest rates. Concerns about foreign exchange management are more active in the Treasury than in the formally independent Federal Reserve, and are related both to trade considerations and to the financing of budget deficits. The record of US interventions in foreign exchange markets has been erratic, and this suggests that there have been persistent difficulties in working for growth without inflation while meeting the expectations of both financial and manufacturing interests.[10] The difficulties have evidently been attributable in part to planning problems, which may well be related to the pluralistic forces influencing the Treasury and to the accommodation of preferences in the politically rather insulated elitist decision-making of the Federal Reserve. Openness to economic advice from elites forming transnational policy communities is probably rather limited in the Federal Reserve, but may well be quite significant in the Treasury, because of its more direct exchange rate responsibilities.

German policy planning capabilities are evolving in a broadly consensual knowledge-intensive decision process focused on the public interest. This is conceptualized as the building of a social market economy with superior structural competitiveness. The degree of consensus, resulting from a tradition of cooperation between the major political parties, the participation of state administrations in the work of the federal government, and the influence of advisory councils, is conducive to long-term planning. This moreover is assisted by stable functional aggregations of interests represented by strong peak economic associations, in a context of general agreement about the efficiencies of the established pattern of macromanagement. The multiplication of collective management issues in the European Union necessitates much intensive interaction with other member governments, especially the French administration, and this makes the formation of domestic consensus sensitive to the interests of Union partners.[11]

Openness to exchanges with regionalized European interest groups, including corporate associations, complements the intergovernmental consultations, and evidently tends to become more significant as deepening integration continues in the Union. The high degree of attention that has to be given to Union issues can, however, limit interest in questions of cooperation with the USA and Japan and, therefore, in responsiveness to transnational elites working for Triad economic cooperation. The concentration of Germany's external economic interests in Europe and the need to assert strong influence in the structuring of the Union's institutions may well cause increasing reluctance to take up issues in the Triad context, although the development of a more active role in that context could strengthen German bargaining leverage in Europe.

Policy planning, to the extent that it relates to Triad issues, evidently has to deal primarily with Atlantic monetary interdependence, in response to American concerns with the international role of the dollar. US requests for fiscal expansion ceased to be feasible when the German government had to resort to deficit financing because of the costs of national unification, but German monetary cooperation has been necessary to reduce downward pressure on the US currency. There have been incentives to extend such cooperation, so as to ensure that German exports will not lose competitiveness, but for German policy-makers it has been clear that the USA's monetary problems will not be solved without fiscal discipline, which is not anticipated. The planning of monetary policy has to reckon with difficult calculations of the likely increasing costs of interventions in currency markets to slow the dollar's falls, and accordingly there is a clear need to work for a stronger German role in the international monetary system. This has to be sought with the cooperation of other European Union states in the building of an effective European monetary structure. To the extent that the anticipated structure will be representative, however, German influence on its operation may be weakened, unless strong bonds are formed with elites in France and several other Union members.[12] The building of such bonds must be expected to have high priority in German policy planning, and may be quite difficult because of the increasing gains by German firms in the Single Market, at the expense of less competitive French, Italian and other European enterprises.

TRANSNATIONAL NETWORKS

In the Triad pattern the most significant transnational elite networks are those formed by business groups within the European Union. The drive for complete market integration resulted in part from the activities of these groups, and deepening integration has caused them to become more active. They endeavour to influence the European Commission, the Council of Ministers and the European Parliament, as well as administrations in member states, taking positions on issues affecting virtually all aspects of the Union's evolution. For effective lobbying the formation of large, regionalized associations has been necessary, and has been encouraged by European Commission quests for dialogue with broadly representative organizations. National groups within these associations have, however, retained their separate identities, as their interests are affected more directly by the policies of their own administrations and by the evolution of their ties with the intercorporate systems of their home economies.[13]

American corporate associations are active in Union lobbying, and the European Committee of the American Chamber of Commerce is very influential, on behalf of about 80 US organizations. This lobbying relates to the interests of American firms in the openness of the Single Market, and can complement but also conflict with the concerns of the European groups. The openness of the Single Market affects all US enterprises producing in, or exporting to, the Union, but as their market shares are strengthened – at the expense of generally weaker European firms – the attitudes of corporate associations in the Union may become defensive. Within the pattern of US business representation, however, there is considerable fragmentation, reflecting the diverse interests of American firms that have gained acceptance in the corporate communities and policy environments of Union members. The potential for effective representation is greater when Union policies are seen to threaten the commerce of large numbers of US enterprises. Support from business associations in the home economy, then, becomes very important, but the fragmentation of corporate interests in these associations limits their capacities for political action.[14] In the total configuration of political activities by assorted corporate groups within the USA, moreover, European issues appear to have only moderate significance.

The Union's elite networks, because of their wide-ranging policy concerns, have a basis for involvement in major issues of Triad economic cooperation. For the present, however, they have few bonds with the American business lobbying groups active in the United States and Europe, and the more issue-specific interests of these groups tend to exclude larger considerations of Atlantic relations. Private initiatives for the development of Atlantic connections have been modest, on each side, and official sponsorship has been lacking. Strains at the governmental level caused by US market-opening leverage in the final stages of the Uruguay Round appear to have discouraged endeavours to promote greater understanding and trust through transnational connections.

Consultations between government officials and staff members in the Organization for Economic Cooperation and Development (OECD) sustain flows of generally discreet economic advice to national administrations and set up informal communication channels between economists in governments and research institutes. Much of the consultative activity deals with Atlantic issues, because of strong European representation, but the organization has no operational responsibilities.[15] The interaction of critical assessments of national policies does not result in the formation of communities of experts committed to advising for the development of wide-ranging collaboration between governments. Ties based on professional interests facilitate communications after government representatives and staff move to other posts, but career interests tend to preclude involvement in forms of transnational political action. Individual connections that may develop with business associations in Europe or the USA tend to be based on issue-specific advising.

In the International Monetary Fund the operational focus on balance-of-payments lending to developing countries allows only consultative activities related to Atlantic and Triad economic cooperation. The formal responsibility is to promote collaboration for exchange rate stability, at the global level, on the basis of assessments of national policies, but the major Triad governments are unwilling to collaborate under the auspices of the Fund. The limited consultative activity on monetary issues in the Triad context is evidently much less significant than the exchanges and reciprocal monitoring in the OECD. Professionals associated with the Fund's exchange rate surveillance functions have little freedom for policy-oriented international networking, and in subsequent careers tend to use their expertise for business or government consulting. For such professionals the perceived incentives to become involved in transnational elite networks are small, especially because of the uncertain futures of such networks.

Global, regional and bilateral interactions over trade and investment involve very large numbers of Triad professionals, but these also are generally not motivated to become active in transnational networks promoting economic cooperation. Their experiences of difficult bargaining in trade negotiations discourage optimism about the prospects for international collaboration but are sources of expertise for consulting. Incentives to engage in such consulting assume more significance than opportunities to collaborate transnationally for trade and investment cooperation that would be expected to be politically difficult, despite the potential economic benefits. Trade relations in the Triad context have involved much more adversarial interactions than those over monetary issues during the past decade and a half, and this, understandably, has affected the attitudes of national groups of trade policy experts.[16]

Altogether, current prospects for the emergence of transnational elite networks committed to the promotion of Euro-Pacific economic cooperation appear to be unfavourable. Failures by governments to engage in integrative collaboration, together with their resorts to conflictual behaviour, have tended to prevent the development of an international political culture and sense of collective identity that would motivate groups capable of acting across borders for the aggregation of interests and the harmonization of national policies. Problems of international political development have thus become evident.

While policy processes have remained distinctly national, the large-scale movement of economic activities across borders has internationalized problems of collective action that have been considered by theorists, and that are still considered by politicians only in domestic contexts. The dimensions of these problems have continued to grow, especially with the expansion of transnational production, but the responses of administrations have tended to be dominated by concerns with domestic contests for power. Efforts to promote international trust and goodwill have not been seen to be politically rewarding, despite awareness that wide-ranging international economic cooperation would bring substantial common benefits. The systemic need for international community formation that would sustain a system of collective management is not being met. The potential political entrepreneurs with talents for such community-building are being drawn into roles within domestic power contests.

Although current processes of high level socialization and selection are not producing sufficient elites committed to international community-building, the need for such elites is becoming greater. The already high levels of structural interdependence are rising, with strains caused by imbalances in gains, which are increasing with the general intensification of competition between firms and between governments. This is a challenge for persons of goodwill with policy expertise and it can be expected that some who will respond will draw inspiration from the Christian tradition which has long influenced social development in Europe and North America. Intensive and highly constructive promotional work will have to be undertaken by new elites united by profound commitments across national borders. These elites will have to stress the obligations of extended accountability which governments must acknowledge in conditions of high structural interdependence, and will have to assert this accountability with reference to the internationalization of market failure problems.

The most urgent task will be to enlist broad support for the stabilization of international financial markets. The growth-retarding volatility which has developed is attributable to gross regulatory failures which have benefited speculators, rather than productive enterprises given wider access to international funding, and which have obliged many of these enterprises, especially in the USA, to emphasize short-term financial management instead of longer-term entrepreneurship. To eliminate the volatility the extremely high volume of speculative activity will have to be brought down: financial markets will then be able to serve productive transactions with larger resources and lower risks. The necessary regulatory activity will have to be comprehensively cooperative, so that there will be no continuation of speculative operations in loosely regulated states.

PLANNING INTERNATIONAL FINANCIAL STABILIZATION

In the current configuration of poorly regulated internationalized financial markets, increased stability will have to be promoted firstly by working for a strong monetary union in Europe, with an effective system of financial regulation that will facilitate extensive global use of the European currency while controlling its movements in relation to the US dollar. The Union corporate associations that have given impetus to the drive for complete market integration could work, under leaderships with broader vision, for the formation of a well-institutionalized and effectively managed European mon-. etary authority.[17]

For full growth in the integrated regional market a single currency will be necessary, that is to serve transaction and reserve functions like those of the dollar in the USA. Current exchange costs and risks in the Union affect efficiencies in the Single Market, to the disadvantage of European firms. The operation of US and Japanese enterprises are also hampered, but the generally larger organizations and resources of these enterprises enable them to cope with the risks and costs more effectively, especially through intrafirm transfers. Energetic advocacy of the basic logic of monetary union will have to be the main line of activity for European elites committed to deepening integration. While motivated by concerns for growth in the Union, these elites will moreover have to be conscious of the importance of their endeavours for the world economy and, therefore, of the need to orient the regional monetary union towards an active global role. Forceful representations from a strong European monetary authority could encourage the development of fiscal discipline, a more functional monetary policy, and more effective financial regulation in the USA.

Incentive conflicts seen to affect the political feasibility of a monetary union could be overcome by planning for a system of weighed voting which would ensure a strong role for Germany in the monetary authority.[18] This would be necessary for responsible management in a regional community that includes weak governments, especially because that monetary authority would have to be a source of budgetary restraint through the Union. Pressures from the less responsible national administrations in the Union for monetary loosening and for less fiscal restraint could have very negative effects if the monetary authority was structured through expedient bargains. These could make effective management in the common interest very difficult, and this prospect could discourage German participation.

The planning would have to emphasize bringing France and Britain into close cooperation with the strong German role. This would be assisted by encouraging cross-holdings between the financial and manufacturing interests of the three countries. French manufacturing managements would then acquire more autonomy, while the divergence between financial and manufacturing interests in Britain would be partially overcome in favour of the latter. This engineering of structural change could be seen to be in conflict with the Union's formal rationale for giving wide scope to market forces, but it would have very positive consequences for interdependent growth in the Union. A core structure for a strong Union monetary authority would have been established, moreover, and as it evolved the pattern of economic power in the region would become less hierarchical. The present trend towards German economic domination would be moderated, and the German intercorporate system would penetrate and be penetrated by those of France and Britain. While there could be reluctance to accept such change, the benefits for each of the three states could be very large, because of enhanced growth and the prospect of regional monetary order.

The effort to promote the development of a strong European monetary authority could be expected to take on an Atlantic dimension because of the involvement of American interests, and especially because of the possibility that European financial institutions could dispose of excess dollar reserves, and that the use of the dollar in intra-union transactions would diminish.[19] On the US side there could be very active interest in consultations, particularly to protect the positions of US institutions in European financial markets. A major European concern would have to be the assertion of sufficiently functional regional monetary sovereignty and, beyond this, the development of a relationship that would encourage changes in the USA, for stability in financial markets. The regional monetary sovereignty would have to be used to promote stability in a well-regulated Union financial system, in which opportunities for currency speculation by financial institutions would have to be restricted. For the building of such a Union financial system much British cooperation would be necessary, because of the size of Britain's financial markets and the extensive scope for speculation which they currently allow.

Advances towards the establishment of a European monetary authority, even if not receiving inputs from elites working for Atlantic cooperation, must be expected to activate US quests for dialogue, especially with Germany. Interaction with the German monetary authorities could assist policy learning by the Treasury and other branches of the US administration, thus increasing awareness of imperatives to bring fundamentals into line with requirements for Atlantic monetary stability, especially through fiscal discipline. Although German exports benefit from American fiscal expansion, there is a basic German interest in the degree of regional monetary stability that could be made possible by budget deficit reduction in the USA, and in the longer-term growth of the US economy that could follow.

German initiatives, hopefully inspired by transnational groups advocating Euro-Pacific collaboration, could bring Japan into the Atlantic monetary dialogue. Thus far Germany and Japan have done little to coordinate their policies on the basis of shared interests in dealing with the USA. French antipathies towards Japan appear to have influenced German decision-making, while Japanese policy has been careful to avoid risking unfavourable US reactions. Germany has relatively greater scope for initiative, as the French antipathies towards Japan have been moderating and German economic links with Japan have been growing substantially. Informal monetary coordination between Germany and Japan could make the Atlantic monetary dialogue more productive. Related consultations within the OECD and the International Monetary Fund could prepare the way for strong persuasion to induce American shifts to fiscal discipline. In this new context of external accountability, moreover, there could be demands for regulatory cooperation by the USA to control speculation in financial markets and to impose more order in the US financial sector.

The increasing fragility of international markets, which makes close cooperation between Germany, Japan and the USA all the more urgent, is a problem for which the USA bears special responsibilities as the top currency state. Much of the instability in these markets is caused by the high volume speculation of US financial enterprises and by stresses in the US financial sector as a whole, particularly in its banking institutions. Opportunities to speculate in the international markets attract US financial institutions partly because of the stresses in their sector. Many of these stresses tend to reduce funding for productive activities, in a context in which credit-rationing is induced by high levels of government and corporate debt. The danger of a financial crisis, which could have severe international effects, tends to increase with rises in interest rates necessitated for inflation control while heavy deficit spending pushes up the level of government debt. As the rates rise, financial institutions tend to make fewer loans (because of declining confidence) but with higher risks (because of information problems). Stock market declines, which can be brought on by reduced investment in productive activity, and losses of confidence, tend to cause further reductions of lending for productive purposes, thus increasing general uncertainties. With such declines numerous banks may fail simultaneously, thus causing further reductions in productive lending and additional rises in interest rates.[20]

Greatly increased general awareness of the need for order in the US financial sector, to ensure more productive funding, will have to be a major objective of Triad networks striving to promote cooperation for stability in international financial markets. The necessity for such order will have to be made evident with reference to the negative effects of stress in the US financial sector on growth, particularly through their influence on the planning of long-term investment decisions, which are related to the continuing risks of a financial crisis. Advances towards monetary union in Europe, it must be stressed, could help to encourage consensus for reform in the USA, especially if regulatory measures are taken in Europe to restrict speculation in financial markets, so as to ensure more funding of productive activity.

PLANNING WIDER COOPERATION

In support of advances towards stability in financial markets it will be necessary to plan for greater cooperation in the management of trade, foreign direct investment, competition and industrial policies. The much more active involvement of business interests in these areas of administration will make the promotion of integrative collaboration more difficult. Concerted efforts at the policy level will require corporate support, with responsiveness by policymakers, so that the intended international harmonization of policies will be aligned with complementary trends in corporate planning, which hopefully will become oriented towards the development of generally more balanced structural interdependencies and the resolution of international market failure problems. To promote such cooperation between governments and firms, the potentially most productive endeavour for highly motivated elite networks will be to enlist Atlantic administrations and corporate groups for the sponsorship of higher technology trade and direct investment planning conferences. Over the long term these could lead to a considerable coordination of national industrial policies and to a spread of relational ties between transnational enterprises cooperating with these policies. General growth prospects would be enhanced through the concerting of entrepreneurship and the evolution of policy mixes more in line with developmental requirements at the national and international levels.

Policy learning conducive to the development of diffuse reciprocity, and thus to integrative cooperation, would be assisted by the proposed trade and direct investment planning conferences. These would multiply intergovernmental exchanges, especially between industrial policy departments, as national administrations would seek much information about the evolution of each other's economic policies and about strategies implemented by transnational enterprises. The strong emphasis on competitiveness in current policy orientations restricts intergovernmental exchanges, thus limiting recognition of opportunities for potentially productive cooperation. Within the European Union the competitiveness at the policy level is moderated in varying degrees by intergovernmental exchanges resulting from European Commission initiatives, notably in the industrial area, and by the activities of interest groups operating across national boundaries; but policy styles are not becoming more integrative.

Managerial learning through participation in the planning conferences would be possible as the potential benefits of wide-ranging cooperation with other enterprises and with national policies became evident. Prospects for more productive operations on a long-term basis would be recognized as constraints posed by the totally competitive behaviour of rival firms were removed through combined shifts to collaborative strategies. Possibilities for the adoption of such strategies can be seen in the numerous strategic alliances formed by US, European and Japanese mature and higher technology firms for market-sharing, complementary and joint investment ventures, risk-sharing and the use of entry barriers. These alliances are managed with cooperation in some areas and competition in others, as managements strive to secure first-mover advantages, undertake investments threatening the market positions of their partners, and emulate innovative moves by those partners. Instrumental orientations persist in many of these alliances as relative gains and losses change bargaining strengths, but there are quests for enduring forms of cooperation that can result from the growth of trust and goodwill. Such cooperation is becoming more and more important for the very large-scale investments in new production equipment that are necessary in higher technology industries.[21] Advances in frontier technology can provide incentives for more integrative cooperation, although this tends to be restricted to the partners whose competitive interests coincide.

The rationale for the planning conferences can be asserted with reference to the current probability of increasing frictions in the world trading system and in the Triad pattern of foreign direct investment policies. Conflicts between the leading industrialized democracies over trade issues and trade-related investment issues are tending to become more serious, because of the import-drawing effects of the USA's fiscal deficits, the large-scale export substitution by its firms manufacturing abroad, the abrasive methods of trade negotiators, the growing pressures for protection of the European Single Market, and the increasing competitiveness of Japanese enterprises. Established trends in the direct investment strategies of US, Japanese and European firms contribute to the trade frictions, activating US and European foreign direct investment policies with local content requirements.[22] In the European Union these are linked with ceilings on Japanese production within the Single Market, as well as quantitative restrictions on imports from Japan. Meanwhile the degrees of informal protection which shelter the Japanese economy tend to provoke continued US and some European opposition. Triad commitments to trade liberalization made during the Uruguay Round must be expected to become more and more qualified, and dispute settlement processes under the World Trade Organization are likely to be dominated by aggressive bargaining.[23]

The ventures in collaborative direct investment planning would encourage the development of more cooperative trade policies, as there would be prospects for more balanced structural interdependence. The favourable shifts in trade policies, moreover, would tend to motivate more active collaboration in investment planning. For all this, of course, the initial emphasis on Atlantic cooperation would have to be sustained, because of the affinities that can help build trust and goodwill, and the lower levels of friction over trade and investment issues. Atlantic relations can be seen as the main area of opportunity for constructive political entrepreneurship by transnational elites and by the policy-makers whom they may influence. The very extensive American corporate interests in Europe and the gradually deepening integration within the European Union constitute a basis for very active consultations about the long-term evolution of Atlantic structural interdependencies. The initial commitments to sponsor the planning conferences could be made principally in the context of such consultations, with understandings that the geographic scope of the conferences would be broadened to include Japan after the utility of the Atlantic ventures had been demonstrated.

Manipulation of the proposed conferences would be an obvious danger, and there could be considerable passive involvement. Government representatives could see possibilities for advancing the interests of national firms while discriminating against foreign enterprises, while managements could have incentives to collaborate with, and also work against, such designs, as well as to restrict information about their projected activities. Reticence about perceived first-mover options is a commonly accepted principle of strategic management. Governments in the more integrated states, with domestic intercorporate cooperation, would be well placed to influence the involvement of other administrations and firms. Decision-makers in the less integrated states could experience difficulties in their efforts to secure effective participation by enterprises based in their countries, but could be motivated to assert their preferences very aggressively, because of resentments at disparities in the gains received by their countries from external trade.

Constructive inputs from highly motivated elite networks could therefore be vital. Their contributions, emphasizing obligations to provide international public goods, could help to initiate successful ventures in collaborative planning that would inspire commitments to further cooperation, with increased trust and understanding. The experiences of productive collaboration could have cumulative effects on government and corporate decision-makers, while the investment planning would set direction for the development of new industrial capacity that would shape future trade flows, although the extent to which this would happen would depend on favourable shifts in the policies of several governments. Initiatives by the European Commission, if they evoked sufficient responses by the US administration, could lead to joint sponsorship of the proposed Atlantic trade and investment planning conferences. Such initiatives could be prepared for partly through the exchanges between the German Council of Economic Experts and the US Council of Economic Advisers suggested in the previous chapter. Economic advice to governments and to the European Commission by transnational elite networks could also encourage the necessary sponsorship. The present flows of advice from national groups seeking to influence policy tend to focus on the advancement of narrowly perceived state interests. In the USA such advice commonly reflects identification with the spirit of aggressively individualistic entrepreneurship (and the tradition of limited government), and would thus discourage endeavours to sponsor trade and investment planning conferences. Some contributions to the policy literature, however, have advocated more cooperation between national firms, on the basis of efficiency considerations with clear international implications.[24]

Constructive contributions to the flows of economic advice would have to stress that governments have shared interests in guiding, collectively, the strategies of large higher technology manufacturing enterprises. These move their principal operations to similar production locations, develop similar trade patterns, shape more and more decisively the evolution of each country's economic structures, assume elements of economic sovereignty, attain greater flexibility in the development of their global strategies, and acquire greater bargaining power.[25] Competition between governments, especially when it leads to investment bidding, enables international firms to act with greater independence for the advancement of their objectives. While all of this must be reiterated, it will also be necessary to emphasize that overall efficiencies in international markets would be increased substantially by the planning conferences. Negative externalities associated with restructuring by large firms would be reduced. There would be pervasive restraints on the growth of oligopoly power. Informational market failure problems would be to a considerable extent overcome. Substantially increased employment would be possible because of general increases in growth. Altogether, an international social market economy would begin to form.

CORPORATE RESPONSIVENESS

General corporate responsiveness, developing in an atmosphere of trust and goodwill, would be essential for the success of the planning conferences. This must be stressed because much economic advice to governments, especially in the USA, assumes that macromanagement is primarily concerned with regulating the activities of firms through arm's length dealings which managements will endeavour to frustrate while advancing their own interests.[26]

In the European Union there are traditions of close cooperation between administrations and enterprises, but deregulatory trends and the prospect of higher unemployment caused by corporate restructuring in the Single Market have evoked warnings that more active dialogue is needed between industrial policy authorities and managements.[27]

In the proposed planning conferences it would have to be expected that US firms would operate very independently, while US officials related distantly to them and to other firms, but that most of the European business representatives would have active links with their own governments and some ties with the European Commission. Japanese managements, participating in the conferences after these had begun as Atlantic exercises, would tend to function in close cooperation with each other and with their own administration. The conferences could thus result in more bargaining than cooperative planning, and there could be more active bargaining outside the conferences between governments and firms intent on their own bilateral or group projects. To promote substantial cooperative planning some concerted steering efforts by participating governments would be necessary, and for this purpose representatives of the European Commission could assume very important functions.

The steering efforts by government representatives could be greatly assisted by peak economic organizations. The development of stronger organizations of this kind in the USA would be encouraged if it were clear that the planning conferences were beginning to function with active European governmental and corporate participation, and that the US administration was becoming committed to a continuing role in the conferences. The collaboration of European and US business associations with officials from their national administrations and the European Commission could be based on responsiveness to projections of sectoral development potentials by US and European officials, and their related projections for infrastructure expansion. The latter projections would tend to induce collaborative location choices by transnational manufacturing enterprises, which in turn would influence location choices by service enterprises. The sectoral development potentials would provide broad contexts for managerial planning, in contexts in which the implementation of plans would be expected to contribute to further projections of these potentials, following the operational logic that has been active in Japan.

The dynamics of the planning conferences would be influenced by general awareness that their contributions to the development of harmonious Atlantic structural interdependencies would later be extended into the Pacific, with the introduction of Japanese participation. The justification for primary emphasis on Atlantic cooperation, because of the magnitude of shared interests, would have to be presented in terms that would be acceptable to Japan, but the competitive challenges of Japanese industry groups would tend to encourage active involvement in the conferences by US and European firms. Japanese corporations could be expected to seek close interaction with these firms, on the basis of prospective interests affected by the conferences, and the resulting exchanges could divert European and US managerial attention from Atlantic concerns.

The steering efforts of participating governments and of the European Commission would be especially significant for the maintenance of a strong focus on Atlantic economic ties, and for the development of shared commitments to wide-ranging cooperation, to link planning processes at corporate and government levels. The transnational elite networks which hopefully would have given some impetus to the sponsorship of the planning conference could contribute to the steering efforts, and thus to the evolution of operating procedures which would enable the conferences to become institutionalized. In this process consultations between high level advisory groups on each side of the Atlantic could be very helpful.

Managerial perspectives, especially in the USA, could be critical of the cooperative planning proposal because of the influence which governments could have on corporate decisions, and because the proposal could be seen to conflict with deregulatory trends in national policies over the past decade and a half. Literature on the utility of government–business cooperation, however, has evidently had some influence on managements in the USA, partly because of references to such cooperation in Japan. In the USA and Europe the deregulatory trends have been followed by microeconomic measures intended to help firms gain increased international competitiveness, and these have in varying degrees encouraged managerial recognition of potentials for productive interactions with the policy level.

Openness to the concept of cooperative trade and investment planning could develop without difficulty among US firms in Europe that have had relatively satisfactory dealings with the German and French administrations and with the European Commission. Consciousness of competitive advantages based on size and technological levels would probably contribute to the openness that might be expected. Support could accordingly be given to European Union proposals for the sponsorship of planning conferences that would initially devote much attention to Europe before assuming a fully Atlantic dimension. Support from European as well as American firms could be elicited, with emphasis by the sponsoring organizations on the importance of a harmonious development of Atlantic structural interdependencies for the building of a more integrated and more dynamic European economy. Current opportunities in the Single Market are being exploited very effectively by US firms, as they are well placed to extend their market shares. If numerous European enterprises are driven into declines, however, resentments will be expressed at the policy level, and disputes between European Union governments will hinder further integration, but may not prevent the adoption of measures to restrict the American corporate presence.

The European Union, it must be stressed, expresses commitments to collective management that have not evolved in the North America Free Trade Area. There is a significant capacity for continuity, moreover, in the institutionalized European system of collective management. Further, while concerns about the effects of unregulated international oligopoly power are understandably quite active in Europe, concepts of governmental economic responsibilities in the Union can be expressed in clear messages to managements about the deficiencies of market forces as providers of public goods. New understandings of market trends are being forced on economic policymakers, especially those in Europe, as problems of market failure are being internationalized and are assuming larger dimensions, straining the capacities of individual governments. These market changes tend to be viewed as challenges to engage in very competitive macromanagement, but are also seen (in Europe) as challenges to shift to more cooperative macromanagement in concert, on the basis of collective identity.[28]

PROSPECTS

Current trends in the Triad pattern are tending to increase the numerous strains associated with asymmetries in the rising levels of structural interdependence. Many problems of international market failure are becoming more serious, mainly to the disadvantage of less integrated and less efficiently managed states, as national patterns of economic activity are linked by trade and international production, with shifts in structural competitiveness. In the core area of the Triad pattern, the import-drawing effects of the USA's fiscal deficits, and the strong orientations of its larger firms towards international production strategies, are tending to motivate increasing reliance on managed trade to reduce adverse balances of payments.

The growth of international oligopoly power, notably in higher technology sectors, is continuing, as the development and application of frontier technology becomes feasible only for very large transnational enterprises linked in strategic alliances, and as these alliances are managed instrumentally in competition for dominant world market shares. While weaker firms are forced into declines, and the exploitation of market dominance becomes more feasible for the more powerful enterprises, negative externalities associated with their continuous restructuring affect sectors and communities transnationally. In this vast process superior advantages tend to be gained, with cumulative effects, by high technology manufacturing firms linked with industry groups:

the Japanese intercorporate system is thus becoming an increasingly significant source of change in North American and European economic structures. While this system benefits from the generation of X efficiencies,[29] it copes with informational market failure problems of international dimensions, yet causes such problems for North American and European rivals.

The provision of international public goods is becoming increasingly inadequate because of market and government deficiencies: intercorporate restraints on oligopoly power are lacking, and international competition policies are not evolving. Transnational sector adjustment to corporate restructuring and relocation strategies is not being promoted. The limited mobility of labour is exploited in the implementation of these strategies, and there is also corporate exploitation of investment-bidding rivalries between national administrations, as well as between states and provinces under those administrations.

Many of the strains associated with imbalances in the spread of gains from production and trade in the Triad pattern contribute to shifts in fundamentals that are exploited in international financial markets. In these shifts the USA's fiscal deficits are prominent factors, and so are its balance-of-payments difficulties. The relatively inferior structural competitiveness of several European Union states is also a significant factor. The volatility in financial markets, meanwhile, tends to add to the problems in the internationalizing markets for tradeables. Smaller firms are disadvantaged more seriously than larger ones by this volatility. Financial uncertainties have the general effect of imposing caution on investment decisions, and thus limit employment prospects. Pressures to ensure profitability, moreover, tend to hinder the development of cooperative efforts to deal with the externalities resulting from corporate restructuring.

The cooperative planning conferences, by offering possibilities for widely coordinated investment decisions and related forms of trade cooperation, would reduce the use of pressures to impose forms of managed trade. Resorts to such pressures would be possible if there were frustrations over the results of the planning conferences, and over the failures of agreements which they had facilitated, but potentials for effective collaboration would have been made evident at the conferences. There would be general recognition of the scope for transnational intercorporate restraints on the further development of international oligopoly power in higher technology sectors, and for supportive cooperation between governments. Sectoral adjustment to the externalities of higher technology corporate restructuring would be assisted, across national borders. The exploitation of labour immobility would become less significant in corporate strategies, in part because of the facilitating roles of governments in the conferences. Investment-bidding by those governments could, of course, become quite active at the conferences, but there would be much sharing of information about it, with reciprocal monitoring that would be a source of restraint. Most of the bidding governments would be administrations in the less integrated and less competitive states, and increased awareness of the disadvantages of their rivalry would encourage them to cooperate.

As completely new ventures in collaboration between governments and firms, the proposed conferences could become prominent in discussions of basic principles of economic policy. For the more integrated states there would be questions about possible losses of cohesion in their intercorporate systems and the weakening of relational ties between these systems and their national administrations, as the assimilative capacities of their political economies could be strained by the entries of foreign firms. For the less integrated states, very independent collaborative strategies by their enterprises in dealings with foreign corporations, and difficulties in evolving designs for optimum national economic structures, would raise questions about the utility of the conferences. National firms, it could be argued, would be more responsive to industrial policy concerns if the conferences were not expanding the ranges of their transnational strategic options.

Yet the less integrated states, being under less efficient national administrations, would have much to gain in the planned corporate and policy cooperation with each other and with the states at higher levels of systemic development. The dynamics of the planning conferences would encourage the development of stronger and more enduring bonds between national enterprises in these less advantaged states. The administrations in these states, moreover, would be challenged to provide supportive planning services on a stable basis, while promoting entrepreneurial consensus on basic designs for industrial development. At a very fundamental level the difficult issue of advanced political development would have to be confronted: limited government, in conditions of highly strained asymmetric structural interdependence, cannot cope with macromanagement tasks without much entrepreneurial cooperation between its managerial elites, and much dedicated technocratic sponsorship and guidance of that cooperation. Reliance on the structuring of incentives, a common principle of economic advice to governments, cannot substitute for solidarity-building on a strong moral basis to serve the common good.

The experiences of cooperative planning would tend to induce policy convergence, towards integrative collective management. The states with greater internal cohesion, capable of acting more competitively as rational actors, would become open to cooperation in the development of their structural interdependencies. The more pluralistic states, less capable of competitive macromanagement, would become committed to collaborative technocratic interaction with transnational enterprises, for more orderly structural evolution. In both types of state the planning experiences would have constructive influences on policies because of recognition of their implications for higher and more balanced growth. The technocratic sponsorship of information-sharing between firms would expand their bounded perspectives, as well as those of the technocrats, thus facilitating recognition of possibilities for long-term intercorporate collaboration, according with responsive industrial policy designs.

At the policy level, initial views about the feasibility of sponsoring effective cooperative planning conferences would be influenced by realist interpretations of state behaviour, the emphasis on incentives in applications of economic theory, and common experiences of idiosyncratic factors in multilateral and multifunctional interactions. Realist thinking discourages optimism about potentials for building trust, goodwill and cooperation in foreign economic relations. Incentive considerations in policy-relevant economic theorizing would raise doubts about the willingness of managements to share strategically significant information and the possibilities for cooperation between technocrats serving different governments. Lessons in the recent history of economic policy interactions between industrialized states, moreover, reflect the frequent and sometimes pervasive influence of high level subjective preferences, attachments and antipathies. Advocacy by highly motivated elites would have to cope with all these problems, but could well be assisted by innovative policy studies produced under the auspices of the European Commission.

Deepening regional integration in Europe is obligating much rethinking about realist theories of state behaviour, especially by giving prominence to the logic of collective management. Meanwhile, emphasis on incentives for firms in economic advice to governments has to be considered with awareness that bounded corporate perspectives can be expanded, through information exchanges and attitudinal changes, to respond to opportunities for cooperation. Uncertainties about idiosyncratic factors in interactions between diverse policy-makers can be sources of concern, in conjunction with realist expectations and anticipations of narrowly focused profit-seeking, but in the planning conferences there would be much critical exposure of dysfunctional subjective preferences.

If the planning conferences can be sponsored, there could be gradual collective recovery of elements of economic sovereignty lost to transnational enterprises. New patterns of collaborative activity by firms could contribute to order and growth in the Atlantic, and later the Pacific, configuration of structural interdependencies. Deeper understanding of imperatives for normative integration at the national and international levels could develop as the planning collaboration continued. Meanwhile, from the experiences of states enduring macromanagement difficulties because of internal divisions, there could come strong affirmations of obligations to engage in comprehensive integrative international economic cooperation. Reciprocal conversions from neomercantilism could begin in the states that have achieved very competitive macromanagement. A long-term process of international community formation would thus be in prospect. Consensus could develop on a doctrine of collective governance, focusing on the orchestration of concerted entrepreneurship in higher technology sectors, and on the social organization of trust across national borders.

NOTES

1. For discussions of the dynamics of European Union decision-making see Andrew Moravscik, 'Preferences and Power in the European Community: A Liberal Intergovernmentalist Approach', *Journal of Common Market Studies*, **31** (4), December 1993, 473–524; Horst Siebert and Michael J. Koop, 'Institutional Competition versus Centralization: Quo Vadis Europe?', *Oxford Review of Economic Policy*, **9** (1), Spring 1993, 15–30; and Juliet Lodge, 'Transparency and Democratic Legitimacy', *Journal of Common Market Studies*, **32** (3), September 1994, 343–68.
2. There are organizational interests in maintaining the strength of established ministerial policy roles. Economists in the Japanese ministries are, moreover, assisted by highly developed information-processing facilities. See Saburo Okita, 'Japan', in Joseph A. Pechman (ed.), *The Role of the Economist in Government*, Washington D.C.: New York University Press, 1989, 173–92.
3. See comments on consensual governance in John O. Haley, 'Consensual Governance: A Study of Law, Culture, and the Political Economy of Postwar Japan', in Shumpei Kumon and Henry Rosovsky (eds), *The Political Economy of Japan*, Stanford: Stanford University Press, 1992, Vol. 3, 32–62.
4. See Kent E. Calder, 'Japanese Foreign Economic Policy Formation: Explaining the Reactive State', *World Politics*, **XL** (4), July 1988, 517–41.
5. The intensive information-sharing in Japanese industry groups and business associations is based on strong commitments to international competitiveness which are reinforced by gains in foreign markets. See Ken-ichi Imai, 'Japan's Corporate Networks', in *The Political Economy of Japan*, *op. cit.*, 198–230; and Yasunori Sone, 'Structuring Political Bargains: Government, Gyokai, and Markets', in Gary D. Allison and Yasunori Sone (eds), *Political Dynamics in Contemporary Japan*, Ithaca: Cornell University Press, 1993, 295–306.
6. See Gavin Boyd, *Corporate Planning and Policy Planning in the Pacific*, London: Pinter, 1993, Ch. 8.
7. *Ibid.*
8. See Mathew D. McCubbins, 'Government on Lay-Away: Federal Spending and Deficits under Divided Party Control', and Gary W. Cox and Mathew D. McCubbins, 'Divided Control of Fiscal Policy', in Gary W. Cox and Samuel Kernell (eds), *The Politics of Divided Government*, Boulder: Westview Press, 1991, 113–54, 155–78.
9. See I.M. Destler, *American Trade Politics*, Washington D.C.: Washington Institute for International Economics, 1992, 2nd ed., Ch. 9. Results from the technology enhancement programme have been dependent on the volume of allocations and the quality of technocratic guidance. See Edward M. Graham, 'Industrial Policy Issues in the US', in Gunnar K. Sletmo and Gavin Boyd (eds), *Industrial Policies in the Pacific*, Boulder: Westview Press, 1994, 129–52.
10. See Keisuke Iida, 'The Political Economy of Exchange Rate Policy: US and Japanese Intervention Policies, 1977–90', *Journal of Public Policy*, **13** (4), Oct.–Dec. 1993, 327–49.

11. See general comments on policy-making in the Union by Moravscik, *op. cit.*
12. See Paul de Grauwe, 'The Political Economy of Monetary Union in Europe', *The World Economy*, **16** (6), November 1993, 653–62.
13. See Andrew M. McLaughlin, Grant Jordan and William A. Maloney, 'Corporate Lobbying in the European Community', *Journal of Common Market Studies*, **31** (2), June 1993, 191–212; and Sonia Mazey and Jeremy Richardson (eds), *Lobbying in the European Community*, Oxford: Oxford University Press, 1993.
14. See William D. Coleman, 'State Traditions and Comprehensive Business Associations: A Comparative Structural Analysis', *Political Studies*, **XXXVIII** (2), June 1990, 231–52.
15. See J.C.R. Dow, 'The Organization for Economic Cooperation and Development', in Pechman, *op. cit.*, 255–78.
16. See Carlo Perroni and John Whalley, *The New Regionalism: Trade Liberalization or Insurance?*, Cambridge: National Bureau of Economic Research, Working Paper 4626, 1994, and David Henderson, 'The World Trading System', in John Llewellyn and Stephen J. Potter (eds), *Economic Policies for the 1990s*, Oxford: Blackwell, 1991, 293–324.
17. See Michael Calingaert, 'Government–Business Relations in the European Community', *California Management Review*, **35** (2), Winter 1993, 118–33.
18. This would influence German concerns noted in de Grauwe, *op. cit.*
19. See Rinaldo M. Pecchloli, 'Policies towards Financial Markets', in *Economic Policies in the 1990s, op. cit.*, 396–421.
20. See Frederic S. Mishkin, 'Preventing Financial Crises: An International Perspective', *Manchester School Papers in Money, Macroeconomics and Finance*, Supplement, **LXII**, 1993, 1–40.
21. See David B. Yoffie, 'Conclusions and Implications', in David B. Yoffie (ed.), *Beyond Free Trade: Firms, Governments and Global Competition*, Boston: Harvard Business School Press, 1993, 429–50.
22. See Henderson, *op. cit.*, and Perroni and Whalley, *op. cit.*
23. The Uruguay Round agreements allow all participating states to become active in structuring the World Trade Organization and in the operation of its dispute settlement system. See *The Results of the Uruguay Round of Multilateral Trade Negotiations: The Legal Texts*, Geneva: GATT, 1994.
24. See W. Carl Kester, 'Industrial Groups as Systems of Contractual Governance', *Oxford Review of Economic Policy*, **8** (3), Autumn 1992, 24–44.
25. See Yoffie, *op. cit.*, and Peter J. Cowhey and Jonathan D. Aronson, *Managing the World Economy: The Consequences of Corporate Alliances*, New York: Council on Foreign Relations, 1993.
26. See Jenny Stewart, 'Rational Choice Theory, Public Policy, and the Liberal State', *Policy Sciences*, **26** (4), 1993, 317–30.
27. See Alexis Jacquemin and David Wright, 'Corporate Strategies and European Challenges Post-1992', *Journal of Common Market Studies*, **31** (4), December 1993, 525–38.
28. See Moravscik, *op. cit.*, and references to European Commission activities in John Peterson, 'Europe and America in the Clinton Era', *Journal of Common Market Studies*, **32** (3), September 1994, 411–26.
29. See discussion of X efficiency in Mark Periman, 'Harvey Leibenstein', in Warren J. Samuels (ed.), *New Horizons in Economic Thought*, Cheltenham: Edward Elgar, 1992, 184–201; and comments on blending bounded organizational visions in Martin Fransman, *The Market and Beyond*, Cambridge: Cambridge University Press, 1990, Ch. 9.

Index

261